The Undead and Philosophy

Popular Culture and Philosophy™
Series Editor: George A. Reisch
(Series Editor for this volume was William Irwin)

Popular Culture and Philosophy™

The Undead and Philosophy

Chicken Soup for the Soulless

Edited by

RICHARD GREENE

and

K. SILEM MOHAMMAD

OPEN COURT
Chicago and La Salle, Illinois

Volume 22 in the series, Popular Culture and Philosophy®

To order books from Open Court, call 1-800-815-2280, or visit our website at www.opencourtbooks.com.

Open Court Publishing Company is a division of Carus Publishing Company.

Library of Congress Cataloging-in-Publication Data

The undead and philosophy : chicken soup for the soulless / edited by Richard Greene and K. Silem Mohammad.
    p. cm. — (Popular culture and philosophy ; v. 22)
    Summary: "A collection of philosophical essays about the undead: beings such as vampires and zombies who are physically or mentally dead yet not at rest. Topics addressed include the metaphysics and ethics of undeath"--Provided by publisher.
    Includes bibliographical references and index.
    ISBN-13: 978-0-8126-9601-1 (trade paper : alk. paper)
    ISBN-10: 0-8126-9601-8 (trade paper : alk. paper)
    1. Demonology. 2. Demonology in literature.
    3. Demonology in motion pictures. 4. Vampires.
    5. Werewolves. 6. Zombies. 7. Ghouls and ogres.
    I. Greene, Richard, 1961- II. Mohammad, K. Silem.
BF1556.U53 2006
398'.45—dc22

                          2006020701

For Henry

Contents

Acknowledgments

We are grateful for the support, advice, and insight we've received from Bill Irwin, David Ramsay Steele, Carolyn Madia-Gray, and all the folks at Open Court. We're also appreciative of the patience, flexibility, and hard work of the contributors to this collection. This has been a long process, and we've been fortunate to have so many fine scholars stick with us over these many months. This work has benefited from the commentary of Nancy Balmert, Dan Fox, Kris Greene, Leo Greiner, Steve Knaster, Joel Morrison, and Rachel Robison, each of whom read early versions of the essays in this collection. Hubbell King and Terry Thiel offered invaluable administrative assistance throughout the process. Finally, we are grateful to our colleagues at Southern Oregon University and Weber State University for generally supporting projects such as this one, as well as providing helpful feedback on particular aspects of this work.

(Un)dead (Un)certainties

The "Undead" have held a firm, steady, icy grip on the public imagination since Bram Stoker first used the word in his novel *Dracula* over a hundred years ago. The introduction of the term, however, merely served to provide a catchy label for an idea that has fascinated us for as long as there have been stories, legends, myths, and superstitions—in short, for as long as there has been popular culture. This fascination shows no signs of diminishing: every year offers new movies and television shows featuring vampires and zombies, books on the Undead continue to top the bestseller charts, and musicians and other artists use Undead imagery in their work. In addition, literary critics, philosophers, and theorists of various stripes have found the theme of Undeath a rich vein to mine (or suck, if you prefer) for their scholarly projects.

For some, it is a matter of controversy that popular culture can provide the basis for serious intellectual inquiry. In fact, there is an enduring tradition in Western philosophy, dating back to Socrates and before, of using examples from pop culture to illustrate difficult or abstract philosophical concepts. Few such concepts have been the object of more persistent inquiry than that of death. For that reason alone, the imaginary state of Undeath is a logical starting point for evocations of central philosophical questions concerning presence, identity, and value. With its double-negative construction (the grammatical negative of *un-* and the metaphysical negative of *dead*), the idea of Undeath problematizes our everyday notions of what it means to be alive in the first place—in a literal sense, we are *all*, as living beings, "Undead." It is only a short step from this idea to the suggestion that the state of non-death (otherwise known as "life") we privilege as authentic might itself be subject to the same doubts that attend our apprehension of Undeath.

One set of frequently debated questions addresses the metaphysical condition of Undeath itself. What does it mean to be Undead? That one is alive and dead at the same time? Neither? Can one be Undead without having first died? Can one be "born" Undead? Is one Undead if one is somehow afflicted so as to be unable to die, as in the myth of Tithonus? Can one have active vital signs and be Undead? The zombie-esque "infected" in Danny Boyle's *28 Days Later*, for example, are living persons who have become mindless killers as a result of a rage-inducing virus—are they Undead? What if one is so stressed out and enervated from working at a McJob and watching hours of television that one loses all or most of one's vital affect and turns into a "zombie"? What about corporate "vampires" who leech off of exploited laborers and consumers? Are these terms purely metaphorical, or is there a true sense in which subjects can be said in such cases to have entered states of death-in-life?

A note on practical terminology: for the purposes of this book, "Undead" will refer to any corporeal beings who are physically or mentally dead, but are in some way not "at rest." [1] This includes supernatural monsters such as vampires and voodoo zombies; it also applies to bodies reanimated by some supposedly natural force, such as George Romero's radiation-spawned zombies, as well as the problematic category of Boyle's infected. One other special case presents itself: over the past couple of decades, philosophers have posited "philosophical zombies" in thought experiments designed to raise problematic counterexamples for various positions in metaphysics. These zombies are respiring, fully functional persons in every sense except that they lack subjective states (that is, consciousness). They look and act like everyone else, but have no thoughts, feelings, or interior life of any kind. Philosophical zombies are technically alive, but there is a sense in which they "shouldn't" be: their existence (a purely fictional existence, presumably) presents a troubling paradox that threatens to upset

---

[1] The editors have elected—largely for the sake of focus—to exclude incorporeal entities such as ghosts, although it is undeniable that they constitute a major category of Undead beings in popular culture.

our most deeply held convictions about what it means to be alive in the first place.

Another line of questioning concerns the persistence of identity: Are we our Undead selves? If I am bitten by a zombie or a vampire and become one as a result, am I still the "me" that was bitten? And if so, to what extent? Entirely? Partly? Not so much? Vampires are usually represented as retaining memories of their mortal lives, and in many cases, the interests and affections that went along with those lives: Bram Stoker's Dracula seems also to be Vlad Dracul, the historical Transylvanian despot, at the same time that he is the Undead Prince of Darkness, and Angel on Joss Whedon's *Buffy the Vampire Slayer* is also a young Irishman (though you wouldn't necessarily believe it from David Boreanaz's screen accent). Vampires may express disdain for the values they held as mortals, and even take pleasure in violating principles they once held dear, but they still exhibit continuity on the level of subjective mental experience. Zombies, in contrast, are generally depicted as unthinking corpses that have somehow retained the ability to walk around and perform basic motor functions. They are subverbal and largely without powers of reason (except for "philosophical zombies" as previously discussed). When they encounter former loved ones, they register no recognition or fondness. The resemblance between the zombie and the person who occupied its body in life would seem to be only an external appearance. And yet this uncanny likeness is so strong that the beleaguered authorities in Romero's films must remind the populace through emergency broadcasts that it is fatal to believe sentimentally that the Undead are our loved ones. They are "just dead flesh." They do, however, occasionally exhibit fleeting and poignant flashes of something like human memory, such as the instinct that brings the zombies in *Dawn of the Dead* to the shopping mall that was an "important place" in their lives. In *Land of the Dead*, one zombie still carries around the gas pump nozzle he operated in life as a filling station attendant, as though out of a residual sense of professional responsibility.

Yet another set of questions involves the ethics of Undeath. Is it bad to be Undead? Is it wrong for vampires to stalk the living? Are zombies somehow less morally accountable than vampires for the havoc they wreak? Are vampires, as a result of having been supernaturally cursed, evil by necessity? Is it wrong for humans to kill vampires or zombies? Since vampires are both conscious and rational, and yet tend to behave very badly, they naturally raise questions about morality and evil. Characters like Louis from Anne Rice's *Interview with the Vampire* and Spike from *Buffy* serve as vehicles for dramatic explorations of internal moral conflict in which the subject's autonomous conscience is set at odds with a force of evil that constantly threatens dominance over his or her soul. Most zombies, on the other hand, are barely classifiable as subjects at all; the individual zombie is often only one unit in a larger collective organism which operates outside most conventional definitions of "intelligence," let alone ethical awareness. Concerning our own obligation to treat these beings ethically, similar distinctions apply: the idea of bringing a vampire into court is on some level slightly less absurd than suing a zombie, and the thought of plunging a stake into a vampire's heart generally pricks the conscience more than that of shooting a zombie in the brain.

Questions like these represent just part of the broad range of perspectives on Undeath explored in this book by writers from diverse academic and theoretical backgrounds. It is our hope that you will come away from the book with an increased appreciation for the ways in which popular culture in general, and depictions of vampires and zombies in particular, can provide a meaningful context for intellectual discourse. We can't promise that you will find any knowledge here that will serve you usefully when the dead do finally walk the earth and pry away the boarded-up slats you've hammered hastily over your windows, but at the very least, as you succumb to the onslaught of those festering hordes, as their fangs pierce your jugular and their cold hands rend your flesh, you will have an expanded philosophical vocabulary with which to describe the horror you feel in those last panic-stricken moments before you too become one of the legions of Undead.

PART I

It's Alive (Sort Of)

1

The Badness of Undeath

RICHARD GREENE

It's an interesting feature of horror films that most people either like them or dislike them for precisely the same reason: they are terrifying. Those who like them enjoy the "rush" of being terrified and those who don't like them find being frightened distressful, unpleasant, or uncomfortable. Few, if any, enjoy horror films but fail to find them frightening to some degree. One reason that horror scares us is because we have an ability to empathize with characters as they are being chased, slaughtered, mauled, impaled, burned, eaten, or tortured. We can easily imagine what it would be like to be hung on a meat hook by Leatherface while still alive or to have one's jugular vein sliced by one of Freddy Krueger's razor-sharp "fingers," and it scares us. Horror films such as *The Texas Chainsaw Massacre* and *A Nightmare on Elm Street* frighten us, in part, by playing on our fear of death. After all death is regarded, at least by most folks, as a bad thing for the person who dies.

While people's emotional responses toward death range from mild anxiety to all-out panic, there is a scenario that frightens us even more. Films about the Undead, such as *Night of the Living Dead*, *Dracula*, *Nosferatu*, and *White Zombie* to name a few, trade on this more terrifying prospect: they threaten us with the possibility of becoming Undead ourselves. There is no shortage of examples in zombie and vampire films of characters that either kill themselves or ask others to kill them so as to avoid becoming Undead. Being Undead is generally regarded as a worse state than being dead.[1] Philosophers have long debated the question of why death is bad for the person who dies. I'd like to address the question of why Undeath—the state of being Undead—is bad for the person who becomes Undead. A successful account of the badness of Undeath must accomplish two things: it must identify the feature or features of Undeath that make it bad, and it must explain why Undeath is generally regarded as being worse than death.

Depending on how one defines it, there are a number of different ways of being Undead. K. Silem Mohammad and I define Undeath as that class of beings who at some point were living creatures, have died, and have come back such that they are not presently "at rest." On this account, all vampires, mummies, and ghosts, most zombies, some skeletons (such as the Lost Skeleton of Cadavra), and miscellaneous other animated corpses, such as the manipulated dead from *Donnie Darko*, would count as being Undead. For simplicity's sake and because when people are queried about the Undead, vampires and zombies come to mind much more frequently,[2] I'll restrict my discussion to the badness of being either a vampire or a zombie.

Some Haunted Housekeeping

As is usually the case when one raises a philosophical question, there is a natural temptation to respond to the question by rejecting it. Rejecting the question of why Undeath is a bad thing for the person who is Undead might take one of two forms: (1) one might cite counterexamples to the claim that Undeath is bad, perhaps by identifying Undead beings whose existence is, intuitively, not bad, or (2) one might take issue with the central arguments for the view that Undeath is bad. While the latter approach is promising and will receive much attention over the course of this chapter, I'd like to quickly dismiss the first strategy. Let's briefly address the notion that for many, being Undead isn't bad.

----

[1] Perhaps it would be more accurate to state that among those who consider Undeath to be a bad thing, it's generally regarded to be worse than death. I have a number of students who think it would be cool to be a vampire. Pretty much nobody, however, wants to be a zombie.

[2] Based on an informal and highly unscientific survey conducted in June 2005 at Southern Oregon University.

There are a number of Undead creatures in recent horror films and television shows who stand out from the crowd by avoiding many if not most of the trappings of being Undead. For example on *Buffy the Vampire Slayer*, the vampires Angel and Spike both have souls by the end of the series. As a consequence they are able to have meaningful relationships, experience strong emotions, perform good deeds, and fight on the side of good. Intuitively, it's not obviously bad to be Angel or Spike. Similarly, in *Interview with the Vampire* Louis is able, albeit with some difficulty, to resist his more basic vampiric urges, and hence, lives on the blood of chickens and rats. In *Shaun of the Dead*, Shaun's best friend Ed experiences no qualitative change in his daily existence upon becoming a zombie—at film's end his normal routine still mostly involves lounging on the sofa, playing video games, and hanging out with Shaun. Count Blah, the muppet-esque vampire on the television series *Greg the Bunny*, thoroughly enjoys all the pleasures that life has to offer ("She went down for The Count, blah"). And Casper the friendly ghost. . . . Well, you get the idea. One thing that all these characters have in common is that they are not in any important sense evil, though one probably wouldn't want to spend more than a few hours in the presence of Count Blah. This raises the question: to what extent do these characters and others like them pose a problem for our more traditional conceptions of the Undead?

Once a fictional concept such as vampirism or zombiedom, or a character such as Dracula or Nosferatu, is established, intuitively it seems inappropriate for subsequent writers to come along and alter that concept or character. It's almost as if a work of art is being altered against the will of its creator, in much the same way that there is something creepy going on when black-and-white films get "colorized." If, for example, a movie were to come out that portrayed Atticus Finch, from *To Kill a Mockingbird*, as a narrow-minded bigot, people would rightly feel that the original work had been harmed or denigrated in some fashion. This line of thought provides us with a reason for thinking that "good" vampires and zombies should not be considered when discussing features of vampires and zombies in general. That being said, the conception that most people have of vampires and zombies is one that has developed over time as various writers have contributed to the legend. For example, some of the more familiar aspects of the vampire story, such as an aversion to holy water and the ability to take other forms, were added later. So we also have good reason for treating subsequent modifications to basic concepts as legitimate. The question is where to draw the line.

My proposal is to treat those modifications to the vampire and zombie mythologies that enhance them without drastically altering our understanding of what it means to be a vampire or a zombie as legitimate modifications, and to treat those modifications that radically alter our concepts, such as the existence of "good" vampires or zombies with whom one can spend quality time playing video games, as interesting hypothetical experiments. It's fun to think about what it would be like if there were vampires with souls or if there were horny muppet-vampires, but these thought-experiments shouldn't then serve to change what we believe about vampires and zombies. For this reason, I'll not consider Angel, Spike, Louis, Count Blah, Ed, and others of their kind to be "real" vampires and zombies. In this chapter all vampires and zombies will be considered to be unfriendly and dangerous. Moreover, all vampires will be considered to be cursed or damned and evil by nature, and all zombies, though not cursed or evil by nature, will be understood to behave in ways that we normally consider to be evil.

Deprivation and Desire-Frustration

Let's begin our search for the badness of Undeath by looking at what philosophers have to say about the badness of death. Since death and Undeath have something in common—they can both be contrasted with being alive—it may turn out that the thing that is objectionable about death is the same thing that makes Undeath bad. At minimum, looking at the badness of death should serve to provide a useful point of departure for our inquiry into the badness of Undeath.

Since it is not obvious that death is a bad thing if there is an afterlife involving some sort of reward for a life lived well, philosophers working on the question of death's badness typically consider death to be an experiential blank. That is, they consider that death doesn't involve any conscious experiences for the person who is dead. On this view, death is not a state in which some part of us lives on after our physical bodies have died. Of course, if philosophers are wrong about this, then the badness of both death and Undeath is easily accounted for. Undeath is bad because one misses out on whatever rewards one has coming in the afterlife. Death, on the other hand, is simply not a bad thing (unless one has misbehaved to such a degree that the afterlife promises punishment instead of reward). Since there is little consensus about whether there is an afterlife, and if there is, about what it's like, it is appropriate to address the question of death's badness by assuming that death is an experiential blank.

If death is simply the cessation of life and nothing more, then it is not clear why death is thought to be a bad thing. As Epicurus points out, "Death is nothing to us, since when we are, death has not come, and when death has come, we are not."[3] If death is considered to be an experiential blank, then the badness of death cannot be accounted for in terms of some sort of unpleasant experience; the badness of death must lie elsewhere. Many (perhaps most) theorists working on this issue today endorse either some version of Thomas Nagel's deprivation view,[4] which is the view that the badness of death lies in its depriving persons of the good things that life has to offer (the *praemia vitae*), or they endorse some version of Bernard Williams's desire-frustration view,[5] which is the view that death is bad insofar as it frustrates certain of our important desires.

While perhaps providing the best hope for accounting for the badness of death, the deprivation view isn't able to account for the badness of Undeath, since the Undead are not deprived of the *praemia vitae*. Vampires, for example, in virtue of being immortal, have the opportunity to experience an infinite quantity of fine things. Of course, there are a number of desirable things that vampires cannot experience, such as the pleasure associated with a fine meal (a glass of warm blood notwithstanding) or the warmth of the sun's rays on one's skin. This, however, doesn't help the deprivation view, as the sheer quantity of positive experiences that vampires will have (in virtue of

---

[3] Epicurus, "Letter to Menoeceus," 124b–127a, in *Epicurus: Letters, Principal Doctrines, and Vatican Sayings*, edited by Russel M. Greer (Englewood Cliffs: Prentice Hall, 1997).

[4] See Nagel, "Death," in his *Mortal Questions* (Cambridge: Cambridge University Press, 1979).

[5] See Williams, "The Makropulos Case: Reflections on the Tedium of Immortality," in his *Problems of the Self* (Cambridge: Cambridge University Press, 1973).

being immortal) will far outweigh those experiences lost due to being a vampire.

Admittedly, the deprivation view fares a little better at accounting for the badness of being a zombie, since zombies seem able to have only a few experiences. Mostly they stagger, grunt, and eat human flesh and brains. If one were to become a zombie, presumably one wouldn't derive a lot of pleasure from listening to the symphony, studying philosophy, or watching a good movie, nor would one have close personal relationships and the like. Still, the badness of being a zombie doesn't seem to lie in the fact that we are being deprived of these things. If it did, then being dead wouldn't be preferable to being a zombie. Being dead would be on par with being a zombie, in terms of badness. Moreover, although zombies do not enjoy many of the finer things in life, it's not clear that they don't experience as much pleasure as do living human beings, or even more. For all we know there is no more satisfying experience to be had than the experience of being a zombie and biting into a fresh living human brain. Until you've staggered a mile in someone's shoes . . . Thus, we can reasonably conclude that the deprivation view does not account for the badness of Undeath.

Proponents of the desire-frustration view of death's badness reason as follows:

(1) If I desire something, then I have a prima facie reason to prefer a state of affairs in which I get it to one in which I don't get it.

(2) Death precludes some desires being fulfilled.

(3) Thus, I have a reason to avoid death.

(4) If something is to be avoided, then that thing is bad.

(5) Therefore, death is bad.

So life is preferable to death, because when one is alive, one's desires can be satisfied, but when one is dead, one's desires are necessarily thwarted. Of course, if one desires death, then this argument doesn't work, but, in such cases, it's not clear that death is a bad thing. Typically people don't desire death, unless life is bad (or at minimum, life seems bad).

Will this line of reasoning also serve to capture the badness of Undeath? At first glance it is a promising strategy. If one becomes a vampire or a zombie at some point in the future, then most of one's present desires will go unfulfilled. For example, my desire to win the first Nobel Prize in Philosophy certainly won't be satisfied if I am a zombie. My desire to spend my retirement lounging in the sun on a beach in Santa Barbara will go unfulfilled if I am a vampire. My desire to be invited to the office holiday party will not be realized if I am either a vampire or a zombie (my colleagues are adventurous and fun-loving, but they have their limits).

Though promising, the desire-frustration account cannot account for the badness of Undeath. The problem is that mere desire frustration is not sufficient for a state of affairs being bad. For example, when I was around ten years old I had a desire to be a major league baseball player when I grew up. When I was in my twenties and thirties, this desire was going unfulfilled. It doesn't follow that because my desire was not being fulfilled, my situation was bad. This is because desires change. When I was in my twenties and thirties I had no desire to be a baseball player. In fact, since I wouldn't have enjoyed being a baseball player, it is plausible to suppose that the situation in which my desire had been fulfilled would have been worse than the one in which it had not been fulfilled.

This does not pose a problem for the desire-frustration account of death's badness. A proponent of the desire-frustration view can hold that as long as a previous desire has been cancelled or replaced by some later desire, then desire-frustration is not a bad thing. So my unfulfilled desire to be a major league baseball player didn't lead to a bad state of affairs, because it was replaced by my desire to be a philosophy professor. Death is bad, on this view, because it is a state that involves unfulfilled desires that have not been cancelled or replaced. Undeath, on the other hand, is a state in which one's desires have been replaced. A desire for scotch has been replaced with a desire for blood. A desire for pork roast has been replaced by a desire for raw human flesh. So Undeath does not lead to desire-frustration; rather, it leads to changed desire, which, as we've seen, is not necessarily a bad thing. So the desire-frustration account is not able to account for the badness of death.

Human Beings, Vampires, Zombies, Pigs, and Fools

As neither of the main views regarding the badness of death is able to account for the badness of Undeath or to explain why Undeath is generally considered to be a worse state of affairs than death, we'll shift our focus to an account of the badness of Undeath that focuses directly on the state of being Undead. Since death is thought by philosophers to be an experiential blank, accounts of the badness of death can't focus on the qualitative aspects of death; that is, they can't focus on the way death feels. If death is an experiential blank, it doesn't feel like anything. Undeath, however, is not an experiential blank. Perhaps the key to identifying the badness of Undeath has to do with the qualitative aspects of Undeath—the way that being Undead feels.

It's not obvious that being Undead feels bad, in itself. As I stated above, vampires are able to have a variety of positive experiences, and it's quite possible that zombies derive great amounts of pleasure from eating human flesh and brains. That being said, it is possible to suppose of some beings that don't experience bad feelings such as pain that one still wouldn't desire to have their experiences. This would hold true whenever the beings under consideration had experiences that are generally less desirable than the experiences that one typically has. John Stuart Mill said, famously, "It is better to be a human being dissatisfied than a pig satisfied; better to be Socrates dissatisfied than a fool satisfied. And if the fool, or the pig, are of a different opinion, it is because they only know their own side of the question."[6] According to this line of reasoning, even though pigs don't necessarily have bad experiences from their own perspective—they appear to enjoy lounging in the sty and slopping around in the mud—it would be bad to be a pig in comparison to being a human being. Similarly, one might argue that, while vampires and zombies are capable of positive experiences, their experiences, when compared to the experiences of human beings, are less desirable. Hence it is bad to be a vampire or a zombie.

---

[6] Mill, *Utilitarianism*, second edition, edited by George Sher (Indianapolis: Hacket, 2001), p. 10.

There are a few problems with this move. First, if successful, this argument only serves to explain why being a zombie is a bad thing. Zombies are clearly lower "life" forms. There is not a whole lot of cognitive activity going on with zombies. Vampires, on the other hand, are frequently portrayed as being quite intelligent, and having a wide range of experiences that humans don't have, such as turning into a bat or a wolf. It is not implausible to suppose that vampiric experiences are more desirable (even from a human perspective) than human experiences. It would appear that the pig analogy just does not hold between humans and vampires. A second and deeper worry about this argument is that it doesn't maintain that Undeath is an objectively bad state. At best it establishes that Undeath is bad when compared to certain alternatives, such as being a living human. Here I want to make a distinction between a state's being objectively bad as opposed to its being comparatively bad. A state is objectively bad when features of that state are bad in virtue of either some qualitative aspect of that state, such as feeling pain or being depressed, or when there is some good lacking in that state that one would not lack under normal circumstances, such as vision or hearing. A state is comparatively bad when it has less total goodness than some other state one might find oneself in. Those who have the intuition that it would be bad to be a zombie or a vampire don't think this because they are comparing it with being a normal living human. In other words, Undeath is not bad because it is thought to be comparatively bad (even though it may well be comparatively bad). Rather, they believe that there is something objectively bad about being Undead, in the same way people think there is something objectively bad about being in pain.

Here an analogy might be useful. If I am battered by some thug on the street, with the result that I suffer a broken leg, I am in a bad state because I have a broken leg. It is objectively bad to have a broken leg. On the other hand, if the thug robs me, with the result that I am left with $6,984.00 in assets, I am only comparatively worse off than before. Having $6,984.00 in total assets is not in and of itself a bad state to be in. Many persons would be happy to be in that state.

A third worry about this line of reasoning is that it doesn't account for the fact that most people would prefer death to Undeath. Almost everyone, if given a choice between being a pig or being dead, would choose to be a pig. Similarly, this argument generates the result that it is better to be Undead than dead. It may well turn out to be the case that Undeath is preferable to death, but a satisfactory account of the *badness* of Undeath can't yield that result. An argument to the effect that Undeath as a state is preferable to death as a state is for all intents and purposes an argument for the view that Undeath is not bad, since death as a state is essentially neutral.

Evil, All Too Evil

One source of the badness of Undeath that we've not yet considered is the fact that the Undead are evil, or, at minimum, perform acts that we tend to view as evil. Vampires and zombies do unspeakable things: they eat human flesh, they drink blood, they destroy property, they maim, they kill, and they cavort with the dregs of hell. The fact that people don't like to imagine themselves doing such things serves to explain why Undeath is generally regarded as being worse than death. Most people would rather be dead than to become some monster that might potentially kill a loved one or burn down their own village. So we've satisfied one of our two criteria that a successful argument for the badness of Undeath must fulfill: we've explained why Undeath is generally regarded as being worse than death. We now must consider whether the fact that the Undead are evil (or do things that are generally regarded as evil) entails that Undeath is bad.

It doesn't follow from the fact that people view certain behaviors as evil that those behaviors are evil. Nor does it follow from the fact that people view certain states as bad that they are bad. As a matter of logic, premises in arguments that refer to people's attitudes don't by themselves lead to conclusions about what is objectively the case. For example, from the fact that many people at one time believed that the earth was at the center of the universe, it did not follow that the earth was in fact at the center of the universe. So the fact that people don't like to see themselves doing things they regard as evil doesn't mean that it is bad to be the sort of being that does those things.

Still, the brute fact that vampires and zombies behave in bad ways (regardless of how we view them) may account for the badness of being Undead. In other words, we need to consider the possibility that the objective badness of Undeath can be accounted for by the actions and nature of Undead beings. Recall that a state is considered to be objectively bad when it either contains some qualitative badness or it lacks some good thing which one would not normally lack. We've already dismissed the argument that being Undead involves being in a qualitatively bad state, so let's consider the possibility that being Undead involves lacking some good thing which one would not ordinarily lack.

Behaving in good ways is generally held by moral philosophers to be a good thing. Some philosophers value performing good acts because of the consequences they bring. Others value good acts because they believe that good acts have intrinsic value—they are valued purely for their own sake. So if being a vampire or a zombie involves lacking goodness in general or lacking the ability to perform good acts, then it seems that being a vampire or a zombie is a bad thing, in virtue of lacking something of value that one would not ordinarily lack.

Notice, however, that any number of creatures may be viewed as lacking goodness or the ability to perform good acts. Crickets, for example, are not able to do good deeds. Yet we don't consider it objectively bad to be a cricket (though for most people it is comparatively bad). The reason it is not objectively bad to be a cricket is because the ability to perform good deeds is not something that crickets ordinarily have. The important thing to note here is that one can't discuss things that are ordinarily experienced (or one can't discuss lacking things that are ordinarily experienced) without relativizing the discussion to a particular kind of thing. It's bad for human beings to lack vision, since it is something we ordinarily have, but it's not bad for bats to lack vision. Conversely, it's bad for bats to lack sonar, but not bad for humans to lack sonar. Thus lacking goodness or the ability to perform good acts would point to an objectively bad feature of being a vampire or a zombie if and only if being good or being able to perform good acts is a feature that vampires or zombies usually have. Of course vampires by nature are not good and are compelled to do evil things (it's part of their being cursed or damned), and zombies are hard-wired to be flesh-and brain-eating predators. One might object that humans are good and upon becoming Undead begin to lack these goods that they ordinarily have otherwise. This, however, only points to a com-

parative badness. Presumably the person who is committed to
the view that it is bad to be Undead would hold that even for
an inanimate object (such as a rock) that suddenly gets transformed into a vampire, there is still objective badness, in virtue
of the evil acts the vampire would perform. It would appear
then that we can't account for the badness of being a vampire
or zombie by appealing to the fact that they are evil or do things
that we generally consider to be evil.

Not to Put Too Fine a Point on It

Let's take stock of our discussion. We've been attempting to do
two things: explain why Undeath is generally regarded as a
worse state than death, and answer the question of why
Undeath is bad for the person who is Undead. We've succeeded
on one count: Undeath is generally regarded as a worse state
than death because of attitudes people have toward evil things.
People don't like to see themselves as potentially performing
evil acts or bringing misery to their loved ones and neighbors.
We've not, however, been able to satisfactorily answer the question as to why Undeath is bad for the person who is Undead.
The badness of Undeath couldn't be accounted for in terms of
the things that make death bad, it could not be accounted for
by focusing on the qualitative aspects of Undeath, nor could it
be accounted for by appealing to specific properties that
Undead beings possess (such as having an evil nature or being
compelled to perform bad acts). Thus we have no alternative
but to reject the claim that it is bad (in the objective sense) to
be Undead. This of course doesn't mean that one should run out
and join the legions of hell. Being Undead may well be bad in
comparison to being a human being. On the other hand, if one
finds oneself sleeping in a coffin, drinking blood, shape-shifting
into a bat or a wolf, or clawing one's way out of a grave in
hopes of dining on fresh brains tartar, one might as well try to
make the best of it. It could be worse, blah.[7]

---

[7] Thank to Nancy Balmert, Kasey Mohammad, and Rachel Robison for helpful comments
on earlier versions of this chapter.

2

Res Corporealis: Persons, Bodies, and Zombies

WILLIAM S. LARKIN

The highpoint of horror in Romero's classic *Night of the Living Dead* has to be when little Karen Cooper, newly Undead, proceeds to devour her father's arm and lay waste to her mother with a trowel. There is something uniquely disturbing about an innocent child turning into a brutal flesh-eating monster. Scenes like this unearth intuitions that bear significantly on the philosophical problem of personal identity. In particular, zombie movies provide a distinctive blend of terror and tragedy that helps reanimate the view that persons are most fundamentally corporeal objects.

Persons

The philosophical problem of personal identity is to determine what, most fundamentally, creatures like us are. We can say that creatures like us are essentially *persons*, but that just gives us the label and not the explanation we are looking for. The question becomes, "What exactly is a person?" Or better: "Under what conditions exactly does a person continue to exist?" Is a human body lying in a coma a person? Is a human body lying in a casket a person? It is tempting to respond to such questions with something like, "Well, it depends on what we mean by 'person.'" That's exactly right; and that's just what we are trying to figure out. We are trying to determine just what we mean when we say that something is a person. The point of philosophy is not to figure out what we *should* say about extraordinary cases *given* the various things we might mean by certain terms. The point is

15

rather to use what we are spontaneously *inclined* to say about extraordinary cases to figure out what we *do* mean even in perfectly ordinary cases by those terms. I want to consider the extraordinary case of the walking dead to figure out just what we mean by *person*.

René "I think therefore I am" Descartes is famous for ultimately holding the view that a person is fundamentally a *res cogitans*—a thinking thing, a certain kind of mind. But he tells us earlier that when he first applied himself to the "consideration of (his) being" what most naturally sprang up in his mind was the following:

> I considered myself as having a face, hands, arms, and all the system of members composed of bones and flesh as seen in a corpse which I designated by the name of body.[1]

On this alternative view a person is fundamentally a *res corporealis*—a bodily thing, a certain kind of material object. Here in Descartes we have the two competing views on personal identity that I want to consider.[2]

The view that a person is fundamentally a certain type of thinking thing takes a *psychological approach* to personal identity. This view claims that a particular person continues to exist so long as her thoughts, memories, character traits, and so forth continue to exist. Granted, one's mind changes from moment to moment; still, there is a clear sense of *psychological continuity* when a human being at some later stage has all the thoughts that it does precisely because some earlier stage had all the thoughts it did. On the psychological approach, psychological continuity is both necessary and sufficient for personal identity. Psychological continuity is *necessary* in the sense that if there were a permanent break in psychological continuity, then a per-

---

[1] René Descartes, in *The Philosophical Works of Descartes* Volume I (Cambridge: Cambridge University Press, 1970), p. 151.

[2] There are other views. Closely related to the psychological view considered here is the memory view of Locke and the dualist view advocated by Richard Swinburne. See Locke, *An Essay Concerning Human Understanding*, Book II, p. xxvii (Oxford: Oxford University Press, 1975). See also Shoemaker and Swinburne, *Personal Identity* (Oxford: Blackwell, 1984). Closely related to the bodily view discussed here is the biological view advocated by Eric Olson in *The Human Animal: Personal Identity Without Psychology* (Oxford: Oxford University Press, 1997).

son would cease to exist: A person could not survive, for example, in a permanent vegetative state in which she has irretrievably lost all higher brain function and all of the psychological contents and capacities that go with it. Psychological continuity is *sufficient* in the sense that if there were no break in psychological continuity, then a person would survive no matter what else might happen: a person could in principle survive, for example, in a nuts-and-bolts robot body with a supercomputer brain into which all of her particular psychological contents and dispositions were downloaded.

The view that a person is fundamentally a certain type of material object takes a *bodily approach* to personal identity. This view claims that a particular person continues to exist so long as some critical mass of her material composition does. Granted, one's body changes from moment to moment; still, there is a clear sense of *bodily continuity* when a human being at some later stage has all the physical traits that it does precisely because some earlier stage had all the traits it did. On the bodily approach, bodily continuity is both necessary and sufficient for personal identity. Bodily continuity is *necessary* in the sense that if there were a permanent break in bodily continuity, then a person would cease to exist: A person could not survive, on the bodily view, in a nuts-and-bolts robot body. Bodily continuity is *sufficient* in the sense that if there were no break in bodily continuity, then a person would survive no matter what else might happen: A person could survive, on the bodily view, in a permanent vegetative state. A person could even survive on the bodily view as a relatively intact corpse—the kind of corpse that might be able to get up and lumber around in search of living flesh.

Bodies

I want to argue for the bodily approach to personal identity over the psychological approach.[3] But before I try to disinter the intuitions that I think support the bodily view, I need to do some ground clearing. I think it is fair to say that the predominant

---

[3] Shameless self-promotion: For a different (more philosophically sophisticated, if not sophistical) defense of the bodily approach over both the psychological and the biological approach see William Larkin, "Persons, Animals and Bodies," *Southwest Philosophy Review*, Volume 20, Number 2

view among ordinary folk and philosophers alike is that some form of the psychological approach to personal identity is correct. In this section I want to weaken the intuitive appeal of that consensus position and motivate the appeal to zombie films that will occupy the rest of the chapter.

The main positive support for the psychological approach comes from the fairly widespread and strongly held intuition that a person could "switch bodies." The idea started when John Locke imagined a cobbler waking up in a prince's body, distinctly perceiving his royal surroundings but clearly remembering his humble past. In an updated version we can imagine a successful cerebral transplant, where a patient wakes up in a new healthy body with memories of her agonizing decision over whether to submit to this new fangled procedure or live out her few remaining days in a body dying of some debilitating disease. Concerning these cases, most people claim that a person will follow her memories, thoughts, and character into a "new" body. If psychological continuity is sufficient, as the psychological approach contends, then that is exactly what will happen. But if bodily continuity is necessary, as the bodily approach contends, then the person will stay with the "old" body while the other body would get a "new" psychology.

I don't think this body-switching intuition settles the issue in favor of the psychological view. First of all, it's a single case, and there might be something funny going on; like a deep-seated survival instinct clouding our metaphysical intuitions. Second, and more importantly I think, one can see through these cases rather easily. It is pretty easy to see what the psychological approach should say about the case. Thus we may be "finding" in these cases just the intuition that we want to find. In other words, philosophically contrived cases are apt to give us biased intuitive data. Instead of people genuinely reacting the way they would were the case real, they may simply be figuring out what the view they unreflectively hold ought to say about the case. It would be better if we could tap into our more natural and spontaneous intuitions, which are at least less likely to be biased by prior theoretical commitments.

This is where I think the value of good fiction comes in. Good fiction can take us off our theoretical guard and thereby allow us to gather better intuitive data. I will argue that good zombie fiction in particular can catch us off our metaphysical guard and thereby reveal some intuitions that weigh strongly in favor of the bodily approach to personal identity over the psychological approach.

One of the biggest problems for the bodily approach, and so one of the biggest considerations in favor of the psychological approach, is another fairly widespread intuition—that people do not continue to exist as corpses. The bodily approach says that bodily continuity is sufficient for personal identity. There is bodily continuity between me and my corpse. Therefore, on the bodily approach I am identical to my corpse. This is something a lot of people just cannot accept. On the psychological approach, I am not identical to my corpse, since that approach claims that psychological continuity is necessary for personal identity, and there is no psychological continuity between me and my corpse. Indeed, my corpse has no psychological properties at all. So it appears we have a pretty strong consideration in favor of the psychological approach.

My main goal in the remainder of this chapter is to defend the bodily approach by urging that, in spite of your initial denials, you really do think that you will survive as a corpse. I know it sounds odd to say that a person will survive as a corpse. But notice how it doesn't sound odd at all to say that a person will one day be dead—be a person who is dead. Of course, a person does not survive as a corpse in the sense that it *continues to live* as a corpse; but on the bodily approach a person does survive as a corpse in the sense that it *continues to exist* as a corpse. On the bodily approach, people can continue to exist without continuing to live. The intuition that people do not survive as corpses may be widespread, but I hope to show that it is not very deeply held. On the contrary, I think that deep down we believe that we will survive as corpses, and I think this comes out when we get sucked into a good zombie movie.

A good piece of fiction draws us in until we find ourselves subtly mirroring the thoughts, emotions, and even some of the actions of the most sympathetic characters. These reactions manifest our natural and spontaneous intuitions regarding the content of the fiction. Our reactions to a couple of the characteristic ploys of zombie movies in particular reveal our deep intuition that people do survive as corpses.

Zombies: The Terror

Zombie movies are distinctively scary. It is not a simple fear of death that a good zombie film exploits. It is not even the horror of being eaten that accounts for what scares us the most about the walking dead. It is rather our fear of being turned into one of them. In addition to our fear of dying and our fear of being eaten, there is our fear of becoming a zombie. That is what really gets to us and provides the distinctive thrill of Undead drama. It is frightening and grotesque when Tom and Judy get burned up when trying to put gas in the old pick-up in *Night of the Living Dead* and then zombies line up to feast on their charred flesh. But a richer chord of fear is struck by the idea, suggested by her catatonic state and awkward reaction to Helen Cooper lighting a match, that good girl Barbara might turn into good ghoul Barbara.

Our fear of being turned into a zombie is brought nearest the surface by the quintessential zombie movie scene in which one of the protagonists pleads with another to not let it happen to him or her. In *Dawn of the Dead*, Roger exhorts his buddy Peter:

> You'll take care of me won't you, Peter? I mean, you'll take care of me when I go. . . . I don't want to be walking around like *that*!

And in *Resident Evil*:

> **RAIN:** I never want to be one of those things, walking around without a soul.
> **ALICE:** You won't.
> **RAIN:** When the time comes you'll take care of it.

We identify with these characters and completely understand their preference for being shot in the head by a good friend over becoming one of the walking dead relentlessly driven to consume the warm flesh of living human beings. We, like them, would rather be simply dead than Undead. But if that's right, then we must think that we would *become* zombies—we wouldn't prefer death to *Undeath* if we didn't think it would be us "walking around like that."

The distinctive terror that grips us when we surrender to quality Undead fiction manifests our deep-seated intuition that we could become zombies. But if it is possible for a person to become a zombie, then a person must be able to survive death. A person could not become a walking corpse without first becoming a corpse. If persons cease to exist when they die, as the psychological approach to personal identity would have it, then it would not be *us* that rise from the dead with a taste for human flesh. But that is precisely what we fear; and so deep down we must believe that people can survive as corpses.

Zombies: The Tragedy

Zombie movies are distinctively tragic. It's not just the travesty of countless innocent deaths that a good zombie movie dramatizes. It's the tragedy of lost innocence that really gets the pathetic juices flowing—the fall from the mild and the mundane to the monstrous. It's disheartening to think how many people would, like Harry Cooper, be reduced to a paranoid, pusillanimous prick in the face of an encroaching horde of monsters. But it is truly harrowing to think of how many mothers and daughters there are, like Helen and Karen Cooper, swelling the rotting ranks of that monstrous brigade.

We are made aware of the tragic dimension of the Undead by another characteristic device of the genre—populating the zombie crowd with recognizable characters and costumes. The zombie crowd is not faceless. The faces may be scabby and decaying, but they are faces we recognize. People from earlier in the film reappear. Barbara's brother Johnny who taunts her playfully at the beginning of *Night* comes back as a zombie to deliver his sister up to his hungry cohorts. We see old ladies in their nightgowns and middle-aged men in their underwear. We see naked people, nurses, and peewee football players. Not too long ago these creatures were on their way to a supermarket or a softball game. Now they are monsters.

It would not be so much tragic as silly to see monsters dressed up like ordinary folk—a funny kind of reversal of Halloween revelry—if these flesh-eaters were not so recently our family and friends. So if zombies are properly pathetic, we must think that these creatures were once quite different from what they are now. That is, if zombies are proper objects of our pathos, we must think that these very same individuals were once something immeasurably better than what they are now. Tragedy requires a fall; but there can be no fall without continuity of person. If zombies are tragic figures, then we must think that it is the very same individuals who were once our neighbors that are now out to gnaw on our entrails.

The distinctive tragic element of Undead drama again reveals our deep-seated intuition that creatures like us could become zombies. But again, if it is possible for a person to become a zombie, then a person must be able to survive death. A person could not become Undead without first being dead. If persons cease to exist when they die, as the psychological approach to personal identity would have it, then it would not be our friends and neighbors that rise from the dead with a taste for human flesh. But that is precisely what we find so tragic about the Undead; and so deep down we must believe that people can survive as corpses.

"They're Just Dead Flesh"

I have urged that our natural and spontaneous reactions to some of the characteristic dramatic devices of zombie films reveal an intuition that persons can *become* zombies and that this intuition supports the bodily over the psychological approach to personal identity. I want now to consider a couple of objections.

First, it might be insisted that zombies are not identical to the people they once were, that those people are gone and have been replaced by the flesh-eating monsters that populate the zombie horde. It might be insisted that there is merely a superficial resemblance between the people who died and their walking corpses. This view is expressly voiced in both *Night of the Living Dead* and *Dawn of the Dead*. In *Night*, a newscaster is asking a supposed expert, Dr. Grimes, what information they have about the creatures that are going around killing and eating human beings. After Dr. Grimes notes that the time between death and "reactivation" is only a few minutes, the newscaster draws what is to his mind the troubling consequence that people will not have time to make any kind of funeral arrangements. Dr. Grimes retorts sharply:

> The bodies must be carried to the street and burned. They must be burned immediately. Soak them with gasoline and burn them. . . .

The bereaved will have to forego the dubious comforts that a funeral service will give. They're just dead flesh, and dangerous.

In the good doctor's mind, zombies are not people who are due any kind of respect; they are just so much "dead flesh." We get the same idea, expressed even more forcefully, by the scientist being interviewed on television in *Dawn* who exclaims,

> These creatures cannot be considered human. . . . We must not be lulled by the concept that these are our family members or friends; they are not.

Here is a clear rejection of the view that zombies are identical to the people they once were. Zombies cannot be considered human, and they cannot be considered as the same people they once were. Those people are gone, and for our own good we must not be taken in by the superficial resemblance between these monsters and the people whom we cared about.

I think these scenes, however, actually serve to draw our attention to and even reinforce our gut-level reaction that these zombies really are our family members and friends. For we intuitively think that the scientists have got it wrong here. These so-called experts are looking at the zombie phenomenon from a safe and clinical distance. They are not out there trying to board themselves up in an old farmhouse or clear out a shopping mall full of monsters. We do not sympathize with the scientists' point of view. We sympathize instead with Ben's hesitation in *Night* when he has to shoot Helen Cooper in the head and with his subsequent remorse. We sympathize too with his relish when he gets to shoot Harry Cooper in the head. It's pretty awful watching zombies gnaw on the burnt-up bits of Tom and Judy, but it's nothing compared to seeing Karen Cooper with a mouthful of her father's forearm. It's pretty frightening when Johnny gets overcome by the graveyard zombie, but it's nothing compared to when Barbara gets done in by her own brother. No matter what the cold logic of the removed scientists tells them, our tingly entrails tell us that it *matters* who these zombies are that are doing the killing and the eating of the people we identify with.

Zombies are dead flesh all right, but not *merely* so. Just because they are dead flesh doesn't mean they aren't also our family and friends.

"This Was an Important Place in Their Lives"

The second objection I want to consider concedes that zombies are people but argues that this does not favor the bodily approach to personal identity. This objection insists that there is psychological continuity between the living and the Undead. People survive as zombies on this view thanks to the preservation of psychology. In *Dawn*, when our heroes first arrive on the roof of the shopping mall and look down through the skylights at the zombies within, there is the following exchange:

> FRANCINE: What are they doing? Why do they come here?
> STEPHEN: Instinct, memory, what they used to do. This was an important place in their lives.

If we emphasize the idea that the zombies have a memory of how important the mall was in their lives, then Stephen seems to be claiming that there is psychological continuity between the living and the Undead.

I think this scene, however, actually serves to drive home the idea that there is no real continuity between the living and the Undead with respect to the kind of high-level psychological features that are distinctive of people. The emphasis in Stephen's line belongs on the idea that we are dealing with an *instinct* here. The sharp satirical edge of Stephen's comment about the zombies in the mall can only be appreciated if we understand that zombies are not psychologically continuous with living humans. The implication is that going to the mall even in living humans is nothing more than a matter of mindless animal instinct.

There is, no doubt, brain activity and some kind of psychology in zombies—they want to eat warm flesh, and they learn how to use rocks and table legs as tools. But it is not the psychology distinctive of people. Zombie psychology is more like that of a non-human animal that is pretty far down the phylogenetic scale. They are driven solely and relentlessly by a single appetitive desire. Moreover, there is really no continuity of psychology from the living to the Undead. Zombies don't remember their family and friends. Johnny shows no sign of recognizing Barbara before he drags her off to eat her. Zombies have to relearn some of the simplest skills or those they were most familiar with. Bub from *Day* and the gas station attendant in *Land* have to relearn what a gun is and how to use it; a softball player in *Land* has to relearn how to swing the aluminum bat that she has been carrying around with her through the whole movie.

What is important to zombies now is very different from what was important to them when they were alive—they probably hardly ever had a hankering for human flesh while they were alive—even though there may be some residual animal instincts compelling them in a purely mechanical way. Just because zombies have some kind of psychology doesn't mean that there is psychological continuity between them and the people they once were.

Dead People

Land of the Dead is the latest in George Romero's genre-defining series of zombie films, and on Romero's authority I am going to take it as the last word on the status of zombies. The distinctive devices to which I have drawn your attention are there in somewhat exaggerated form (an indication, I think, that the genre has reached a fairly late stage in its development). The movie opens with a humorous survey of zombies in their daily routine, including a trio of musicians playing in a gazebo bandstand, a gas station attendant who instinctively responds to the distinctive ding of the pneumatic bell, and a pair of teenagers out for a lover's stroll. A little later on a zombie-bitten protagonist takes the burden off his buddies by shooting himself in the head to avoid turning into a zombie.

When we first meet our hero, Riley, he tells a neophyte zombie hunter and the audience that zombies have started to adapt to their new situation and behave "just like us." The zombies end up organizing after a fashion and proceeding on something like a mission to take down the last bastion of power and privilege for the select few living at *Fiddler's Green*. Indeed, the zombies and some of the less-than-select living humans have this mission in common. At the end of the movie Riley is faced with a dilemma. A zombie horde has overtaken a crowd of humans clamoring to get out of the gated city and one of Riley's gang is wondering whether to shoot into the crowd. She is unsure what to do because there are "people out there," and it is clear that she is referring to the humans and means to exclude the zombies. Our hero decides she should not shoot into the crowd and replies with perhaps the best line of the film:

RILEY: Those people are all dead.

It's clear in contrast that Riley means to include both zombies and humans under the heading "people." So here the most sympathetic character in the most mature treatment by the undisputed master of the genre refers to zombies as people. And it feels right. We are relieved that Riley chooses not to fire into the crowd at the security fence or to pursue the Undead who are slowly escaping across a bridge out of the city in search of place to call their own. We are relieved because we too think those zombies are people.

We are attracted to zombie films by the distinctive terror and tragedy that the Undead evoke. Zombies are peculiarly scary because we think that we could be turned into one, and zombies are peculiarly tragic figures because we recognize the innocent people that these monsters once were. Our responses to the distinctive ploys of Undead drama reveal our intuition that zombies are people—our intuition that people who were once alive and relatively innocent could continue to exist as walking corpses.

This intuition that zombies are people too betrays our preference for the bodily over the psychological approach to personal identity. If zombies were once our friends and neighbors, then bodily continuity must be sufficient for personal identity and psychological continuity must not be necessary. If creatures like us could turn into zombies, then persons must be able to continue to exist so long as their bodies do. To the extent that we can be taken in by a good zombie film, we must think that a person continues to exist so long as some critical mass of her material properties does and that a person can survive without any distinctively human psychology. To the extent, therefore, that we can appreciate the distinctive terror and tragedy of the Undead genre, we must think that a person is most fundamentally not a *res cogitans* but rather a *res corporealis*.

3

"She's Not Your Mother Anymore, She's a Zombie!": Zombies, Value, and Personal Identity

HAMISH THOMPSON

The Value of a Zombie

Why do we have so few qualms about killing zombies? The Undead's aggressive anti-social behavior usually involves an insatiable lust to eat, kill, or transform us. This no doubt creates a justification for zombie decapitation on the grounds of self-defense. Another reason, retribution, hardly seems a relevant justification given their largely mindless state. Retribution as a justification for punishment presupposes some kind of moral agency that at a minimum requires some substantial notion of self that zombies appear to lack. In *White Zombie*,[1] some of the zombies are guilty of hideous crimes before their transformation. If zombies possess a minimal self and their zombified identity is continuous with their prior identity, and the zombie in the pre-zombie state is guilty of a heinous crime, we might think that we are still justified in punishing him or her on the grounds of retribution.[2] But what if the zombie before zombification was an innocent child, a girlfriend, a boyfriend, a fiancé, or your mother?

Another reason proposed for the limited moral worth of zombies might be their largely absent mentality, their altered personal identity, or some combination of both. Zombies clearly appear to have something going on "upstairs," but not much, and presumably what they have is very different from their prior

---

[1] Directed by Victor Halperin, 1932.
[2] Granted, this is a rare case.

state. Brain diseases such as Alzheimer's and disorders such as autism also raise questions about absent and altered personal identity. For example, at what point is the person no longer "at home"? Or at what point is a person no longer the same person I once knew? Zombies clearly bring to mind the ravages of brain damage and serious cognitive disorders. Good horror exploits our deepest fears and issues that we rarely like to bring to the surface. To understand these fears it is necessary to explore the metaphors for and analogies to our own general condition.

Another attempted justification for the moral devaluation of zombies, other than an absent mentality, is their altered personal identity. This altered identity perhaps releases us from prior obligations to the pre-transformed individual. If this identity is altered to such a degree after zombification, we might think that out of a certain respect for the prior identity of the individual we are obligated to terminate the zombie.

Three general justifications for zombie termination appear to be as follows: a) they are (or are very close to being) brain-dead; b) because of their radically altered life goals, what personality is left lacks the same personal identity as the original individual, releasing us from prior obligations; and c) after zombification they are usually homicidal cannibalistic killers.[3]

The Philosophical Challenge of Zombies

Each one of these justifications, however, poses a philosophical conundrum to our desire for absolute and sharp distinctions. If zombies are only partly brain-dead, how much is left and does this matter? Is what remains of the personality of zombies after zombification an altered personal identity? If we remove the homicidal tendencies by training the individuals, as in *Day of the Dead*,[4] or chaining the individuals up, as in *28 Days Later*[5] and *Shaun of the Dead*,[6] presumably the justifica-

---

[3] In *White Zombie*, zombies are not the cannibalistic killers we often take them to be today, but "dead" persons brought to life and controlled after application of a drug to fulfill a role as slaves on a sugar plantation on Haiti, murderous thugs, or a sex slave. This first zombie film was based on a non-fiction account of Haiti, *The Magic Island* by William Seabrook, 1929.

[4] Directed by George Romero, 1985.

[5] Directed by Danny Boyle, 2002.

[6] Directed by Edgar Wright, 2004.

tion for termination on the grounds of self-defense is removed. However, we are still left with questions as to how we should treat these individuals.

Should we use them in service industry jobs or as entertainment on game shows, as depicted in *Shaun of the Dead*? Do we have an obligation to terminate them out of a respect for their past identity? If your spouse is zombified, should you divorce him or her? Even if we grant the status of "dead" to the zombie, issues arise concerning our perceived obligations to the body alone.

Obligations to the body are instrumental to the Marine's absolute commitment to "leave no man behind" (meaning by "man" a dead body), even at the potential expense of other living persons. This apparent obligation is apparent in the massive investment humans have in rituals of burial and cremation. If one takes literally a hoped-for resurrection of the body, the initial mutilation causing zombiehood might be troubling, but the future mutilation required in "finishing off" the body often leaves little of the original. Nobody usually stays behind to bury a decapitated zombie.[7]

The sharpest moral challenge often arises when a character is faced with the realization of the altered state of a loved one and the choice of either terminating the loved one, who is thus transformed, or being transformed oneself. In *Invasion of the Body Snatchers*,[8] the girlfriend's personal identity is substituted when her psyche is replaced by an alien psyche in a physically identical body.[9] The father of the girl in *28 Days Later* gets "the disease" as an infected droplet of blood falls into his eye. In *Shaun of the Dead*, Shaun is confronted with the required termination of his mother, whose zombie transformation is hardly great given her somewhat mindless previous state.

Dead or Alive?

Zombies, often described as the "living dead," confront us directly with the question whether they are alive or dead. If we

---

[7] Except in *Dawn of the Dead*, 1978.

[8] Directed by Don Siegel, 1956; remake directed by Philip Kaufman, 1978.

[9] Clearly alien personality substitution is not the same as zombification, but it is nicely illustrative of a substituted personality that results in altered moral obligations.

can classify them as dead, any moral question about termination is largely resolved. Zombies, however, challenge this dichotomy. Zombies present us with beings who appear to be alive, but who lack the rich mental life that we associate with "normal" persons. Their decay and disintegration is rather more indicative of death than life, but on the other hand, their dogged animation and lumbering groaning is more indicative of life than death.

The flicker of awareness that appears to be present in these beings may or may not be sufficient for some semblance of rationality as a criterion for personhood. This limited awareness may or may not be sufficient to argue for a continuity of personal identity in the individual. We get a clear acknowledgment of zombie memory, and even a hint of revenge (and perhaps affection), when the trained zombie in *Day of the Dead* uses a gun to shoot the killer of his trainer. In *White Zombie*, we get the striking image of the zombified heroine playing piano despite her complete failure to recognize her new husband. In *Shaun of the Dead*, Shaun's best friend at the end is depicted as perhaps capable of playing video games.

Alternatively, we might describe zombies as more dead than alive. In years past, one proposed criterion for death was the absence of a soul. This sharp distinction between being ensouled or not, as separate from the distinction of being alive or dead, allows for the consistent imagined possibility of being alive but soulless.[10] According to this criterion an oak tree satisfies the "in between" condition of being alive but soulless. But souls are a little hard to measure and not just a little metaphysically dubious.

Current debate regarding a brain-based criterion for death tends to focus on what might be termed "total brain death" or, alternately and more controversially, "partial brain death." If we opt for a brain-based definition of death that considers death as only the loss of the higher cognitive functions while leaving the lower cognitive functions intact, then zombies might be legitimately classified as "dead."

But what higher cognitive functions are sufficient for claiming that an individual is alive? One possible requirement might

---

[10] We get this explicit analysis from the minister in *White Zombie*.

be a functioning cerebellum. This allows for consciousness, personality, memory, reason, enjoyment, and worry, as well as a variety of other higher-level cognitive capacities.[11] Lower brain functions such as those that allow for breathing and a heartbeat do not allow for such capacities. The absence of higher cognitive functions and the presence of only the lower would therefore result in a state classifiable as "death." Zombies appear to lack individual personalities and rich conscious lives. They do appear, on the whole, to possess "behavioral" memories, high levels of aggression, and a rather insatiable hunger. If this distinction between higher and lower cognitive capacities is sound, and zombies are categorically determined to lack the higher, we might legitimately classify zombies as "dead."

This loss of higher cognitive capacities in zombies is very loosely analogous to real cases of brain damage, in which involuntary motor actions such as spasms and blinking may create the terrible illusion of conscious awareness. A person in such a medical condition is sometimes described as being in a "permanent vegetative state," or more specifically, when automatic behaviors such as blinking occur, as "awake but unaware." In these cases there are no specific responses to varied stimuli, despite what individuals might desire to see in otherwise random spasms of behavior. Zombies, however, have fairly sophisticated responses to environmental stimuli. They can recognize non-zombified humans clearly as potential food. They also respond to lights, or a jukebox playing Queen's "Don't Stop Me Now," as in *Shaun of the Dead*.

Since we see motion and goal-directed behavior as indicative of "life," the behavior and rather zealous focus of zombies makes it hard just to automatically classify them as "dead." When Shaun and his friend witness a zombie in the backyard, they mistake her for being simply drunk. This over-simplistic classification of zombies as dead is also complicated by the rather miraculous recovery of the heroine in *White Zombie*, which suggests the possibility of reversal of the zombification process. The scientist in *Day of the Dead* hopes to find a way to effect such a reversal. However, just as zombie films pose a

---

[11] Robert Veatch, "The impending collapse of the whole-brain definition of death" in B. Steinbock, J. Arras, and A. London, eds., *Ethical Issues in Modern Medicine*, sixth edition (New York: McGraw Hill, 2003), p. 270.

problem with arriving at a clear criterion for death, they do not give us a clear criterion for personal identity.

Self as Fiction

In assuming zombies' possession of somewhat limited mentality, popular representations pose a problem for us in attributing to them anything like a coherent identity. One solution might be to reject the notion of a personal identity that a being either possesses absolutely or absolutely does not. Perhaps we could opt for a more fluid concept of self that admits of degrees. This strategy mirrors a tradition in philosophy of rejecting absolutist notions of self.[12] The Scottish enlightenment philosopher David Hume challenged such absolutist conceptions when he identified the self as essentially a "fiction" rather than an essence. What we describe as the self is in his account really a continuous series of perceptions and experiences that we bundle into a unity and describe as "me."

According to Hume, when our psychology ceases, we cease. To think otherwise is to go beyond "serious and unprejudiced reflection." Thus Hume concludes that mankind is "nothing but a bundle or collection of different perceptions, which succeed each other with an inconceivable rapidity, and are in a perpetual flux and movement. . . . The man is a kind of theatre, where several perceptions successively make their appearance; pass, re-pass, glide away, and mingle in an infinite variety of postures and situations." He goes on to conclude that there is no simple essence which constitutes our basic identity, however tempted we are to mistakenly imagine such a basic essence, or as he describes it, "simplicity."[13] Once an absolutist notion of self (and hence, a personal identity that is either possessed or not) is abandoned, this raises the intriguing possibility of degrees of psychological continuity.

Contemporary philosopher Derek Parfit takes up where Hume left off. Once all talk of souls and essences is abandoned in terms of the richer notion of degrees of psychological conti-

---

[12] This is also apparent in certain interpretations of Buddhist thinking.
[13] David Hume, *An Enquiry Concerning Human Understanding* (Chicago: Open Court, 1971), p. 259.

nuity, then we are in a position to evaluate zombies more carefully. As Parfit remarks, "if there will be one future person who will have enough of my brain to be psychologically continuous with me, that person would be me."[14] If zombies have some form of psychological continuity, then we have an idea of personal identity that will presumably give zombies a basic potential for psychological continuity which unites their present identity to a previous one. According to Parfit, bodily continuity alone is not sufficient for personal identity—psychology matters. Furthermore, valuing a human in a permanent unconscious state, yet alive, ignores the importance of psychological presence and degrees of continuity.[15]

Curiously, in *Invasion of the Body Snatchers*, all the memories of the original persons remain intact in the physically duplicated body. This demonstrates some considerable psychological continuity. In the duplicate body, however, the original person's life goals are replaced with a new mission and a personality apparently devoid of emotion. The prior values and intentions of the original person are entirely replaced in the duplicate with a new objective—to replace all the remaining original humans with "pod people." This raises the analogous possibility that in addition to acquiring an insatiable hunger for human flesh, zombies' life goals change. Perhaps this alteration in life goals is sufficient to warrant the claim that the individual after zombification is no longer the same person, despite their limited mental continuity.

"Not Your Mother!"

Of what does remain of the zombies' mental life, does their personal identity remain constant? We might place a higher demand on psychological continuity and memory for personal identity that goes beyond simple non-autonomous abilities such as how to play the piano, play a video game, or shoot a gun. But even if we grant a limited psychological continuity between the pre-zombified person and the zombie, we might also require a cer-

---

[14] 'The Unimportance of Identity', in N. Rauhut and R. Smith, eds., *Reading on the Ultimate Questions* (London: Penguin, 2005), p. 237.
[15] *Ibid.*, pp. 227–28.

tain continuity of life goals in order to be able to claim strict continuity of personal identity.

Invasion of the Body Snatchers demonstrates an example of a clear substitution of personality in individuals. As humans sleep, they are duplicated in pods, but in such a way that despite considerable psychological continuity between the original person and the duplicate person, there is a radical alteration of personality. This altered personality and adoption of new life goals makes it easier for us to judge that the replaced individual is indeed a new individual.

This is closer to the thought experiment posed by John Locke, another enlightenment philosopher. In this experiment he proposes the possibility that the soul of a prince that carries with it the conscious memories of its past life enters and informs the body of a cobbler. The soul of the cobbler departs as soon as the soul of the prince enters. Locke argues that it is obvious the cobbler would now be the same person as the prince, despite having the cobbler's body, and that he would now be accountable only for the actions of the prince.[16] This alteration would presumably absolve us of all prior obligations to the cobbler. So can we argue that the zombies' personality has changed to such a degree that we could treat them as if their personality has been substituted for another personality?

Aspects of zombies' personalities clearly do change. The hungry animalistic snarl of Shaun's mother in *Shaun of the Dead* at the point of transformation appears to indicate an altered personality complete with different life goals. One reason for the moral devaluation of zombies partly arises from the lack of mentality in the new identity after zombie transformation. However, if the zombie is a loved one or friend, then the change in personal identity is crucial, entailing the release of the old obligations created by the prior interpersonal relationship.

Because of the altered personal identity of individuals who undergo radical transformation, the argument runs, obligations to the original individual become moot. Apparent changes in identity allow for Shaun's killing of his flatmate and mother in *Shaun of the Dead*, to be at least justifiable, if not easy, given

---

[16] John Locke, 'On Identity and Diversity' in L. Bowie, M. Michaels, and R. Solomon, eds., *Twenty Questions*, fourth edition (Belmont: Wadsworth, 2000), p. 347.

the release from prior obligations. But still, our sympathy with Shaun's trauma at the killing of his zombified mother is caused by a doubt we might legitimately have about these distinctions. For example, a friend of mine in college professed to be "born again." His behavior certainly changed in combination with distinct attitudes and life goals.[17] If I made a promise or borrowed money from him before he was "born again," perhaps afterwards I no longer have an obligation to keep my promise or repay my debts to him despite his bodily continuity. This would make as much sense, I might argue, as repaying a debt to Robert after borrowing the money from Jane: I obviously have no obligation to repay the debt to Robert, and therefore, I have no obligation to repay my debts to my "born again" friend.

Parfit's account of personal identity in terms of psychological continuity explicitly admits of degree, and this raises serious questions as to the continuity of self as well as the constancy of personality in the zombified individual. This is particularly hard for Shaun, when confronted by his zombified mother, because of her somewhat zombie-like character prior to zombification.

Zombies and Us

Finally, there is the question of "normal" persons' similarity to zombies. Once sharp distinctions between "dead" and "alive," "self" and "non-self," are rejected, and if these concepts are admitted in terms of degree, what then are we? For the "research and development" in writing this chapter, I decided to undergo some video-gaming experiences. After getting hooked, to my horror, it was six in the morning, and I had lectures to prepare the next day. I was in a state of partial zombiehood, with continuous responsive behavior to a visual stimulus, but a state of self-awareness that could hardly be described as present. The portrayal in *Shaun of the Dead* of the line of checkout assistants who mindlessly (if rhythmically) "beep" the purchases of customers, or of Shaun's best friend as he whiles away the hours

---

[17] In the 1978 version of *Invasion of the Body Snatchers,* the psychiatrist Dr. Kibner, played by Leonard Nimoy, makes a direct reference to the "born again" phenomenon when after transformation he tries to convince Dr. Bennett that transformation is for the best. He argues that after transformation Bennett will be "born again into an untroubled world free of anxiety, fear, and hate."

paying video games followed by a rapidly induced drunken stupor at the local pub, raises the terrifying possibility of our own general normal condition of zombiehood.

What distinguishes us from zombies, however, is our potential for brief intermittent actualizations of imaginative goal-directed action. Zombies appear to lack this capacity. One such actualization of self is presented in *Shaun of the Dead* when Shaun and his best friend are finally popped out of their humdrum existence by the full realization of the violent circumstances of their environment. For the first time in the film they make a conscious decision and plan for their future. This is depicted in the film by a break in the continuous narrative and the portrayal of three possible futures imagined by Shaun and his friend: first, go to Shaun's mother's house to get his mother, kill his zombified stepfather, pick up his ex-girlfriend, go over to her place, and have a cup of tea; second, go to Shaun's mother's house to get his mother, kill his zombified stepfather, pick up his ex-girlfriend, return to Shaun's house, and have a cup of tea; third, go to Shaun's mother's house to get his mother, kill his zombified stepfather, pick up his ex-girlfriend, go to the pub and have a pint, and wait for the whole thing to blow over. As Shaun's girlfriend says at the end of the film: it is not so much what Shaun eventually chooses, but the fact that he makes a decision—and presumably actualizes his autonomous self—that matters.

Zombie films challenge the dichotomies that we often take for granted. Just as these films challenge the distinction between being dead or alive, they challenge overly simplistic conceptions of the "soul." A more reflective analysis of zombies should perhaps lead us to reject the notion that zombies are simply soulless or dead. Presumably our consciences are partially salved as we decapitate or kill them due to the threat they pose to our own survival. A more subtle justification for zombie termination might be offered when we consider their absent or limited "animalistic" mentality in an attempt to classify them as more dead than alive. But they clearly fall above the criterion of death when we consider them in contrast to severely brain-damaged individuals. Zombies can clearly respond to basic environmental stimulation albeit in a somewhat anti-social and ponderous manner.

Perhaps most subtle of all is an attempt to justify their termination on the grounds that they have an altered personal identity given a radical change in life goals and aims. This absolves us of responsibilities we might have to the prior individual. It also opens up the possibility that we might be justified in terminating the zombie out of a respect for the prior identity that is no longer present after transformation. However, none of these justifications are entirely satisfactory, given open questions such as how much of a personality change is required for there to be the categorical claim that a zombie is no longer the "same person." Perhaps we ought to respect the "new person," despite the hostility issues. I am not really advocating the implementation of PETZ, a society for the Protection and Ethical Treatment of Zombies. But perhaps a more complex analysis of the relation between personal identity, mentality and value should at least give us pause for concern the next time we bash out the brains of a zombie with a cricket bat.[18]

---

[19] I would like to thank Walter Ott, who in discussion posed some of the philosophical questions raised by zombies, value, and personal identity.

4
Dead Serious: Evil and the Ontology of the Undead

MANUEL VARGAS

I don't know whether Undead beings exist. I also think it is an open question whether anyone is evil in, say, the way bad guys are depicted in supernatural horror films and serial killer movies. I do think it's nevertheless puzzling that the Undead are frequently portrayed as evil in that way. I'm inclined to think that *if* we were to stumble across any Undead they would be *less* likely to be evil than any random live person we stumble across. Consider this a call for some Undead understanding.

Some Puzzles about Undeath

Common-sense conceptions of the Undead aren't perfect, but they are a good place to start. Without a good supply of Undead to study, it simply isn't possible to proceed by studying them as scientists might. I'll therefore begin with our ideas or concepts of the Undead.

Some philosophers (the editors of this book, actually) have proposed this account of what we mean by *Undead*: it refers to "that class of beings who at some point were living creatures, have died, and have come back such that they are not presently 'at rest.'" This definition seems like a good place to start. It is a perfectly reasonably construal of how we tend to think about the Undead, to the extent that we do, and it is consistent with how the Undead are portrayed in literature, movies, television, video games, and other aspects of popular culture.

On the account we've started with, it is a requirement that there be some death involved prior to Undeath. Something

Undead can't have stayed alive. An interesting thing about these elements of our working definition is that we don't have to have experimented on the Undead to know these things. We just have to have an adequate grasp of the concept of "Undead" to recognize that anything that is going to count as Undead has to have died (and thus lived), in at least some recognizable sense of having died. Because they are grounded in our concepts, let's call these truths about the Undead *conceptual truths*.

Conceptual Truths about the Undead

There can be conceptual truths about things that do not exist. There can be conceptual truths about unicorns, even though unicorns surely do not exist (unlike the Undead, perhaps). One such conceptual truth might be that under normal conditions an adult unicorn has a horn. This truth doesn't require that unicorns exist in any substantial sense. The same goes for any truths about the Undead.

All I mean by the notion of a conceptual truth about the Undead is the idea that from where we currently stand, there are some things that would have to be true of an entity for us to treat it as even a candidate for being Undead, at least right here and right now. Our experiences might give us reason to change our concepts, and thus the conceptual truths about something, but nothing in what follows turns on these sorts of details.

This definition does rule out some things that we might be tempted to think of as Undead. There is a category of creatures called "philosophical zombies." These are beings who, apart from lacking consciousness, are like normal human beings in their outward appearance. Although the name might distract, I believe that we should hold that philosophical zombies are no more Undead than is the rock musician and horror movie director Rob Zombie.[1]

Most interesting truths aren't conceptual. Non-conceptual truths require that we learn something about the way the world is put together. Our common-sense concept of a twenty-first birthday party may require that there be someone (or some-

---

[1] For a groundbreaking piece of zombie ontology, and further reasons to think that philosophical zombies simply are not zombies in the Undead sense of the word, see David Chalmers's classification of zombies at http://consc.net/zombies.html.

thing) for whom the party is intended (a conceptual truth), but this does not settle when and where a particular party is held, nor whether twenty-first birthday parties are generally good or bad. Concepts don't settle these things by themselves. Similarly, that there are conceptual truths about the Undead does not mean that all truths about the Undead are purely conceptual. We may discover that the Undead are somewhat different from what we expected, just as we might learn that particular parties are better or worse than we expected.

Sometimes we find that a concept is just not decisive on some issue. Consider the idea that the Undead are not "at rest." Presumably this means that the Undead are not straightforwardly dead. But are they alive? Are they some other thing? I suspect that we will not find agreement in common sense thinking on this issue.

When common sense is unsettled about something, we have to recognize that any attempt to "clean up" or unify our thinking about some concept will require changing how at least some (and maybe even all) of us think about this issue. In the case of the Undead, this might mean that any attempt to decide whether the Undead are alive, dead, or something else entirely will require departures from the way some or all of us tend to think about these things. These departures might be motivated by things we learn from studying Undead specimens, were we to find any. And, these departures might be motivated by reflecting on accounts we have of life. If, for example, some of the things we thought about the Undead relied on erroneous understandings of what life means, then we should expect that a suitably informed understanding of life might change how we think about the Undead.

For now, it is enough that we acknowledge that (1) there are some conceptual truths about the Undead, (2) these conceptual truths provide partial characterizations of the nature of the Undead that require further supplementation, and (3) what supplementation is provided may change the way we think about the Undead.

Kinds of Undead

I now want to turn to one way of supplementing the way we think about the Undead. It's helpful to think about two different kinds of things, *nominal kinds* and *natural kinds*. What makes something a nominal kind is that it is what it is in virtue of our having defined it that way. "The stuff on my desk" is a nominal kind, in that I can think of or treat it as a kind, but the sense in which it is a kind of thing is very loose and largely (perhaps entirely) dependent on my thinking or stipulating that it is a kind. On the other end of the spectrum are natural kinds, things like water and electrons, which are (let us suppose), roughly, real, non-artificial, non-socially constructed kinds of things. In between, there are presumably lots of kinds of kinds, such as *social kinds* (ethnicity, and maybe race and gender) and *artifactual kinds* (computers, toasters, and chairs), and so on.

I believe that the Undead do not make up a natural kind (or an unnatural kind, for that matter). Instead, the term *Undead* refers to something closer to a nominal kind, a motley crew of different things whose unity is more a function of how we happen to have constructed the category and less a function of any unity in the universe's own organization. For example, apart from being both thought of as "Undead," there seems to be little that connects zombies and vampires. One lacks higher mental capacities and the other has them. One requires a diet of brains and the other a diet of blood. One has a body that is rotting and the other has a body that is capable of repairing itself from a wide range of injuries. Indeed, whether an Undead creature is identical to the creature associated with the body prior to death seems to vary. Vampires seem to be their old selves (albeit with a case of vampirism). Zombies, while sporting the rotting bodies of former people, do not themselves seem to be the persons who once were in those bodies. It's not even clear whether a body has to remain even mostly intact in order to count as Undead. At least in principle, there doesn't seem to be any reason to rule out the possibility of composite Undead, something constructed out of disparate parts, each of which was attached to a different body, each of which died. Perhaps the Frankenstein monster is an instance of an artificially created composite Undead.

If I am right, the Undead do not make up a single natural kind. To put the point somewhat technically (bear with me for two sentences), the Undead make up something like a nominal kind, where various members of that nominal kind (vampires, zombies, composite Undead, and so on) may themselves be further nominal kinds or in some cases natural kinds. What determines the limits of the overarching nominal kind (the borders demarcating Undead and not Undead) is largely fixed by what conceptual truths there are about the Undead, and any constraints imposed by the universe on the reality of the Undead. In other words, there are lots of ways to be Undead, and some of those ways may be more and less a product of our way of thinking about things.

I now want to shift from discussing what we might exaggeratedly call "purely conceptual" issues about the Undead to ways in which some otherwise perfectly boring facts about the world should shape our understanding of the Undead. In particular, I believe we can learn something about the Undead by canvassing some of the possibilities of how Undead creatures might come to be.

First, we must acknowledge Undead of supernatural origin. This would include any Undead brought about by the work of magic. A zombie created by the spell of a sorcerer would be an instance of something Undead of supernatural origin, as would be one created by the will of a demon. Prior to the last part of the twentieth century, this may have been the predominant way of thinking about the origins of the Undead. You might be tempted to think that *all* instances of the Undead must have supernatural origins (perhaps you think this is a conceptual truth). But this does not seem plausible. Indeed, the trajectory of popular culture has increasingly been to emphasize the origin of the Undead in viruses or biological weapons programs initiated by entirely non-magical agents (see, for example, Max Brooks's excellent book *The Zombie Survival Guide*, and movies such as *28 Days Later*, *Resident Evil* video games and movies, *Blade* comic books and movies, and so on.). Although we might discover that the Undead are entirely of supernatural origin, this is a contingent empirical fact, something we would have to learn from the field and not from the philosopher's armchair.

A second important class of Undead origin is *artificial*. These would be Undead who were created by agents (whether human, divine, demonic, or other) by entirely non-magical means. The bioweapons program gone awry in *Resident Evil* or the accidentally released virus in *28 Days Later* would be an instance of the creation of Undead by artificial origin.[2]

The third possibility would be Undead whose creation is by entirely natural forces, devoid of the intervention of agents. Some accounts of vampirism seem to have this structure, treating it as a virus that developed by mutation on its own, as opposed to, say, the intervention of a lab of genetic engineers or the infernal actions of the devil.

Once you realize that the Undead might be of natural origin, you might also wonder whether we have already encountered some Undead and just not recognized them as such. Consider that there are a range of mysterious, "quasi-living" entities that we do not yet understand well. These include viruses and the even less well known viroids. It's unclear whether these entities count as living. At least for some of them, it is possible to introduce conditions that stop all quasi-living functioning but then to change those conditions so that their functioning is restored. If we come to count viruses and viroids as living, then those capable of ceasing and recovering their quasi-living functioning might be candidates for the Undead. And, given what we know, these might well make up the largest chunk of the Undead population. Moving up several levels of biological complexity, there are a range of plant and animal entities whose biological functions can be brought to a complete halt and then restored or "restarted." It is natural to think of many of these things as living throughout the process—seeds are commonly taken to be alive, even when frozen or put in some context where all metabolic activity ceases—but this raises interesting questions about the extent to which being alive is not merely a feature of an entity (the seed) but instead an entity and a context together. Maybe whether you are alive or dead depends on facts about more

---

[2] As I was writing this essay, news reports about re-animated dogs ("Zombie dogs!" screamed a few headlines) were surfacing, in light of work done at Safar Center for Resuscitation Research in Pittsburgh. The researchers were horrified that their work on resuscitation was being represented in this way. I wonder if part of the problem is that the researchers have prejudicial views about Undead, of the sort this essay is meant to dispel. The existence of these dogs and the headlines they provoked lend credence to the idea of there being Undead by artificial means. For a useful summary of the media flurry about it, see Jennifer Bails, *Pittsburgh Tribune-Review* (18th July, 2005), available at: http://pittsburghlive.com/x/tribune-review/trib/regional/s_348517.html.

than you, but also facts about the environment you find yourself in.

Working out all the possibilities of a context-sensitive account of life is too big a project for this essay, but it does suggest a few possibilities for our reflections on the Undead. If we acknowledge that contextual features play a role in determining what counts as living, we would have to say a great deal more about what those features are if we are not to count the Undead as living. In turn, this would open up the possibility that some of the living are Undead. Consider that some people (including baseball player Ted Williams) have been cryogenically frozen soon after their death, in hopes that at some later date they might be revived and restored to life. Should we think of this as a case of someone becoming Undead? What about someone who "dies" in the emergency room but is then revived? Puzzling cases abound for supernatural forms of the Undead as well. Was Lazarus of biblical fame Undead? How about the resurrected Jesus? How about everyone whose body is resurrected on Judgment Day? Resurrection somehow seems different from becoming Undead, but maybe this judgment is a result of our piecemeal understanding of both of these categories.

A useful way to sort out some of these complexities is to suppose that there is a multi-axis continuum of phenomena with poles that include alive, dead, and not-ever-having-been-alive-at-all (NEHBAA). Different kinds of beings, Undead or otherwise, will occupy different places along this multi-axis continuum. That is, lots of everyday stuff will cluster in a range of spaces near one end or another of the alive, dead, and NEHBAA poles (see the diagram below). Your current pet is hopefully alive, but depending on its health it might be more or less close to the dead pole. Your great-great-great grandfather is probably at or very close to the dead pole and remote from the alive pole. Viruses and other unusual creatures rest somewhere between alive and the NEHBAA pole.

If we think about things in this way, it becomes natural to think of Undeath as including a wide range of states that fall in between all of these poles. Vampires may be alive enough to be counted as alive. Zombies might fall on the other side of a vague line demarcating life and death. Composite forms of the Undead (think Frankenstein's monster) might turn out never to have been alive as a unit (although many and maybe even all parts will have been parts of different entities that were themselves alive), and thus they would be somewhere approaching the NEHBAA pole. Depending on their construction, composite Undead might also come in various degrees of livingness. In sum, the class of Undead creatures is likely to occupy a large and diverse state space, with different kinds of Undead clustering in different areas in that state space. There's more diversity among the Undead than the usual catalog of vampires, zombies, and so on might lead you to believe.

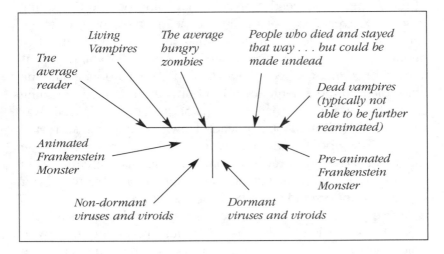

A Touch of Evil

People use the word *evil* in a lot of different ways. The sense of evil I'm interested in is perhaps most familiar to us from fictional representations, reserved for a kind of person who has a disregard for morality and a special desire to see others injured. Hannibal Lecter may be the clearest example. Sauron and Iago might also be cases, depending on your interpretations of them. Serial killers, or at least our representations of them (think of John Gacy or Jeffrey Dahmer), tend to fit the bill. This sort of evil (although maybe there are varieties of evil here, too) seems to be recognizably different from other things we sometimes describe as evil.

I want to acknowledge up front that there are other senses of the term *evil*, senses I am not interested in for present purposes. For example, philosophers and theologians sometimes use *evil* as a trumped up way of meaning "anything bad from a moral standpoint," as in when they discuss "The Problem of Evil" (roughly, how could an all-good, all-knowing, all-powerful God allow bad things to exist?). However, this usage is a very large departure from how we ordinarily talk about evil, to the extent that we do. If you sneak a cookie from a cookie jar, you might have done something morally bad, but it is a stretch to call what you did evil in the sense in which we think of movie serial killers as evil. The sense of evil I am interested in is something closer to how a wide range of people—religious believers and atheists alike—might describe an extraordinarily malicious or cruel individual.

Let us call the more restricted sense of evil with which I am concerned *the malevolent sense of evil*. What makes something evil in this sense is having motives to harm others, to damage the welfare or well-being of others, and acting on these motives. Agents are evil to greater and lesser degrees depending on the extent to which they have and act on these motives. An agent who only acted on evil motives would be pure evil. An agent who almost never acted on these motives might be said to be hardly evil at all.

This characterization of evil requires some refinement. Sauron wouldn't turn out to be evil in the malevolent sense if the reason he aimed to conquer Middle Earth was to secure equality and equal dignity for all races. Although it might be morally wrong to kill innocent humans, hobbits, dwarves, and elves, and generally misguided to try to secure political and social equality for orcs and trolls, it wouldn't be profoundly, truly, or genuinely evil in the malevolent sense of the term.

In the jargon of philosophers, the motive has to be non-instrumentally held. Non-instrumental motives are motives that cannot be explained by appeal to other beliefs or desires that I have. I just have them. Contrast this with an instrumental motive: my desire to arm myself with holy water and my belief that there is holy water to be gotten at the local church can generate in me an instrumental motive to get out of the chair, to get to church, and to secure holy water from, say, the baptismal fount at the church. Non-instrumental motives don't depend in that way on other desires and beliefs I have. My desire to be happy is a good candidate for a non-instrumental desire: I don't want to be happy because I think it is going to satisfy some other set of beliefs or desires; I simply want to be happy.

Something that is evil in the malevolent sense has to have a non-instrumental desire to damage the welfare of others. There may be other things required as well. Perhaps a creature incapable of consciousness cannot be evil in the relevant sense. Still, I will leave aside other conditions that may be required but which seem less distinctive of evil in this sense.

Again, I do not intend to deny that there are other, less demanding senses of evil. We might also learn that there are surprisingly few instances of malevolent evil in the world. Even if we were to discover this, however, it would not mean that there are not other senses of evil. It would simply mean that what evil there is is rarely, if ever, malevolent.

Evil and the Undead

Despite its potentially small range of actual cases, malevolent evil is a sense and perhaps the dominant sense of evil that we associate with the demonic and the Undead. What makes the vampires, zombies, and ghosts of fiction malevolently evil is that they are apparently motivated by non-instrumental desires to do us ill. At least part of what makes the Undead of horror movies so horrific is not merely that they wish to kill us—it has to do with *why* they wish to kill us. They do not wish to kill us for some further, recognizable cause we can imagine ourselves sharing but do not happen to share. Rather, it is that they have some basic desire to harm us and that's it.

We might find that the Undead are somewhat different from what we imagine them to be. In particular, we might learn that the Undead, despite what we tend to think, actually lack the motives required for evil in the malevolent sense. This might well be difficult to determine. There are, however, several reasons why we should, on reflection, be skeptical that the Undead will typically turn out to be evil.

First, if it turns out that there are naturally occurring Undead, it seems plausible that a good many of them will not be sophisticated enough to have desires at all, much less desires of the relevant sort. If zombies don't really have motives (maybe their brains have decayed too much for them to really have motives, even if they preserve certain functions that we might have once called "instinctual"), then they cannot, strictly speaking, be malevolently evil. They would be more like a deadly virus—the kind of thing we have reason to avoid and to try to control, but nothing that is really evil. Moreover, if it turns out that there is a range of naturally occurring Undead from viroids up through insects (assuming these lack motives), then as a matter of numerical considerations it may well work out that most Undead simply lack the mental machinery to count as evil.

Second, even if many archetypal forms of the Undead have motives, it is not obvious that they have the special kind of motive required for evil. Suppose zombies are motivated to, say, eat fresh brains. Would these motives count as non-instrumental desires to see the welfare of others harmed? Nope. To the extent that zombies do have desires to eat fresh brains, those motivations likely depend on a more basic desire to get food, and the belief that fresh brains constitute food. That would make an instrumental and not an evil-constituting motive. Even if the desire to eat fresh brains is non-instrumental, it does not look as if it's really a desire to harm the welfare of others. If there were a way to get fresh brains without harming the welfare of anyone, I suspect zombies would be perfectly satisfied. Contrast this to Hannibal Lecter—presumably he would reject harm-free brains as a mediocre substitute, at best. At any rate, there is no evidence to suggest that harm-free brains would be rejected by zombies. In the absence of such evidence, we should conclude that zombies lack the desire that marks out malevolent evil. In short, zombies are not evil—they are just misunderstood.

Even if we find that a majority of the Undead have the relevant mental machinery to be capable of non-instrumental desires to harm others, there does not seem to be any reason why they would have those motives in greater frequencies than you or I tend to have them. If they are Undead of a sort that suffers from advanced physical decay, this seems to diminish the chance that they could have the relevant sorts of motives (or motives at all). On the other hand, if they don't suffer from advanced physical decay, it does not seem likely that they will have motivations significantly different from the ones we currently have. And, as far as I can tell, most people don't seem to be malevolently evil.

Consider the case of vampires. A vampire simply seems to be the person who was in the body prior to becoming a vampire. There is no obvious reason why having become a vampire would suddenly add non-instrumental motives to harm others. To the extent that vampirism introduces new desires, they don't (necessarily) seem to be of the problematic sort. That is, on becoming a vampire you might want to suck blood and so on, but it is difficult to see why this should make you want to do bad things to other people when you did not want to do them before. We should not simply assume that vampirism brings with it non-instrumental desires to harm others.

What makes vampires a complicated case, however, is the often-held idea that they are damned or in some sense "fallen." Perhaps damnation does the work of introducing the relevant non-instrumental desires, making vampires necessarily evil in a way that other forms of the Undead might not be. It is an interesting question whether damnation could/would/should have the effect of introducing desires that give rise to malevolent evil, and I am uncertain about the matter. The vampire as *necessarily* evil in light of damnation or something like it has received reinforcement in comparatively recent popular culture from at least the early seasons of the *Buffy the Vampire Slayer* television show. Despite its influence, the view of vampirism as necessarily evil (which the show seems to abandon in later seasons, anyway) does swim against an enormous tide of recent popular culture that holds that vampires are not necessarily evil in the malevolent sense, and for that matter, not necessarily damned. See, for example, a good number of Anne Rice's vampire novels, Tanya Huff's *Blood* series, Charlaine Harris's *Southern Vampire Mysteries*, Laurel Hamilton's *Anita Blake* series, and the recent vampire-mystery novels by Kim Harrison. Indeed, I am told that in at least one genre, the contemporary romance novel, a vampire is *never* evil. In many contemporary comic books vampires are just people with a condition where they live a long time and need to suck blood (the vampire Cassidy in *Preacher* fits this mold). Something similar can be said for vampires in popular culture outside of fiction, ranging from movies (think *Underworld*) to video games (for example, *Morrowind: The Elder Scrolls 3*). So, even if something about vampires brings with it malevolent impulses, it is important to recognize that this problem is apparently rooted primarily in supernatural vampires, and to acknowledge that these impulses might be overcome by other motives or values.

The preceding reflections suggest that vampires never really fail to leave behind a basic fact of the human predicament: We've all had bad motives, but with the right upbringing, friends, or environment, most of us tend to do a good job keeping it under control. If so, then even if it turns out that vampires necessarily have malicious motives, it does not follow that they are evil to any great degree, or that they are even evil at all. After all, a vampire might never come to act on any of his or her non-instrumental motives to harm others.

I suspect that the reason why vampires have been associated with irredeemable, malevolent evil is a function of two things. First, there is the need for blood. Wanting to suck someone's blood can seem pretty creepy, and we may be tempted to think that *creepy* equals *evil*. But creepy isn't necessarily evil. And, if popular representations of vampires are any indication, when a vampire finds a way to circumvent the need for blood we don't tend to think of the vampire as straightforwardly evil. So maybe the creepiness of needing blood makes it easier to interpret the average vampire as having non-instrumental desires to harm us. After all, if they wished us well, surely they wouldn't want to suck our blood? (For what it's worth, I think that in reasoning this way we are reasoning badly. But I also think bad reasoning is widespread. However, I *also* think that there are oftentimes good reasons for reasoning badly.)

There is also a second reason, connected to the first, which provides some culturally influential impetus to the thought that at least vampires are typically evil. The original vampire of fiction seemed to act out motives that are easiest to make sense of as non-instrumental desires to harm others. And, at least in some chronicles, the figure Dracula was modeled after—"Vlad the Impaler"—committed atrocities on a scale that we seem to find easiest to explain by appeal to motives of the malevolently evil sort. Ascribing non-instrumental desires to harm others to someone gives us a way of making sense of what otherwise tends to seem radically senseless. By appealing to non-instrumental motives we can "explain" certain horrific acts: he is someone who wishes us ill *for no good reason—he simply wants us to hurt.*

Resting in Peace

So what have we learned about the Undead?

- First, if there are Undead, the largest number of Undead are likely to be of natural origin. Comparatively simple entities (biologically speaking) such as viruses, virons, or even more complex things like seeds and insects, likely make up the largest chunk of the Undead, much as they do among the not-yet-having-died living.

- Second, there is no reason to think that among the most-likely-to-exist forms of the Undead (the comparatively biologically simple), many will have the capacities required to be evil in any genuine or profound sense.

- Third, even among more sophisticated forms of the Undead, many of the Undead of classical lore seem to lack the capacities required to be evil.

- Fourth, even if there were Undead agents with the right capacities to be evil, there is no special reason to think that they have the motives that make one evil in any greater frequency than we find in regular, not-previously-dead humans. Even if they did have those motives, there is no reason to think that they would be fundamentally different from us in the capacity to act against those motives.

It's time for us to abandon our prejudices about the Undead. It may not be evil to portray them as we tend to, but it is wrong.[3]

---

[3] My thanks to Diego Nieto for advice on some of the biological issues I raise, and to Katherine Denson, Shaun Nichols, and the editors of this volume for helpful discussions or comments about the material in this paper.

5
Zombies, *Blade Runner*, and the Mind-Body Problem

LARRY HAUSER

RACHEL [TO DECKARD]: Or we could live in sin, except that I'm not alive.

—PHILIP K. DICK, *Do Androids Dream of Electric Sheep?*

Zombies and Replicants

J.R. SEBASTIAN [TO ROY BATTY]: You're so perfect!

—*Blade Runner*

Zombies are Undead. Something animates them, but whatever it is—whether voodoo or science run amok—it's not their departed souls or, as philosophers (not wanting to prejudge the theological question of souls) would have it, their conscious selves or minds. Zombies enter philosophy where horror fantasy and science fiction meet dawning scientific fact. Robots, many believe, are unconscious, soulless automata. Many further believe robots will remain unconscious and soulless no matter how convincingly human their appearances and behavior become, even robots able to fool the most careful unaided observer—like the androids in *Blade Runner*.[1]

---

[1] All quotations and references to characters and situations refer to *Blade Runner* (directed by Ridley Scott, 1982) a film adaptation of Dick's 1968 novel, *Do Androids Dream of Electric Sheep?*

That zombies enter philosophy in this vicinity partly explains the peculiar way in which philosophy zombies are Undead. Much like computers (according to the general supposition), typical philosophy zombies are unfeeling, but capable of sophisticated thought (or at least the appearance of it). This is quite unlike the stereotypical zombies of George Romero's *Living Dead* series which are severely cognitively and emotionally diminished, if not completely unthinking or unfeeling. Maybe they have sensations—maybe brains taste like something to them. Who knows? On the other hand, they are certainly intellectually challenged. One can't reason with a *Living Dead* zombie.

In Romero's *Land of the Dead* zombies develop rudimentary communication and tool-use skills. Philosophy zombies' intellectual abilities are imagined to be even further developed—typically, as well developed as yours and mine. "As human as human" is the rule with zombies in philosophy: zombies in philosophy are more akin to the wives in *The Stepford Wives* or the pod people in *Invasion of the Body Snatchers* than to the brain-munching ghouls of *Night of the Living Dead*. Still, with Stepford wives and pod people there's something discernibly, albeit subtly, amiss. Philosophy zombies resemble normal humans more perfectly still. In philosophy, zombies are typically, outwardly, indistinguishable from normal humans, at least to the naked eye, like the Replicants in *Blade Runner*. A Replicant can only be detected by a special test measuring "capillary dilation of the so called blush response, fluctuation of the pupil, involuntary dilation of the iris" and other involuntary emotional responses. They call it "Voigt-Kampff," for short. Some philosophers have even imagined zombies literally identical to humans; some philosophy zombies *are* humans. We'll return to that.

Zombies that haunt philosophers' imaginings these days are fully humanoid agents, information processors, and even organisms. Outwardly, or objectively, philosophy zombies appear to be typical individuals. Inwardly, or subjectively, however, there's no conscious "light" behind their eyes, however much they seem to shine. Objectively, philosophy zombies are *perfect* human replicas, as human as human; subjectively, however, there's "nobody home."

Despite their seeming intelligence—or rather precisely because of it—philosophy zombies do eat brains . . . in a sense.

And herein lies their horror for materialistic philosophies of mind and, consequently, for scientific psychology. In the philosophy of mind, *materialist* theories maintain that mental functions can all be accounted for in physical terms, or identified with material processes, without recourse to immaterial entities like souls. In philosophical thought experiments, however, zombies seem to "devour" everything *about* brains that various materialist theories might suppose thoughts and sensations to be. Philosophy zombies "eat brains" by seeming to be counterexamples to every attempt to identify thoughts and sensations with the things about brains materialists propose to identify them with. *Behaviorists* propose to identify mental states with adaptive behavioral output. *Functionalists* propose to identify mental processes with computations that produce such output. *Mind-brain identity theorists* propose to identify minds with the underlying neurophysiology that, perhaps, implements such computations. All these alternatives seem to be ruled out by zombies. In philosophy, zombies eat behavior, programs, and brains.

And Bears! Oh No: Zombies Invade Philosophy

DECKARD [TO ZHORA]: Is that a real snake?

The first reported sighting of what philosophers have since come to call "zombies," however, was not of humanoid zombies, but of zombie animals.[2] In the wake of William Harvey's discovery that the heart is a pump, René Descartes proposed in 1637 that every life function could be explained materialistically on mechanical principles. Even adaptive intelligent-seeming behavior, such as birds' nest-building and navigational abilities, Descartes argued, could be explained as the activities of unreasoning, unconscious mechanisms. Proposing to regard animal bodies as machines, Descartes concluded that all animals are "automata," furry (or scaly or feathery) robots, totally lacking reason and consciousness. Shades of *Pet Sematary* . . . except in *Pet Sematary*, the resurrected pet corpses—like Romero's zombies and unlike philosophers' zombies—are manifestly not

---

[2] The first to actually give the name "zombies" to the unconscious or soulless automata philosophers have imagined was Robert Kirk, in "Zombies v. Materialists," *Aristotelian Society Supplement* 48 (1974), pp. 135–163.

themselves. They've changed, turned vicious. Zombie animals, as conceived by Descartes, on the other hand, are indistinguishable from our pets, wildlife, and cattle, because they *are* our pets, wildlife, and cattle!

Descartes, notably, did seem to glimpse humanoid zombies once. Having introspectively assured himself of his own consciousness, looking out his window to see other "men crossing the square," he still wondered whether what he saw were "any more than hats and coats which could conceal automatons."[3] What do I really know about anyone else's inner life—or lack thereof—except what their words and acts seem to reveal? Zombies are us! Oh no! Or, rather, since I know from my own first-person experience that I am conscious (or so Descartes taught) zombies might be *you*. Philosophers call this the "other minds problem." Descartes, however, dismissed the possibility of humanoid zombies. The variety and flexibility of human actions "guided by the will," he reasoned, could not be mechanically replicated. Since the infinite variety of conscious reason outstrips the necessarily finite resources of material devices, Descartes concluded that no machine could ever use words or other signs to "produce different arrangements of words so as to give a meaningful answer to whatever is said in its presence"; neither could a machine "act in all the contingencies of life in the way in which our reason makes us act." Whereas "reason is a universal instrument which can be used in all kinds of situations," Descartes reckoned such scope of application and flexibility of operation would be "impossible for a machine."[4] Only the presence of an immaterial principle or soul in us (a theory called "dualism") could explain the virtually infinite variety of human behavior. Whereas life-processes could be mechanized, thought-processes could not.

Descartes, it now seems, dismissed the possibility of humanoid zombies too soon. He underestimated the potential of machines. In 1937 Alan Turing demonstrated the theoretical possibility of fully programmable devices, or "universal machines,"

---

[3] *Meditations on First Philosophy, Discourse on Method*, Meditation. II, in Cottingham, Stoothoff, and Murdoch, eds., *The Philosophical Writings of Descartes*, Volume 2 (New York: Cambridge University Press, 1984).

[4] *Discourse on Method*, Part 5, in Cottingham, Stoothoff, and Murdoch, eds., *The Philosophical Writings of Descartes*, Volume 1 (New York: Cambridge University Press, 1985).

paving the way for the development of digital computers and showing how the infinite variety of behaviors "guided by will," such as speech, might be, in principle, explained as mechanical effects of computation. Much as the heart is a pump, and biological inheritance is DNA replication, Turing-inspired "functionalists" (or "cognitivists") hypothesize that the brain is a computer. Thought is computation.

Zombies Ate My Brain!

RACHEL [TO DECKARD]: Have you ever "retired" a human by mistake?

Just when everything seemed to be going materialism's way— just when it was finally dawning what sort of mechanisms minds might be and what sort of material processes thought might be—along came zombies. At first materialists were in denial. They wanted to say, "A thought experiment—the mere *possibility* of zombies—proves nothing. Only if there really were NEXUS 6 units like Rachel, and they really weren't conscious, would it refute behaviorism; only if there really were NEXUS 7 units (say) that computed the same subfunctions as brains, yet unconscious, would it refute functionalism; only if there really were NEXUS 8 units (say) with brains physiologically indistinguishable from human brains, yet unconscious, would it refute mind-brain identity theory. That such units conceivably *might* not be conscious proves nothing." It was here that zombies in philosophy turned ugly. Modern materialism says that everything mental is identical (and scientifically identifiable) with something physical, just as water is identical (and scientifically identifiable) with H_2O. Such scientific identification, however, entails that water is not just *actually* H_2O ("in this possible world," philosophers say); water is *necessarily* H_2O ("in all possible worlds," philosophers say). It has to be H_2O, or else it wouldn't be water. Essential scientific identifications such as that of water with H_2O, when true, are not possibly or conceivably otherwise. So the best philosophical opinion, following Saul Kripke, now has it.[5]

---

[5] *Naming and Necessity* (Cambridge, Massachusetts: Harvard University Press, 1972). To imagine the stuff filling our lakes and streams to be other than H_2O, Kripke pointed out,

But to imagine the presence of adaptive behavior, or under-lying computational processes, or even brain processes as such, is not *ipso facto* to imagine conscious experience. Zombie thought experiments seem variously to imagine beings with humanoid behavior, programs, and brains, without subjective experiences. Zombies, so conceived, seem possible in ways inconsistent with the truth of all would-be materialist identifica-tions. So the story goes.

"And since subjectivity can't be identified with any sort of material processes—and I am directly aware in my own case that it exists—it must be essentially separate and immaterial, confirming dualism. On the main point, Descartes was right after all!" So, it seems, the story would continue—if zombies really are conceivable. Alas, it seems they too readily are.

To evoke zombies, John Searle instructs, "always think of [the thought experiment] from the first-person point of view": you have to imagine yourself as the zombie. As Searle sets the stage, suppose that doctors gradually replace your brain with silicon chips, perhaps to remedy its progressive deterioration. From here, you may conjure yourself a zombie by imagining as follows:

> . . . as the silicon is progressively implanted into your dwindling brain, you find that the area of your conscious experience is shrink-ing, but that this shows no effect on your external behavior. You find, to your total amazement, that you are indeed losing control of your external behavior. . . . [You've gone blind but] you hear your voice saying in a way that is completely out of your control, "I see a red object in front of me" . . . imagine that your conscious experience slowly shrinks to nothing while your externally observ-able behavior remains the same.[6]

You have imagined yourself gradually becoming a zombie. And no sooner are such zombies conjured, of course, than they're off on their rampage. Against behaviorism, "we imagined . . . the behavior was unaffected, but the mental states disappeared." And there's no way to stop them before they transmogrify.

---

is not to imagine water not being H_2O; it is imagining the stuff so described (and so called) not being water! To imagine the presence of H_2O is *ipso facto* to imagine the presence of water, and *vice versa*.

[6] *The Rediscovery of the Mind* (Cambridge, Massachusetts: MIT Press 1992), pp. 66–69.

Suppose the replacement chips implement the same programs, maintaining all the same *internal functions* as the brain cells replaced. The replacement chips perform exactly the same computations as the brain. There goes the functionalist idea that thought is computation—zombies ate its program.

Here Searle, himself hoping to spare some vestige of materialism, leaves off. But zombies are not so easily stopped. Suppose silicon-chip-replacement therapy is unavailable. The medical doctors are powerless. You have heard of a certain witch doctor. Desperate, you fly to a remote isle, voodoo rites are enacted, and *voilà*. The deterioration of your brain is magically reversed. To the amazed medical doctors back at the clinic, your brain is indistinguishable from your very own predeteriorated brain. But wait! As your brain is being magically restored . . . it's just as before. Your conscious experience slowly shrinks to nothing. You're a zombie. There goes mind-brain identity. Zombies ate its brain. Though some (including Searle himself) deny that such fully human bio-zombies really are conceivable, none have shown the contradiction in it. Indeed, it is just this that possibility that philosophers who have raised the "other minds problem" seem to be conceiving.

Plan B from Inner Space: Revenge of the Zombies

TYRELL [TO DECKARD]: "More human than human" is our motto.

Since they do seem to be conceivable, bad brain-eating zombies must be stopped before they destroy civilized philosophy of mind and scientific psychology as we know it. I have a plan. Much as Earth enlisted Godzilla to battle Ghidrah in *Ghidrah the Three Headed Monster*, I propose to create new breeds of zombies to battle their evil cousins. Familiar zombies, conjured, as it were, from the second-person familiar perspective, increase our attachment: there's I and thou and thou art zombie. Super-smart zombies are not just as smart as us, but smarter. Being in these ways superlatively human, such zombies resist dementalization. Their imagined or stipulated lack of subjective experiences seems not to impugn the genuineness of their apparent intellectual endowments. These zombies can battle their evil cousins to a standoff, at least, and perhaps even defeat them.

To conjure familiar zombies, put yourself in Deckard's shoes. Imagine your own true love to be a zombie. Imagine your beloved has no subjective experience of sensations, no inwardly felt experiences (what philosophers call "qualia") whatsoever. Yet your beloved, we're imagining, behaves in every way just as your real-life beloved (who, presumably, is not a zombie) really behaves: smiles as warm; kisses as sweet; loyalty as steadfast; words as tender; love as true. Only the "light" isn't on. No qualia.

I submit that you should not deny your true love's cognitive abilities and attainments. He or she still wants you to prosper, still knows your preferences, still prefers scotch to bourbon, and so on. To strengthen the intuition, extend the fantasy to your mother, your father, your children, all your friends, siblings, colleagues, teachers, everyone you know. They're all zombies! Should you conclude that your beloved and the rest don't think, that they know nothing at all and don't understand English? It was from Mother, Father, and the rest, in particular, that you got your English, and such words as *think*, *know*, and *understand*. I think you should conclude, "How odd! I alone have these peculiar subjective experiences besides the wants, beliefs, and so forth, that others have." The thought of mental life without subjective experiences may be horrible, but it's conceivable. Familiar zombies show this.

As for super-smartness . . . since the NEXUS 6 Replicants were "at least equal in intelligence to the genetic engineers who created [them]," let us suppose, off-world, they undertake genetically re-engineering themselves or their descendents. Suppose these descendents, NEXUS 9s, are decidedly *more* intelligent than the human genetic engineers who created their forebears (except, still no qualia). Suppose these NEXUS 9s return to earth. They show us how to make our microwaves synthesize food out of thin air and how to turn our Ford Tempos into time machines. They show us how to achieve peace on earth, with liberty and justice for all. What should we say? That our NEXUS 9 benefactors didn't really know how to turn Tempos into time machines? That they didn't really understand the revolutionary physical principles involved, but now we do? I think we're not as ungrateful and conceited as that. We'd say our subjective-experience-bereft benefactors *knew* how to turn Tempos into time machines.

Finally, imagine zombies both smart and familiar—or, rather, venerated. Imagine it is discovered that many, most, or even all of the leading contributors to our human intellectual heritage(s) were zombies (Descartes, especially, included). Nevertheless, I submit, we should not deny their mental attainments. Despite not meeting the would-be dualistic essential condition for thought, despite being bereft of subjective experiences or "qualia," these famously smart zombies remain paradigm thinkers on the strength of their achievements. Intelligent is as intelligence does, absence of itches, aches, tingles, visual images, and such, notwithstanding. Indeed, the surpassing greatness of their intellectual attainments makes super-smart venerable zombies especially easy to imagine, especially given the well-known antipathy between thought and feeling. No one ever solved an equation or proved a theorem in the throes of agony or orgasm.

How I Learned to Stop Worrying and Love the Zomb

DECKARD [TO BRYANT]: And if the machine doesn't work?

It seems that intuitions about thoughts (cognitive states like belief and inference) and feelings (sensations such as itches and afterimages) diverge under different zombie-thought-experimental conditions. Brain-eating zombies like Searle's undermine materialist accounts of sensation; qualia-eating zombies like mine undermine dualistic accounts of thought. Furthermore, the supposition that thought somehow *requires* feeling—besides being contrary to the well-known antipathy just noted—would be indecisive in its upshot. Even assuming this no-thought-without-feeling "Connection Principle" (as Searle dubs it), the question remains: should we conclude that intelligent-acting androids are not really thinking (given their imagined lack of feelings); or should we rather conclude (given their evidently thoughtful behavior) that they have feelings after all?

Is it a standoff, then? Does dualism rule the experiential realm and materialism the intellectual? Yet, even this partial "triumph" of dualism would seem to be strangely empty and inconsequential. As *pure sensations* or experiences, shorn of every

concomitant physical (behavioral, functional, neurophysiological) element, qualia are "saved" from materialistic identification
precisely by being conceived as ineffectual; as events lacking
further effects, what philosophers call "epiphenomena." This is
suspicious. Not everything thought to be conceivable really is
so. Materialists who were in denial thought they could conceive
of water not being H_2O, but they were mistaken. Perhaps it's the
same with the supposed conception of beings "which are physically and functionally identical [to us], but which lack [subjec-
tive] experience": perhaps such "phenomenal zombies," as
David Chalmers calls them, likewise, only seem to be conceivable, but really are not. Chalmers notes parenthetically, "It is not
surprising that phenomenal zombies have not been popular in
Hollywood, as there would be obvious problems with their
depiction." "Problems" to say the least! They look and act
exactly like you and me. In the case of NEXUS 8 bio-zombies
(imagined above), neither CAT scans nor MRIs nor any other
conceivable objective tests could distinguish phenomenal zombies from ordinary human beings. This being the case, the
"problems with their depiction" that Chalmers notes, are likewise problems with their conception. What exactly are we supposed to be imagining when we imagine beings "physically
identical to me (or to any other conscious being), but lacking
conscious experiences altogether"?[7]

Here we are in a position to appreciate Searle's observation
that the conception of phenomenal zombies has to be done
"from the first-person point of view"; but who is that first person? Whose point of view is it? It must be the zombie's, but the
zombie, "lacking conscious experiences altogether," is supposed
to lack a "first-person point of view"! Like mad scientists in the
movies who are destroyed by their own creations, it seems that
the zombie-spawning thought experiments destroy the experi-
menters themselves, and with them the experiments. If qualia
are required for a first-person point of view, the experiment
abolishes the viewpoint on which it depends. It seems that zombies, then, are not coherently conceivable after all.

So is that the end? Have zombies been defeated? Has Plan A
prevailed after all? Has thoroughgoing materialism been saved?

---

[7] *The Conscious Mind: In Search of a Fundamental Theory* (Oxford: Oxford University
Press, 1996), pp. 94–96.

I wouldn't be too sure. First, it seems we can imagine the process of zombification (as in Searle's evocation) even though we can't quite see our way to the end. So long as the subject's awareness hasn't shrunk to zero, there's a first-person point of view that can be imaginatively taken. Perhaps, where imagination leaves off, we extrapolate ("and so on") our way to the end. Furthermore, the incoherence of a first-person narrative minus the first person only arises where qualia are totally absent: for so-called "absent qualia" scenarios. "Inverted qualia" (I-see-red-where-you-see-green type) scenarios would still seem conceivable, and pose similar challenges to materialism. If either green experiences or red experiences might conceivably "supervene" (as philosophers say) on the very same state of the brain, then that state cannot be identified with either experience.

Fortunately, while good, qualia-eating zombies, do not provide full immunity, they do provide a measure of protection, like flu vaccine: you still get zombies, but a milder case. It is only *so far as the mental states in question depend on qualia for their existence*, only so far as they are inconceivable without qualia, that bad, brain-eating, zombies show that the mental states cannot be identical with brain states. Good zombies show that this is not that far for mental states involved in cognitive thought. For a good portion of our mental life (the whole cognitive part, it seems), qualia are inessential; so good zombies seem to show.

As for sensations (itches, aches, afterimages, tastes, and the like), though prospects for materialistic identifications of these remain in jeopardy, even here, good zombies diminish the havoc brain-eaters would otherwise wreak. Computers equipped with sensors, for instance, are "sentient" in a sense. They get information about their surroundings from ambient light (as in vision), vibration (as in hearing), and chemistry (as in taste) even if not in the sense of having subjective visual, auditory, and taste experiences. They can still be said (I think unequivocally) to "see" things they visually detect, "hear" sounds they aurally discern, and "taste" flavors they chemically differentiate.

What about consciousness? How can zombies behave intelligently if they're unconscious? Good zombies are conscious in the sense of being cognizant *of* things (registering their presence) or being cognizant *that* certain things are or aren't the case (representing them as so being) despite not being "phenomenally conscious" (possessed of qualia). Conceivably, your imagined zombie lover is in this manner aware of your presence: he or she registers it, and responds just as your real lover would. Conceivably NEXUS 9 astro-zombies are aware that Tempos are gas-powered: they represent that fact and respond accordingly. This much is cognitive. It's the specifically phenomenal (subjectively felt), not the cognitive (rational representational) aspect of consciousness that's supposed to be lacking.

As for self-consciousness and subjectivity, good zombies, it seems, can even be "self-aware" in the sense of having access to their own internal states. Some computer programs, for instance, maintain state variables. Good zombies, it seems, can have points of view both literally (the loci of their visual sensors) and figuratively (in the form of unique overall representations of reality).

As for the soul, being pure sensations or "raw feels," qualia seem very far removed from that spiritual concept and from actions "guided by the will." Even if they *do* lack raw feels (as we have been imagining), Replicants still realize they are all-too mortal, fear death, and "want more life," or so they say. And they say it with feeling. Or so it seems.

Do Androids Dream of Electric Sheep?

DECKARD [TO TYRELL]: How can it not know what it is?

Much as philosophy zombies are supposed to copy human beings in every way except their feelings, *Blade Runner* Replicants were "designed to copy human beings in every way except their emotions." However, "the designers reckoned that in a few years they might develop their own emotional responses. Hate, love, fear, anger, envy" (Bryant to Deckard); and in the film, it seems their designers were right. From hot-headed Leon ("let me tell you about my mother!") Kowalski, to Blake-misquoting Roy ("tears in rain") Batty, *Blade Runner* Replicants seem far from emotionless; indeed, they are almost overwrought. Perhaps they protest too much. The question Leon asks Deckard—"Painful living in fear, isn't it?"—is repeated by Roy in the climactic scene. Is it just a canned response, simulating emotion? When Rachel says to Deckard, "I love you . . . I trust you," is that a lie?

In *Blade Runner* it takes Deckard more than a hundred questions to determine that Rachel is inhuman. Being inhuman, she is denied moral standing. She can be summarily "retired" without trial or justification. To be morally disenfranchised on the basis of barely discernible differences in involuntary emotional responses—"capillary dilation of the so-called blush response, fluctuation of the pupil, involuntary dilation of the iris"—seems like picky grading, unless these involuntary emotional response differences are indicative of some deeper lack. But how would we know that?

We do have evidence, in the inhuman way Pris convulses when shot through the solar plexus, that *Blade Runner* Replicants differ from humans in their internal wiring, their subfunctional architectures. Plausibly this makes a difference in the way it feels to be them. But how would we know that? And why should it be supposed to be the difference between having feelings and having none? Perhaps Rachel's loving feeling is merely different from ours, not absent.

We have further evidence in the way Leon reaches into the beaker of liquid nitrogen and Pris into the beaker of boiling water, without sustaining bodily damage, that Replicants are made of different stuff. Perhaps rather than being made of carbon-based stuff, like humans, *Blade Runner* Replicants are made of silicon-based stuff, like computers. Plausibly this makes a difference in the way it feels to be them, also. But why, again, should it be supposed to be the difference between having feelings and having none? And how, again, would we know that? Again, perhaps Rachel's loving feeling is merely different from ours, not absent.

And if she has no feelings whatever—if she really is a philosophy zombie—what then? "I love you," she says. And if she not only talks the talk, but walks the walk ever after, if she wishes him well, and wants to be with him, is it all a lie for lack of some subjective amatory itch?[8] And if it was no subjective feeling that moved her to pull the trigger, killing Leon, to save Deckard's life, doesn't Deckard still owe her? Deckard says he has never retired a human by mistake, but it seems he has been

---

[8] And if she has some such feeling, but wishes him ill, wants him gone, and betrays and despises him ever after, has she spoken truly?

"retiring" *persons*—intelligent and possibly sentient beings—all along.

But wait! Even if qualia are required for true love, and Rachel has none, her profession of love is no lie. She will have spoken untruly, but she will not have knowingly done so. What she *thinks*—including what she thinks about her feelings—is supposed to be unchanged. Good zombies, among other things, enforce this supposition. Lack them though she may, she still *thinks* she has feelings; as does Deckard. As do I. Conceivably, I too am deluded! Based on Descartes's intuition of infallible self-awareness (the first person point of view) as the zombie thought-experiments are, yet seeming to undermine that very intuition, philosophy zombies may not be coherently conceivable after all. Plan B has led us back to plan A.[9]

---

[9] Parts of this paper are based on a paper, "Revenge of the Zombies," that I presented at the American Philosophical Association Eastern Division Colloquium: Philosophy of Mind, December 29, 1995 (accessible online at http://members.aol.com/lshauser/zombies.html).

PART II

Undead White Males

6

Heidegger the Vampire Slayer: The Undead and Fundamental Ontology

ADAM BARROWS

Sympathy for the Vampire

Count Dracula has proven the most persistently adaptable and resilient of popular icons, retaining his power to intrigue and frighten audiences across generational and cultural divides. While Bram Stoker didn't invent the vampire, his treatment of the monster in his 1897 novel, *Dracula*, was immediately more compelling than earlier English fictional attempts, like *Varney the Vampire* (1847). Stoker's many original additions to vampire lore have now become inextricably bound up with our popular imagination of the creatures. Among these additions were the use of garlic as a protective charm, the location of the neck as the privileged site of blood-sucking, and the Count's ability to shapeshift, particularly into bats.

Stoker's greatest innovation, though, was his use of the vampire story to explore deeper metaphysical questions about the true nature of humanity. Far from representing the vampire as a coldly grotesque monster, Stoker explored the pathos and psychological terror of a human being, with a core of goodness, becoming trapped inside a godless and eternally Undead body. As the original working titles for the novel suggest, the terror of becoming Undead captured Stoker's imagination far more than the personal figure of the Count himself. Stoker's working title for *Dracula* was *The Dead Undead* and, only weeks before publication, the novel was to be called simply *The Undead*. The Count, in fact, only physically appears as a character in roughly forty of the book's three hundred pages. The rest of the book is occupied with the other characters' fear of Dracula and what he represents. The fear of becoming Undead makes the Dracula story consistently compelling.

Compare Stoker's killing of a vampire with the killing of a vampire in the sensational anonymous serial, *Varney the Vampire*, published fifty years before *Dracula*. Here is the killing of Clara Crofton in *Varney the Vampire*:

> The eyes of the corpse opened wide—the hands were clenched, and a shrill, piercing shriek came from the lips—a shriek that was answered by as many as there were persons present, and then with pallid fear upon their countenances they rushed headlong from the spot. (*Dracula*, p. 338)[1]

And the killing of Lucy Westenra in Stoker's *Dracula*:

> The thing in the coffin writhed, and a hideous, blood-curdling screech came from the opened red lips. The body shook and quivered and twisted in wild contortions. . . . Finally it lay still. The terrible task was over. . . . There, in the coffin lay no longer the foul Thing that we had so dreaded and grown to hate that the work of her destruction was yielded as a privilege to the one best entitled to it, but Lucy as we had seen her in her life, with her face of unequaled sweetness and purity. True that there were, as we had seen them in life, the traces of care and pain and waste; but these were all dear to us, for they marked her truth to what we knew. (*Dracula*, p. 192)

Note how strikingly different is Stoker's approach to the killing. In the earlier novel, we witness the slaughter of an animal. In Stoker's novel, we witness the liberation of a human soul. The author of *Varney the Vampire* plays the stake through the heart for pure grotesque shock value, with a screech that draws the narrative away from the evil scene along with the crowd of onlookers, so that we are not allowed to look at the results of the killing. Stoker borrows the scream but does not pull away from the coffin. If we were to represent the two killings cinematically, we might use for the *Varney* scene a quick cut from

---

[1] This quotation from *Varney the Vampire* comes from the "Contexts" section of the Norton Critical Edition of Bram Stoker's *Dracula* (New York: Norton, 1997). All my quotations from *Dracula* are from this edition.

a close-up on the face of the screaming Clara to a long shot of the crowds fleeing the tomb. For Stoker's scene, in contrast, our camera would linger on the impaled vampire, zooming in on her transfigured features. Stoker describes the change in attitude of the killers from a hatred and bloodlust for the "foul Thing" to an appreciation of Lucy's "truth." To kill a vampire, for Stoker's "vampire-hunters," is not just to satisfy blood-lust or to combat evil, but to liberate a "true" humanity which is trapped inside a "false" inhumanity.

In her rally to the troops as they prepare to hunt the Count in Transylvania, Mina Harker reminds the hunters that they have to pity the poor soul stuck inside the Count's Undead body:

> I want you to bear something in mind through all this dreadful time. I know you must fight—that you must destroy even as you destroyed the false Lucy so that the true Lucy might live hereafter; but it is not a work of hate. That poor soul who has wrought all this misery is the saddest case of all. Just think what will be his joy when he too is destroyed in his worser part that his better part may have spiritual immortality. You must be pitiful to him too, though it may not hold your hands from the destruction. (*Dracula*, pp. 268–69)

For Mina, humanity is "true" and vampirism is "false." Her friend Lucy Westenra, killed earlier by the hunters, has been cured of vampirism by a stake through the heart, as if murder were an antidote for the "false" orientation of vampirism. The dead Lucy is the "true" Lucy, while her Undead manifestation is the "false" Lucy.

Stoker's greatest contribution to the vampire legend is to focus our attention not only on the physical grotesqueries and violence of blood-sucking, but also on the far more troubling psychological fear of becoming "false," of having one's death, a fundamental part of one's natural being, taken away, leaving the core of "true" humanity encased in a pallid deathless shell of skin and bone. What is endlessly compelling about Dracula is the monster's subversion of our most deeply held metaphysical beliefs. "I know now the span of my life," writes Jonathan Harker in Transylvania (p. 45). Although the knowledge is frightening for him, it distinguishes him from Dracula, whose life, being endless, has no span. It stretches from endlessness to endlessness, from abyss to abyss. The life of the vampire is an unpunctuated succession of feedings, denied the common human bond of death. In an early conversation with Harker, Dracula explains his desire to come to London:

> I long to go through the crowded streets of your mighty London, to be in the midst of the whirl and rush of humanity, to share its life, its change, its death, all that makes it what it is. (*Dracula*, p. 26)

It's possible to understand this speech as a glimpse of Dracula's buried "true" self, struggling to become a part of humanity, a plea for the changeless to know change, for the deathless to feel death, for the Olympian outsider to share in a common humanity.

The Philosophy of Death

Death teaches us to be "true" humans. This lesson of Stoker's *Dracula* will be repeated exactly thirty years later by a German philosopher named Martin Heidegger (1889–1976). Nowhere in the western philosophical tradition does Death play such a key role as it does in Heidegger's book, *Being and Time* (1927). The key insights that ground Heidegger's study of Being are that 1) death cannot be public but must be faced alone, and 2) life without death is existentially meaningless.

Heidegger didn't just modify Western philosophy, but hoped to radically refocus it. For Heidegger, what was wrong with Western philosophy was that it was epistemological and not ontological. These are fairly daunting terms, but they can be defined quite simply. Epistemology is the study of *how we know*. Ontology is the study of (among other things) *what we are*. The entire philosophical tradition from Plato through Descartes to Kant, Heidegger wrote, focused on *how* we acquire knowledge about the world. Kant's landmark *Critique of Pure Reason*, for instance, concluded that we always confront the material world with the help of certain categories like Time and Space, ideas that are not learned but rather are hard-wired. This is all very fine, Heidegger felt, but its failure was that it put the cart before the horse. How can we talk about *how* we know things until we have decided what the word "we" is referring to in the first place? What is the "being" that knows Time and Space? Does it have any fundamental characteristics that can be agreed upon?

Heidegger's ontology was "fundamental ontology," he argued, because it cut thorough all biological and social explanations of human nature to get to the more primordial, deeper, metaphysical core of *what we are*. In order to understand what is fundamental to being, Heidegger suggests that we must separate what is truly "authentic" about our being from the common, everyday, "inauthentic" knowledge of being. We already know deep down what we are, but that knowledge is clouded and distorted by all the distractions and deceptions of everyday life. Throughout *Being and Time*, then, Heidegger explains that there is always a true and a false way of "being." In our everyday, run-of-the-mill, nine-to-five existence, we are "cut off from the primary and primordially genuine relations of our being" (p. 159).[2]

What do we learn about ourselves when we cut ourselves off from our immersion in the "inauthentic" daily round of routines? For Heidegger, the key revelation for humanity is that it *ends*— it will die. Without death, we could understand ourselves only as existing forever in a succession of empty moments. Instead, death provides us with a temporal arc—an experience of being thrown forward towards an indisputable end. The problem of existence, however, is that inauthentic, everyday experiences act relentlessly to conceal and obscure death. It's not, of course, that there is some conspiracy to hide the biological fact of death. Tombstones abound and it is a truism that everyone dies. But these public acknowledgments of death only act to obscure the fact of one's own personal death. Consider the following excerpt from *Being and Time* in which Heidegger explains how the "they" (his term for inauthentic, everyday beings) try to trick a dying person into not facing his death:

> . . . the "neighbors" often try to convince the "dying person" that he will escape death and soon return again to the tranquilized everydayness of his world. . . . This "concern" has the intention of thus "comforting" the "dying person. . . ." But basically, this tranquilization is not only for the "dying person" but just as much for "those who are comforting him. . . ." Even "thinking about death" is regarded publicly as cowardly fear, a sigh of insecurity . . . and a dark flight from the world. (*Being and Time*, pp. 234–35)

---

[2] All my quotations from Heidegger's *Being and Time* are from Joan Stambaugh's translation (Albany: SUNY Press, 1996).

For Heidegger, a confrontation with death is not simply some kind of perverse morbidity. It is an act of "courage." Inauthentic beings ("they") cover up death and are thus always partial and incomplete, living blindly and deludedly into a future that will be an endless succession of present moments. Since the life of "they" has no end, it has no borders or limits and is unable to be grasped by the mind. "True" being, in contrast, is a bordered whole, with Death making it a complete entity. For Heidegger, this state of being is described almost ecstatically as a "passionate anxious freedom toward death which is free of the illusions of 'the they' . . . and certain of itself" (p. 245). Societal pressures try to "tranquilize" or "veil" this freedom, but authentic beings reject such pressures.

"Inauthentic" beings live forever in an endless succession of moments. What better example of this "inauthentic" being is there than the vampire? To kill the vampire is to teach him to understand his life as a bordered whole, to teach him to confront and accept his own death. Vampire-hunting, in the light of *Being and Time*, becomes a kind of philosophical task—making "true" dead humans out of "false" deathless vampires.

Dracula as Inauthentic Being

Dracula's entire existence gives the lie to death, presenting a possibility of life without end. Stoker, in the early 1890s, wrote a checklist of Dracula's most important characteristics in preparation for writing the novel. Number four on the list was: "absolutely despises death and the dead" (p. 343).[3] Stoker conceived of Dracula as a sworn opponent not of humanity, but of the very idea of death itself. The vampire's promise is to give life without end to chosen beings. His promise to the wretch Renfield is to give him the life force of thousands of rats. "All these lives will I give you, ay, and many more and greater, through countless ages" (p. 245). In this instance of vampiric seduction, Renfield is like the dying person in Heidegger's scenario and Dracula acts as "they," convincing the diseased mind that death is only what happens to other lowly forms of life, like rats.

---

[3] Christopher Frayling provides this list in "Bram Stoker's Working Papers for *Dracula*" in the Norton Critical Edition of *Dracula*.

Dracula's attitude toward death is "inauthentic." His notorious inability to be reflected by mirrors is a metaphor for his inability to "reflect" on his own true state of being. There's a veil of inauthenticity drawn over Dracula that the mirror only makes painfully obvious. Dracula, as compelling a figure as he is, resembles Heidegger's "they" in his lack of a stable self-image. In the same checklist of Dracula's attributes, Stoker wrote, "painters can't make a likeness of him—however hard the artist tries, the subject always ends up looking like someone else" (p. 344). Even though it was undeveloped in the final version of the novel, this aspect of Dracula nevertheless clarifies Stoker's understanding of Dracula's lack of "reflection." A painting of Dracula would end up "looking like someone else." Dracula has no distinct character himself. He is sometimes like you and sometimes like me. When Mina sees him in Piccadilly, he is a young thin man with a dark mustache (p. 155), while Harker knows him in Transylvania as aged and white-haired (p. 51) Francis Ford Coppola's adaptation, with its use of elaborate makeup, makes much of this aspect of Dracula's fluctuating appearance. Dracula is not distinct, but shifts from one form to another. He is mist as well as beast, old as well as young, masculine as well as feminine (his conquest of Mina, as many critics have noted, places him in the feminine role, with Mina at his breast). Despite what Van Helsing constantly asserts about Dracula's "selfish child-brain," Dracula is in actuality self-*less*. He is a kind of perverted communal force that transforms victims into his own likeness, a likeness that is, we are reminded, indistinct and unstable. Lucy, when she becomes a vampire, is not a *self*, but a pale imitation of Dracula. When Dracula smashes Jonathan's shaving mirror, he calls it "a foul bauble of man's vanity" (p. 31). The vanity of self does not translate into vampiric terms, in which self is unfocused and indistinct.

Dracula is self-less, and the vampire-hunters despise selfless people. This attitude comes out early in the novel, when Dr. Seward makes the following observation in his diary about Renfield:

> . . . a possibly dangerous man, probably dangerous if unselfish. In selfish men caution is as secure an armour for their foes as for themselves. What I think of on this point is, when self is the fixed point the centripetal force is balanced with the centrifugal; when

> duty, a cause, etc., is the fixed point, the latter force is paramount, and only accident or a series of accidents can balance it. (*Dracula*, p. 62)

Seward's point here, which is clouded with his odd Victorian language of weights and balances, is that the self is a "fixed point" that balances the various potentially dangerous forces we contain. "Unselfishness," far from being a goal for noble altruistic behavior, is here seen as a pathological condition. To put all this bluntly, Stoker sees self as good and selflessness as evil. It is the loss of one's self as a "fixed point" that constitutes the vampire's main seduction. The hunters, keeping as dispassionate and "selfish" as possible, militate against this seduction. Note how Van Helsing, confronted with one of the female vampires in Transylvania, characterizes their power:

> . . . in old time, when such things were, many a man who set forth to do such a task as mine, found at the last his heart fail him, and then his nerve. So he delay, and delay, and delay, till the mere beauty and the fascination of the wanton un-dead have hypnotize him, and he remain on, and on, till sunset come. . . . I was moved to a yearning for delay which seemed to paralyse my faculties and to clog my very soul . . . certain it was that I was lapsing into sleep, the open-eyed sleep of one who yields to a sweet fascination. (p. 319)

To yield to the vampire is to lose one's self-consciousness and self-preservation. One is reminded here of Heidegger's description of how "they" *tranquilize* the invalid, making him think his death is always far away—too far to worry about. The sensual pleasure that the vampire promises is a prolonged time of drugged delay, of constant waiting, as if one were suspended forever in the moment between sleep and wakefulness. For both Stoker and Heidegger, this moment is dangerous because the self loses its focus and centrality. The vampire hunters strip away this veil of inauthenticity, exposing it to the harsh and sober sunlight, courageously plunging a stake of authenticity through the heart of the inauthentic vampire, asserting the sheer force of self against selflessness. Their selves are "fixed points" which sharpen readily into vampire-slaying stakes.

Bram Stoker's *Dracula* was unique among vampire novels in its focus on the metaphysical condition of vampirism and its evocation of pity for the "true" human trapped in the false deathless state of the vampire. With a philosophical orientation towards death that would later be repeated in Heidegger's *Being and Time*, Stoker insisted that only an authentic self, claiming death as its indisputable freedom, could have the strength and courage to destroy the false seduction of the self-less "they," symbolized as a potential horde of vampires who all resembled each other while paradoxically resembling nothing.

Heil Heidegger? Dracula's Willing Executioners

Is Heidegger's philosophy a sound one? Are we willing to embrace his language of "authenticity"? To answer this question, I believe, is at the same time to decide whether we really *like* Stoker's vampire hunters. Isn't there something dogmatic, right-eous and brutal about Van Helsing and crew? Are there danger-ous implications in asserting that only a certain type of being is "true" or "authentic"?

As readers familiar with Heidegger will be aware, the philosopher's career was marred by controversy over his mem-bership in the Nazi Party. While many prominent German intel-lectuals fled the Nazi regime, Heidegger remained and enjoyed great prominence in the Third Reich. After the war, he was stripped of all his professional duties for his involvement in the Nazi Party. That Heidegger was technically a Nazi is indis-putable. What remains a subject of controversy is whether his program of fundamental ontology can be divorced from his own involvement with fascism or whether it is inherently implicated. In other words, is there something about *Being and Time* that, even in the Weimar period before the Nazis took power, was pointing Heidegger towards fascism? I can only begin to approach this controversy here, but the reader is directed to a particularly useful collection entitled *Martin Heidegger and the Holocaust* which presents the views of both Heidegger's sup-porters and detractors.

The most troubling aspect of Heidegger's ontology for our purposes here is its sometimes Olympian dismissal of the every-day and the ordinary. The simple designation of "idle chatter" to signify everything from advertising slogans to the consolation one finds on a deathbed, seems frighteningly contemptuous. The move from contempt of the everyday to brutality towards those who "chatter" can hardly be far. Further Heidegger never attempts to describe the possibility for a social and communal relationship *between* individual authentic beings. So, if I tune out the chatter and confront my death, how do I go about forming an "authentic" community, for instance? Would privileged beings build a gated community? Wouldn't it be something of a drag to have to live there? Though Heidegger makes clear that "authentic being" is not a biological designation, his failure to answer these objections allows a sizable gap in his philosophy for racial and cultural prejudice to creep in, even if it wasn't already there in the first place. Heidegger's later writings are chockfull of nationalistic paeans to the hale and hearty German peasantry, particularly from his own region, the Black Forest. In these later works, authentic being is used less as a metaphysical category and more as a marker for racial purity. Perhaps Heidegger took the ideas of *Being and Time* in the wrong direction, or perhaps *Being and Time*, with its language of "authentic" and "inauthentic" beings, was hopelessly open to racial and cultural prejudice from the start.

How we interpret Heidegger will largely reflect how we interpret Bram Stoker, with his opposition of a "true" humanity against a "false" vampirism, or his embrace of a fierce self-possession that fuels what Van Helsing himself describes as "butcher work" in the novel's most chilling description of vampire slaying. Read the following passage and imagine how it was possible for Nazi concentration camp doctors, guards and Hitler's other "willing executioners" (to borrow a controversial phrase) to slaughter men, women, and children:

> Oh, my friend John, but it was butcher work; had I not been nerved by thoughts of other dead, and of the living over whom hung such a pall of fear, I could not have gone on. I tremble and tremble even yet, though till all was over, God be thanked, my nerve did stand. Had I not seen the repose in the first face, and the gladness that stole over it just ere the final dissolution came, as realization that the soul had been won, I could not have gone further with my butchery. I could not have endured the horrid screeching as the stake drove home; the plunging of writhing form, and lips of bloody foam. (*Dracula*, p. 320)

I am not the first to reflect on the troubling implications of the vampire slayer's brutality. The vast majority of interpretations of

Dracula over the last fifty years have focused on the vampire as a victim (sometimes guilty, sometimes innocent) of wildly disproportionate violence. He has been interpreted as a symbol of the Jew, the homosexual, the Oriental, the victim of patriarchy, the victim of imperialism—the list goes on and on. The clearest example in film of a revisionist interpretation of *Dracula* is John Badham's 1979 version, with Frank Langella as an attractive and sympathetic Count, killed by Laurence Olivier's bumbling and dogmatic Van Helsing.

While vampires can and do serve as markers for a universally applicable terror, as marketable in the early twenty-first century as in the late nineteenth, the novel which first made their terror evocative did so on the basis of a philosophy that many have found utterly tainted with the same stain that created the horrors of Auschwitz and Dachau. In adaptation after adaptation, we become Dracula's willing executioners, ritualistically expelling the "inauthentic" beings from our zone of ontological purity. Can we justify our gleeful involvement in the ritual?

7

When There's No More Room in Hell, the Dead Will Shop the Earth: Romero and Aristotle on Zombies, Happiness, and Consumption

MATTHEW WALKER

The flesh-eating zombies of George A. Romero's *Dead* films turn stomachs—sometimes by twisting them right out of mangled bodies. Like vampires, they're creatures of hunger, human beings who've returned from the dead to feed on the living. Yet unlike those Undead whose razor-sharp fangs complement their razor-sharp refinement, Romero's zombies (un-)live not in some foggy Transylvania, but in an all-too-contemporary America. They have nasty table manners and are bad conversationalists. They are the *mindless* Undead, living corpses who'll surround you *en masse* in search of a warm meal. And that hurts.

In his apocalyptic zombie masterpiece, *Dawn of the Dead* (1978), Romero hints that the Undead are around us, as close as the local shopping mall. Doubt it? Go and you'll see them, shuffling down the aisles, staring vacantly into space, consuming without end. At Christmastime, you'll find them pressed against store windows, hell-bent on hot bargains.

In depicting zombies as the ultimate consumers, Romero satirizes consumerism—the search for happiness through material acquisition. Although consumerism's rise as an unofficial secular religion began after World War II and reached its apex in the "I shop, therefore I am" yuppie culture of the 1980s, human beings have long been acquisitive animals. Indeed, it's striking that Romero's sly criticisms of consumerism echo certain arguments offered nearly two thousand years ago by the Greek philosopher Aristotle (384–322 B.C.E.).

At first blush, Aristotle might seem an odd guide to elucidate the character of our contemporary zombification. After all, the philosopher whom Dante called "the master of those who know" lived and thought long before the advent of shopping malls, global market economies, and the sort of large-scale manufacturing that made mass consumption a viable possibility. And nowhere does Aristotle ever mention creatures like "zombies" or "the living dead." While some spurious pseudo-Aristotelian works offer reports of iron-eating mice, you won't find any commentary about flesh-eating corpses.

Despite the historical distance that separates Romero from Aristotle, though, we can still imagine the two sharing a Cinnabon at the local food court. Like Romero, Aristotle isn't above providing gross-out descriptions of cannibalistic mayhem. For instance, in the fifth chapter of Book VII of the *Nicomachean Ethics*—Aristotle's major treatise on ethics—the philosopher serves up some memorably gag-inducing accounts of "bestial" vice so far beyond the pale that it seems simply to fall outside the boundaries of humanity. In these odd pages, Aristotle introduces us to feral women who devour unborn fetuses, Black Sea tribes who sacrifice babies and munch on raw human flesh, and mad slaves who feast on other people's livers.

Okay, so maybe this bestiary would be more at home in the low-rent gore-shockers of some of Romero's Italian imitators— think Lucio Fulci or Joe D'Amato—but the point remains: Aristotle finds a philosophical role for the disgusting if it can help clarify the nature of the human good. And even if the ancient agora is no match for the modern mall, reading Aristotle can help us understand the motivations and desires that Romero's zombies share with today's devotees of consumerism. It can also help us get clear about why a life organized around material acquisition might constitute the sort of "living death" that Romero suggests.

"Let's Go Shopping First!": We Are the Zombies

In Romero's *Dawn of the Dead*—unlike Zack Snyder's 2004 remake, which I won't discuss—a zombie plague has been ravaging the world for years. With the ranks of the living dead steadily swelling, and with humanity's petty squabbles only making things worse, society faces imminent meltdown and collapse. Fleeing Philadelphia, a quartet of survivors hole up in an abandoned but fully stocked shopping mall in suburban Pittsburgh. Although the foursome initially plan only a short stay, they end up remaining once they discover all the mall has to offer. The chirpy Muzak notwithstanding, everything they could ever want seems to be there for the taking—and all under one roof.

Seizing the mall for themselves, the survivors pick off the zombies who continue to stagger down its cold white corridors. Having sealed off the entrances, the quartet set out to shop till they drop. They try on clothes, watches, hats, rings, cosmetics, coats; they load up on candy, cheeses, salamis, coffees, spices. One of the survivors, Peter, says it all when he breaks out in a big grin and holds up a giant loaf of bread: *"Mangia!"*

Eat!

Consume.

But after their Hickory Farms and J.C. Penney orgy, the quartet grow finally and unshakably *bored.* The mall, despite its endless supply of material goods, ultimately fails to confer happiness. The survivors soon kill their time playing records on high-end stereo systems, getting sloshed on gin, skating aimlessly at the mall rink, gambling with worthless piles of cash lifted from the mall bank. Their life degenerates into glitzy despair, until they show all the vitality of the zombies in the outside parking lot. From behind her deluxe '70s vintage fondue kit, Fran asks, "What have we done to ourselves?"

Romero is fairly explicit about the parallels between the living and the Undead. In one scene, the survivors—absurdly overdressed in fancy furs—survey their maximum-security consumer utopia. While the groaning hordes of zombies try to claw their way back into the mall, the survivors wonder what drives them.

PETER: They're after the place. They don't know why. They just remember. Remember that they want to be in here.
STEPHEN: What the hell are they?
PETER: They're us. That's all.

As the hero and moral center of the film, Peter isn't just speaking about himself and the other survivors in the mall. He's speaking about *us* the viewers as well, consumers in our own right, viewers tempted by the fantasy of unlimited access to a mall full of stuff. And presumably, he's speaking for Romero as well. Yet Peter's words also have a sense of implied criticism. By equating "us" with the walking dead outside the mall, Peter hints that we the living might not be so much better off than the zombies.

"I Don't Want to Be Walking Around Like *That*!": Living versus Living Well

So what might we consumers have in common with the living dead? Why might we both have ceaseless desires to *consume things*?

In *Nicomachean Ethics*, Book V, Chapter 1, Aristotle calls the overreaching desire for the goods of fortune *pleonexia*. In ancient Greek, the word *pleonexia* literally means "the disposition to have more," but carries the sense of "graspingness," of "grabbing for extra when you have your share." In *Politics*, Book I, Chapter 9, Aristotle tries to explain *pleonexia* by reference to people's unlimited desire for sheer survival: "The cause of this disposition is being serious about living, but not living well. Now with their desire for living extending into infinity, so too they desire without limit the things productive of living." In other words, *pleonexia* is motivated by an excessive desire to hold on to life. By taking more than their fill of the goods of fortune—which Aristotle identifies in *Nicomachean Ethics*, Book V, Chapter 2 as honor, wealth, security, and the like—those who "grasp" seek to keep at bay the inescapable bad fortune with which death confronts us. To this extent, the grasping differ from those whom Peter says "still believe there's respect in dying."[1]

In *Dawn*, graspingness is probably best personified by Stephen (a.k.a. "Flyboy"), the well-meaning, but tragically flawed, proto-yuppie who convinces his girlfriend Fran to take off with him in a stolen TV news chopper. When she expresses ethical reservations, he interrupts with an appeal to the ultimate,

---

[1] My discussion of plexonia and mortality has benefitted from Thomas W. Smith, *Revaluing Ethics: Aristotle's Dialectical Pedagogy* (Albany: SUNY Press, 2001), pp. 136–140.

brute value of sheer self-preservation: "We've got to survive, Fran. Somebody's got to survive." Later on at the mall, Stephen rhapsodizes to Fran about his virgin "shopping trip" with Peter and Roger. "You should see all the great stuff we got, Frannie," he says. "All kinds of stuff! This place is terrific. It really is. It's perfect. All kinds of things. We've really got it made here." Thus, when an outlaw biker gang invades the mall toward the end of the film—"We don't like people who don't share!" yells their leader—it's Stephen who takes to his rifle and fires the first shots in a final battle to defend his spoils. "It's ours," he mutters. "We took it. It's ours."

One of the great mysteries of Romero's zombie films is just *why* the dead return. In the first, *Night of the Living Dead* (1968), newscasters speculate that radiation from a returning Venus space probe is somehow involved. In *Dawn*, there's some chat about a virus, and at one point, Peter proposes that hell is full, but no one *really* knows. No answer is ever settled upon.

Perhaps *pleonexia* plays a role. To desire living without limit is to desire immortality, or in ancient Greek, to be *athanatos*. But one might be *a-thanatos*—literally, without death, deathless—in at least two ways. On one hand, one could be immortal by living like the gods to whom Aristotle alludes in *Nicomachean Ethics*, Book X, Chapter 7, the divinities who spend eternity in the exalted contemplation of the cosmic order. On the other hand, one might be immortal simply by continuing to metabolize, simply by *surviving*, even if the resulting survival left much to be desired. To be without death in this sense might count simply as *not* being dead, or as being *un-dead*. So maybe one "explanation" for the dead's return to life is that their graspingness *in* life—rooted in their unlimited desire *for* life—knows no bounds. From beyond the grave, they grasp for more living, even if such survival fails to count as living *well*. As Stephen speculates, the walking dead haunt the mall out of "a kind of instinct . . . memory . . . what they used to do." As the Undead, the zombies continue to act on the desires that governed them during their lives. It's not surprising, then, that once the walking dead have turned him into dinner, it's the now-lurching, Undead Stephen who leads the zombie army upstairs into the protagonists' makeshift penthouse.

"Attention All Shoppers: If You Have a Sweet Tooth, We Have a Treat for You!": The Limits of Hedonism

Even if both zombies and consumers are driven by grasping-ness, why join Romero in thinking that consumerism should turn us into zombies? Or, to put it another way, why should *Dawn's* hard-shopping quartet zombify *themselves* through unlimited acquisition?

Once again, Aristotle offers a clue. Immediately following the *Politics* passage quoted earlier, he argues that the unlimited desire to consume for the sake of *mere* living typically assumes a certain picture of *good* living. In his trademark crabbed Greek, Aristotle writes, "And as much as they aim at living well, they seek after bodily enjoyments, so that since these also seem to find their source in acquisitions, all focus is on obtaining wealth." In other words, those who grasp after material goodies are prone to identify the good life with a life of enjoyment, a life devoted to the kind of pleasure that we can procure through consumption. (In *Nicomachean Ethics*, Book V, Chapter 2, Aristotle calls such gratification "the pleasure from gain.") In fact, so far as such a pleasure-focused life promises to be free of suffering, it might seem to offer the same insulation against fate that mere living does (see Smith, *Revaluing Ethics*, pp. 142–46).

It's fitting, then, that Romero's original screenplay for *Dawn* describes the mall's "bright store fronts, with their displays of goods designed to attract shoppers to the sweet life the items pretend to represent." Romero's use of the term "sweet life" is revealing. In ancient Greek, the word "sweet" translates as *hêdus*, which also means "pleasant." *Hêdus* is the word from which we get the English "hedonistic." The sweet life that Romero thinks the mall advertises, we might guess, is a hedo-nistic life—a life of enjoyment like the one Aristotle talks about. But given what happens to his gang of four, Romero seems skeptical about the sweetness of this life. It wouldn't seem to be so sweet after all.

In Book I of the *Nicomachean Ethics*, Aristotle examines the sweet life as a model for good living, or what he calls "happi-ness" (*eudaimonia*). When Aristotle talks about "happiness," though, he doesn't do so in a narrowly "psychological" way.

He's not using "happiness" the way I might if I were to say, "I was so happy when I found a limited first edition Japanese pressing of Goblin's *Dawn of the Dead* soundtrack!" Our modern notion of happiness usually refers to a transitory elevated mood or feeling. Aristotle, by contrast, is speaking about something like the *best possible life* for human beings, the life in which human beings *flourish* most, the life in which they most fully *shine forth* as the kinds of beings they are.

To see what Aristotle's driving at, consider plants and animals. While neither can be "happy" in any strict sense, they can still live better or worse *as* plants or animals. The best life for a spider plant will be the life in which it flourishes most as a spider plant, blossoming forth with sturdy green shoots and photosynthesizing without a hitch. The best life for a bulldog will be the one in which she flourishes most as a bulldog, with all the barking, tail wagging, slobbering, and eating that should entail. In turn, Aristotle's *Nicomachean Ethics* searches for the best mode of life for human beings. Aristotle wants to spell out the features of a life in which the highest capacities of human nature most fully come to light.

Although he ultimately rejects the life of enjoyment as a model of happiness, Aristotle tries to give it a fair hearing in *Nicomachean Ethics*, Book I, Chapter 5. After all, he notes, this is the life in which most people—"and the most vulgar"—think that happiness consists. Even if he's a bit snobbish here, Aristotle doesn't think common opinion about the life of enjoyment is totally wrong or crazy. Surely, we'd all agree pleasure should have *some* place in happiness. No doubt we're tempted by the lives of those who possess the material resources to enjoy whatever sensual indulgences they wish. If we're honest with ourselves, part of us is probably tempted to say, "*That's* the life!" Aristotle considers the life of Sardanapallus, a mythical Assyrian king who spent his palace days eating, drinking, and loving. In *Dawn of the Dead*, we might think of Roger, who finds the mall's master keys and quips, "Keys to the kingdom."

But can happiness really be reduced to a life of enjoyment through consumption? Like Romero, Aristotle thinks not. He dismisses the life spent in the pursuit of pleasure as "fit for cattle." Aristotle's not just being a prig here: he really means it. As he argues a few chapters later, such a sensation-focused life might actually do the trick for horses, oxen, and other animals, which lack capacities for reason and which flourish by living in accord with their sensitive capacities. But such a life cannot fit the bill for human beings, organisms best defined by their capacities for practical and theoretical reason.

To put the point another way, Aristotle thinks the life of enjoyment gets its priorities wrong. Neither the unlimited pursuit of stuff, nor its use in a life devoted to bodily enjoyment, grants sufficient weight to our key capacities. At best, a life of enjoyment treats these capacities as purely instrumental means for getting more stuff and more bodily pleasure. Like the flesh-eaters who always fall for Peter and Roger's diversionary tactics—mindlessly following their tap-tap-tapping against store windows—those devoted to enjoyment through consumption ultimately get tugged around by whatever pleasures and wayward distractions come their way. So described, the life of enjoyment is not one somebody can truly *lead*. And since it leads to the atrophy of those capacities that most fully manifest our humanity, Aristotle believes that it can't fully satisfy us. As the path to frustration taken by *Dawn*'s characters, it proves a kind of living death.

"Hey, Let's Get the Stuff We Need!": Putting the Mall in Its Place

That's not to say that Aristotle thinks material goods and sensual pleasure have no place in the best human life. As he argues in *Nicomachean Ethics*, Book I, Chapter 8, we need material goods because they provide the equipment necessary for performing those noble and virtuous actions that best display our rational capacities at work. If we lack these goods, the happiness we obtain through our virtuous activity is apt to be stunted and deformed. Moreover, sensual pleasure can and should be enjoyed in a happy life—temperately, in a virtuous manner guided by practical wisdom. So even if he challenges the goodness of unbridled acquisitiveness, Aristotle defends some forms of consumption after all, provided that they stay within reasonable limits. In *Politics* Book I, Chapter 9, he insists that these limits are set by the good life itself. Acquisition that supports such a life is beneficial; acquisition that hinders it is bad.

Likewise, we go astray if we see Romero as a cranky scold in high Puritan mode, tsk-tsking us for being enticed by the day-dream of living in a shopping mall. Romero's satire of consumerism, while sometimes savage, is never nihilistic, never merely cynical. More than anything, Romero's treatment of this life is melancholic. Although the zombies horrify us, they are sad creatures, lost souls condemned to wander the mall in search of an elusive satisfaction.

While he's clear that the mall encourages a false view of the good life to the extent that it encourages passive consumerism, Romero doesn't necessarily reject the mall completely. Although the mall misleads us by identifying the good life with "gadget-oriented affluence" (as Romero's script calls it), the mall at least offers temporary sanctuary for the film's main heroes, Peter and Fran. For Romero, then, the mall is at least instrumentally valu-able as a place where you can get useful goods—and surely, *that* value is nothing to scoff at. Ultimately, however, Peter and Fran have to leave the mall at *Dawn*'s conclusion if they're going to preserve any of their humanity. As their helicopter ascends the shopping center teeming once more with zombies, Peter asks how much fuel is left. "Not much," Fran says. The film ends on an ambiguous note: while the dawn sun brings with it the prospect of a happier day, even if Peter and Fran have to face it empty-handed, these last survivors ultimately have no place to go. To the extent that a life of unlimited means has blinded them to the ends that make a life worth living, it has left them without a clear destination.[2]

---

[2] For helpful comments, I'd like to thank Marissa Walsh, Christian Bauman, and the edi-tors of this volume. For a more in-depth (though somewhat technical!) discussion of Aristotle's views about the value of "external" goods, see John M. Cooper, "Aristotle on the Goods of Fortune," in his *Reason and Emotion: Essays on Ancient Moral Psychology and Ethical Theory* (Princeton: Princeton University Press, 1999). Translations in this chapter are my own.

8

Zombies, Rest, and Motion: Spinoza and the Speed of Undeath

K. SILEM MOHAMMAD

Zombies are, one might say, the deadest of the Undead. In the classic Hollywood depiction, they are shambling, cadaverous beings whose creeping, halting motions are one of the most unsettling aspects of their appearance. Even in cases where a zombie is not technically dead, but hypnotized like Madge Bellamy in *White Zombie* (Victor Halperin, 1932), or in a coma—arguably—like Christine Gordon in *I Walked with a Zombie* (Jacques Tourneur, 1943), the eeriness of the cinematic spectacle consists in the separation of the person from her consciousness at the same time that she continues to walk and perform simple actions. A similar dread infuses the replacement of living persons by alien pod people in *Invasion of the Body Snatchers* (Don Siegel, 1956) or by androids in *The Stepford Wives* (Bryan Forbes, 1975): the body looks the same, but the consciousness is gone or transformed into something inhuman.

We don't want the dead to get up and walk, even—or especially—if we loved to see them moving in life. Nor do we want to see our loved ones acting slowed-down and emotionless as if they were "dead," even in a figurative sense: it creeps us out. In the absence of what we think of as the vitality of conscious existence, the ability to walk or clutch or even eat amounts to little more than the grisly reflexive spasms of rigor mortis. Either what ought to be vivacious and spirited has become still and lifeless, or what ought to be dead somehow, uncannily, is not. Either way, we react with horror.

But why exactly does slowness or stillness play so central a part in the horror we associate with zombies? Often invoked in this context is Sigmund Freud's famous theory of the "uncanny" (*unheimlich*), derived from Friedrich Schelling's idea that "everything is uncanny that ought to have remained hidden and secret, and yet comes to light." Freud describes the uncanny as "that class of the terrifying which leads back to something long known to us, once very familiar." Whatever we perceive as uncanny, he argues, is connected with memories that we have repressed since childhood and that are reawakened by unexplainable, disturbing *recurrences*. Things that we have shoved back into a dark corner of our awareness—even things that were initially familiar and comforting—undergo a disturbing transformation when they reemerge, especially if they reemerge by some means other than an exertion of our own will.

"Many people," Freud observes, "experience the feeling in the highest degree in relation to death and dead bodies, to the return of the dead, and to spirits and ghosts." Vampires, zombies, and other Undead beings, accordingly, are often represented as (un)living embodiments of the return of the repressed. Their sluggishness replicates the motionlessness of death, but at the same time enacts a suppressed wish: that the dead might return to us, move among us again as they did in life. In its new, uncanny manifestation, however, this once-familiar motion terrifies us rather than giving us comfort or joy.

This dynamic of the uncanny is not limited to human bodies, or even to animate beings. Terms like "zombie" have enjoyed increasing currency in both theoretical and popular discourse as ways of referring to any attenuated modes of existence in which an original presence is supplanted by a phantasmic placeholder, as when Bulent Diken writes that the World Trade Center survives after its destruction as a "spirit, zombie, or fetish" in media consciousness.[1] In this image, perhaps, we see the ultimate emblem of Undeath: an edifice endowed with consciousness by public sentiment only after its destruction, at which time it becomes a kind of inanimate zombie. Or it has in a sense been animated, but only as a set of phantom tombstones for itself. A stillness that in "life" was in no way remarkable (all skyscrapers are still) becomes uncannily inextricable in "death" from our association of it with a haunting and haunted absence.

---

[1] "'We Are All Migrants': Immigration, Multiculturalism and Post-Politics after September 11" *Third Text* 57 (Winter 2001–02).

Recently, however, popular-culture developments have thrown a spin on this traditional equation of zombies with creeping slowness and stillness. A new zombie walks—or rather runs—among us. Zombies (some of them, at least) are now scary in a speedier way.

Slow Zombies

Zombies of the original Caribbean variety, as depicted in films like *White Zombie* and *I Walked with a Zombie*, only move when bidden, or when set by some external cause into automatic motion. It may never occur to them, accordingly, to cease from such motion until they are commanded otherwise or stopped by some accidental force. They are, that is, only contingently animate. It is significant that these voodoo-charmed slaves first struck the popular imagination of western capitalist society at the dawn of industrial automatization: they are the perfect metaphor for an utterly alienated modern workforce.

In the intervening years of the twentieth century, however, a host of social and technological innovations conspire to create the conditions for a new evolutionary phase in the un-life of this figure, chief among which are the pervasive specter of nuclear annihilation and the increasing spasms of unrest among various underclasses. By the 1960s, a different kind of zombie rears its rotting head: one that does not merely shamble obediently, but pursues its own gruesome agenda.

The archetypal incarnation of the radicalized postmodern zombie emerges in George Romero's 1968 film *Night of the Living Dead*. Like its predecessors, this zombie is dull, slow-moving, and low on affect. Unlike them, it acts on its own initiative, a seemingly inexhaustible compulsion to devour the flesh of living humans. Perhaps more accurately, whereas the voodoo zombies are under the control of human masters who manipulate them in order to achieve their own ends, these ghouls are under the control of an impersonal force that nevertheless manifests itself in the zombies' uniform compliance. That force is radiation, supposedly released by a satellite that has crashed to earth.

Romero's radioactive Undead are aggressive, relentless, and highly efficient. By the end of *Night*, the living characters have all either been overpowered by them or killed trying to escape them. This is due in part, to be sure, to the protagonists' isolation: recurring emergency broadcasts indicate that although the zombie menace is widespread, law enforcement and military authorities have been able to contain the outbreak in populated areas to some degree. Homegrown armies equipped with rifles, gasoline, and metal hooks manage to surround and demobilize great numbers of the walking dead with minimal difficulty, owing chiefly to one liability on the Undead's part: like the voodoo zombies of the past, they are *slow*. As a rural sheriff proclaims during a televised news report, "They're dead, they're all messed up."

In Romero's later films, however, containment of the Undead has not been so successful. By *Dawn of the Dead* (1978), the first sequel, it is clear that the crisis is global, and that there is no clear solution in sight. In *Day of the Dead* (1985), the third film in the series, it appears that humanity has been driven almost entirely underground. *Land of the Dead* (2005), the most recent installment, hints that while civilization has regained some of its foothold, the threat of zombie rebellion indicates what may be a permanent state of crisis for two competing "class" structures: the privileged but besieged living and the disenfranchised but ever-more organized Undead.

The slowness of these zombies, then, does not necessarily result in failure. Like ants, they are relatively easy to kill, but as soon as you turn your back there are more of them. Romero's message at the end of *Land* appears to be that the Undead, like Mother Theresa's poor, are always with us. In fact, the Undead in this fourth film are in many ways indistinguishable from the living poor: they are hungry, unruly, and unattractive, and no one wants to become one of them. They are no longer really even truly scary, so much as a grim, intractable nuisance. From a certain perspective, *Land* is the most "optimistic" film in Romero's tetralogy: despite all the horror and slaughter, there is still, it suggests, something like a choice to be made, and accordingly there is a potential solution. What this solution might be is unclear, but at least there is still some time to work towards it. This much at least the leaden pace of the zombie masses allows.

Before we move on to the sped-up zombies of more recent cultural productions, let's take a brief look at Spinoza's *Ethics* (1677), wherein he derives a theory of ethics from the natural physical relations of acting and being-acted-upon that obtain between bodies, and of the speeds at which those relations occur.

(De)composing Bodies

In order to apply Spinoza's thought to the concept of Undeath, it may be helpful first to examine his account of the difference between life and death itself. He argues that death is by no means a cut-and-dried state, and that the body might in fact "die" though certain vital signs persist:

> I understand the Body to die when its parts are so disposed that they acquire a different proportion of motion and rest to one another. For I dare not deny that—even though the circulation of the blood is maintained, as well as the other signs on account of which the Body is thought to be alive—the human Body can nevertheless be changed into another nature entirely different from its own. For no reason compels me to maintain that the Body does not die unless it is changed into a corpse.[2]

To talk about life and death as points on a continuum in this way rather than as absolute states of existence, and to define life itself as a set of relations between moving parts rather than as a mystical force that exists independently of the body, is to posit a radical definition of consciousness or soul.

In his earlier book, *The Emendation of the Intellect* (published posthumously with the *Ethics* in 1677), Spinoza describes the soul (or mind) as a "spiritual automaton" (II/18), a mechanism that is autonomous but subject to fixed laws of thought in the same way that material bodies are subject to physical laws. In the *Ethics*, Spinoza treated mind and body as two separate modes of the same essence, and was especially concerned to refute dualist theories that attempted to explain the motions of the body by positing the dominance of mind:

---

[2] IV, P39 Schol. In *The Collected Works of Spinoza* Volume I, edited and translated by Edwin Curley (Princeton: Princeton University Press, 1985), pp. 408–617. When Spinoza refers to "the Body," he does not mean only an assemblage of mechanical organs; he means the entire person whose physical and mental states taken together comprise the Body. For Spinoza there is no meaningful distinction between such states: he asserts that "the Mind and the Body are one and the same thing, which is conceived now under the attribute of Thought, now under the attribute of Extension . . ." (III, P2, Schol.).

And of course, no one has yet determined what the Body can do, i.e., experience has not yet taught anyone what the Body can do from the laws of nature alone, insofar as nature is only considered to be corporeal, and what the Body can do only if it is determined by the Mind. . . .

Again, no one knows how, or by what means, the Mind moves the Body, nor how many degrees of motion it can give the Body, nor with what speed it can move it. So it follows that when men say that this or that action of the Body arises from the Mind, which has dominion over the Body, they do not know what they are saying, and they do nothing but confess, in fine-sounding words, that they are ignorant of the true causes of that action, and that they do not wonder at it. (*Ethics* III, P2, Schol.)

From a Spinozist point of view, we might observe, there is no *material* difference between a zombie and, say, a ghost. Both are the mobile, uncanny residue of living subjects, toxic complexes of actions that continue past the point when they should be able, or when none desire them to. A Spinozist would then reject any idea that they are opposites, that one is "body" and the other "mind." Such distinctions finally amount to little: both move, both touch, both bring death to life. What is a body, if not a presence that imposes itself on experience? What is a mind, if not the principle that translates the actions of such presences into intentions and desires?

Spinoza's emphasis on bodily autonomy, as well as on motion, rest, and speed, goes some way toward demonstrating why he is an ideal writer from whom to derive a philosophy of zombiedom. One of the things that made it difficult for him to publish his theories in his lifetime was the tendency for his thought to challenge the tenets of scriptural theism, suggesting as he does that the soul can be conceived as a complex of determinate actions and reactions—that is, in much the same way that he conceives the physical body. For Spinoza, we are all, in at least one sense, automatons or zombies.

Spinoza conceives of death as a disruption or redisposition of parts, or of simple bodies within composite bodies, wherein "the simplest bodies … are distinguished from one another only by motion and rest, speed and slowness" (II, P13 A2"). Deleuze refers to the process here described by Spinoza as one of "composition" and "decomposition": certain bodies make themselves faster and more complex (that is, more powerful) by decomposing the relations between parts of other bodies and absorbing those relations so that they are recomposed as their own.

When a bird eats an insect, or when a person eats a bird, the relations conducive to life are absorbed by the consuming body, and that body is thereby made stronger. When a zombie decomposes the relations of a living human by consuming its flesh, it not only thereby gains sustenance for its own body, it also facilitates a larger process of de- and re-composition wherein the victim's body itself becomes a zombie body which in turn seeks other living bodies to de- and re-compose. Because by far the greatest amount of energy expended by zombies goes toward this process of assimilation, in some ways it makes more sense to think of the zombie's body not as the individual, animated human corpse it occupies, but as the larger mass of bodies that constitute the total zombie organism.[3]

One might wonder where ethics comes into all this. Just as Spinoza got in trouble with the religious authorities of his day by espousing a theory of *pantheism* (God is everything, everything is God) that in their minds—and, more approvingly, in the minds of later readers—amounted to atheism, he also courted endless recrimination by anticipating Nietzsche in rejecting the moral concepts of good and evil in favor of the more narrowly ethical (or ethological) concepts of good and *bad*:

> Those things are good which bring about the preservation of the proportion of motion and rest the human Body's parts have to one another; on the other hand, those things are evil which bring it about that the parts of the human Body have a different proportion of motion and rest to one another. (IV, P39)

From this point of view, that which is good or bad is so only from the perspective of the body that is either composed or decomposed by other bodies. Accordingly, concepts such as "evil," considered in an absolute sense, are merely abstractions that get in the way of our achieving the the greatest fulfillment possible in our lives; they cause us to tend toward sadness rather than towards joy, and therefore should be avoided. Phenomena like poisoning, sickness, and death, in this ethical

---

[3] For an entertaining virtual illustration of this process and its alarming rapidity, visit the Zombie Infection Simulation web-game at http://kevan.org/proce55ing/zombies/.

system, are no more than what Spinoza, as rendered by Deleuze, calls "bad encounters":[4] bad for the body that gets decomposed, good for the decomposing body (in the case of zombies, decomposing in more sense than one).

A workable ethics, then, consists in finding out what relations are possible between different bodies, and in what way those relations can most effectively contribute to our well being both as individuals and as a collective community. Deleuze frames the questions relevant to a Spinozist ethology as follows:

> How do individuals enter into composition with one another in order to form a higher individual, ad infinitum? How can a being take another being into its world, but while preserving and respecting the other's own relations and world? . . . In what order and in what manner will the powers, speeds, and slownesses be composed?[5]

I want to suggest that zombies represent the progress of an imaginary counter-human ethology: one in which questions such as Deleuze's have failed to be adequately considered, and accordingly, in which another more powerful body (or body of bodies) steps in to enact its own process of recomposing its decomposing self by decomposing *our* compositions.

We say that zombies are "mindless"—it is practically part of the definition. What we mean, a Spinozist would say, is that they are very focused ("single-minded"). They have no time to spare on abstract reflection or moralizing. Or they are not permitted that privilege. Zombies, whether they are the will-sapped slaves of Haitian voodoo lore, or the bloodthirsty ghouls of Romero's living dead movies, are radically task-oriented beings. They have a job to do, and nothing else. And herein lies their true difference from ghosts: ghosts are often highly imaginative, even fanciful. They can afford to be, as they are far less subject to the constraints of time—that is, to the relations of rest and motion. A ghost, as a result, need hardly move at all. Zombies, on the other hand, are the products of imaginations in the grip of tremendous and immediately present real-world anxieties. And

---

[4] Gilles Deleuze, *Spinoza: Practical Philosophy* (San Francisco, City Lights, 1988), p. 22 and passim.
[5] *Spinoza: Practical Philosophy*, p. 126.

if they were at one time apprehended as a sluggish but steadily progressing horde on the horizon, symbolic of some vaguely imminent but still dormant catastrophe, they are now a violently swift and powerful explosion of nightmares spawned by our actual daily headlines.

Fast Zombies

As though sensing that Romero's relatively hopeful political idealism has overtaken his grasp on the severity of crisis, younger filmmakers have instituted a new modification of the Undead mechanism: the fast zombie. Two recent films get maximum mileage out of this innovation: Danny Boyle's *28 Days Later* (2002), and Zack Snyder's 2004 remake of *Dawn of the Dead*.

In *28 Days*, we are to understand the force driving the "zombies" as chemical, not radiological: they are impelled by a virally induced "rage" that apparently has nothing to do with hunger or any other bodily desire beyond the will to inflict harm. This compulsion is so strong that the actions of the infected ultimately lead to their own demise, as they do nothing to sustain their bodies, which finally break down. Contributing to this breakdown, no doubt, is the frantic pace with which they pursue the uninfected. Shots in which huge crowds of the infected chase the film's protagonists through the streets of London are chilling in their suggestion of real-life scenes of politically and religiously motivated mob violence, and even more chilling in that the social impetus for the violence is absent; there is no specific social grievance, only the mayhem that generally attends such grievances.

Similarly, in *Dawn*, rioting swarms of Undead surrounding a suburban shopping mall break windows, overturn burning vehicles, and shriek with what sounds like the extremist fervor of revolutionaries (but is in actuality brute blood lust). As with Boyle's infected, there is some suggestion that Snyder's zombie epidemic is virally or otherwise biologically induced, but unlike the former ghouls, these zombies don't wear out; they rot and break apart, but keep on coming. In both cases, there is a pronounced swerve from the "classic" model in which zombies are relatively easy to evade once one has gained a little distance and secured some fortification. It finally matters little whether the zombies in these films are "really" Undead or merely "sick": the physiological conditions they have entered fundamentally change their ethological composition, and thus their status as persons or nonpersons.

The first few minutes of *Dawn* constitute what should come to be considered one of the premier set pieces of zombie cinema. Ana (Sarah Polley) is a hospital nurse who drives home one evening at the end of what seems like a normal day, except for largely ignored media reports in the background (car radio, TV) of some vaguely developing crisis. Ana distractedly switches the station and turns the channel. When she pulls into the driveway of her suburban tract home, she is greeted by Vivian, the neighbor girl (the name connotes life and innocent vigor). Ana and her husband Luis go to bed.

In the next scene they awaken to see that Vivian is standing in the dark doorway to their bedroom. She is bloody and crazed. She hurls herself forcefully at Luis and tears out a big chunk of his flesh. Ana shuts herself in the bathroom. Luis, now also a zombie, batters down the door, and she manages to escape through the window. In a subtle visual shock, we see that it is not night-time, as the scene has seemed to suggest, but broad daylight. As Ana gets in her car and flees, pursued by the now-running Undead Luis, we see first that the neighborhood is in a state of chaos, and beyond that the entire city.

There are flames, sirens, and people running in the streets. Frantic residents run from sprinting zombies only to be struck down by speeding ambulances. As Ana makes her way onto the open road, the camera pulls back to give us wider panoramic views of the catastrophe. The city skyline is a haze of smoke and helicopters. In a computer-enhanced aerial shot, Ana's car narrowly escapes another car coming at her from a cross street at a T-shaped intersection, and the second car goes on to crash into a gas station, which explodes spectacularly. Ana's car goes off the road, into a secluded woodsy patch, where it collides with a tree.

Coinciding with Ana's implied unconsciousness, the credits begin. Documentary images of global unrest are montaged against news reports of the unfurling zombie crisis, to the accompaniment of Johnny Cash's jangling end-times anthem "The Man Comes Around." Shots of rioters in the streets and Muslims bowing their heads at prayer in mosques are juxtaposed with Undead faces and limbs gaping and clutching at the camera. Talking heads on TV inform us that no one knows any-thing and that there is no end in sight to the terror.

At this point the viewer may already be exhausted, and indeed, although there are other memorable moments in the film, nothing quite compares to these first nightmarish minutes in terms of sheer adrenaline-surging shock. These fast zombies, unlike Romero's, are never presented as poignant embodiments of desire, whether for food or for lost identities. When Luis pounds on the window of Ana's car with his fist, he seems more angry than hungry. There's no indication that Snyder's zombies bite their victims in order to eat them rather than just to attack; like Boyle's infected, they are driven primarily by naked, irra-tional aggression.

If, at the end of Romero's *Land*, there is the implication that the class of the living must find some way to adjust its own all-consuming demands in order to accommodate the irresistibly emerging class of the Undead and thus avoid annihilation at its hands, the implication of Boyle's and (especially) Snyder's films is yet more alarming: the living have had their chance and blown it. More to the point, the alarming shift from representa-tions of zombies as slow-moving to fast-moving predators sig-nals a mass awareness that these Undead figures, without losing their fierce relevance to our contemporary condition of perma-nent crisis, have changed the visceral referent of their terror-inducing power from the relatively placid, yellow- to orange-alert realm of the Uncanny to the full-bore red-alert level of the Real.

Zombies, we might conclude, are the monsters *par excel-lence* of late-capitalist culture. If voodoo mind-controlled zom-bies translate the uncanny into a twentieth-century context of alienated labor and an oppressed third world, postmodern and postnuclear zombies such as Romero's—and to an even greater extent, fast zombies like Boyle's and Snyder's—push us beyond uncanniness. They are not just symbols of repressed desire or anxiety; they are the radically embodied, limit-breaking conse-quences of repression in its social totality, the inevitable erup-tion of crisis on a global rather than personal level. The increase in zombie velocity we see in recent films is an extreme expres-sion of a Spinozist-Deleuzean bad encounter which outstrips humanist imagining. The perspective from which we view these zombies is one we cannot rationally assume: the perspective of the Body transitioning into the greater composition of the Body by which it is decomposed.

Vampires play to a fantasy of quasi-imperialist dominance, of identification with Evil as a force of powerful immortality (and accordingly, of Good as a convenient escape hatch). Zombies afford no such flattering binary constructions of morality. They confront us with a world reduced to the elemental valences of good and bad, bodies in motion and bodies in faster motion. If we identify with zombies, it is an impossible identification with the dissolution that must inevitably ensue in the failure of our species to assimilate other bodies into ourselves in a mindfully ethical way.

PART III

Dirty Rotting
Scoundrels

9

Zombie Gladiators

DALE JACQUETTE

> Those unmindful when they hear for all they make of their intelligence may be regarded as the walking dead.
>
> —HERACLITUS, Fragment 3

On the Prowl

Hollywood zombies are easily distinguished from ordinary civilians like you and me. They are ravenous, stalking, reanimated dead people with superhuman strength, overturning cars and breaking through doors. They feed on the living flesh of hapless victims, and with a single infectious bite they can turn others into zombies in a growing mob of the marauding Undead. We know them by their rotting limbs, sunken dull lifeless eyes, and gnashing teeth. The classic Hollywood zombie stagger gives them away even from a distance as we flee in our SUVs from one ravenous horde to the waiting maws of another hulking throng blocking the street at the edge of town.

Often we do not know even by the end of the movie where zombies come from. It's a virus, or a curse, or just something that happens every once in a while. Filmmakers can cook up the flimsiest plots about why the Undead are loose, or they can just picture the world of today as though it suddenly had to barricade itself against an onslaught of the predeceased. It scares the pants off of us in the theater to watch these ghouls rampaging on the screen, just as it is meant to. The point, dramatically, is to portray these unfortunates as a frightening life- and even civilization-threatening menace, and then to blow their heads off in interesting ways. They are, after all, already dead, and they will thoughtlessly destroy us all if we don't destroy them first. Hollywood zombies nevertheless are not the most frightening kind of zombie that might be encountered.

Philosophical Zombies

We need to distinguish Hollywood from *philosophical zombies*, the latter of which are still more insidious than their Hollywood prototypes, even though as a rule they do not feed on human flesh. They terrify precisely because they are so difficult—practically impossible in many contexts—to discern from ordinary human beings.

Philosophical zombies were dreamed up by philosophers as a thought experiment to test concepts and illustrate a variety of theoretical problems about the nature of consciousness and the mind's relation to the body. Philosophical zombies look and act just like you and me, so that, in contrast with Hollywood zombies, there is often no way to know the difference. Indeed, the only difference between philosophical zombies and non-zombies is the stipulated fact that the former have no conscious states of mind such as feelings of pain, joy, belief states, desires, or the like.

A rock presumably has no conscious mental states, whereas a dog probably does. Philosophical zombies are more like rocks than dogs in this regard, even though they behave and even talk in a manner indistinguishable from that of normal conscious persons. David J. Chalmers proposes in this light "to consider the logical possibility of a *zombie*: someone or something physically identical to me (or to any other conscious being), but lacking conscious experiences altogether."[1]

If we look around at the persons in our community, standing in line at the bank or grocery store, or even members of our family and friends we have known for many years, we should consider the logical possibility that any of them might be philosophical zombies. The problem is that we would have no way to know it from their external appearance or behavior. You and

---

[1] David J. Chalmers, *The Conscious Mind: In Search of a Fundamental Theory* (Oxford: Oxford University Press, 1996), p. 94.

I, on the other hand, can rest assured that we are not zombies, and in a sense we could not be, as long as we are thinking thoughts such as these.[2]

Automata Among Us

How is it possible for human beings who look and act just like you and me to exist without any conscious states? It may be conceivable for such a thing to occur, if all motor actions including a subject's verbal behavior are governed autonomically by those parts of the brain that in normal individuals are solely responsible for such unconscious functions as heartbeat, breathing, digestion, and the like, over which we do not generally exercise volitional control.

Suppose, then, that all aspects of zombie behavior are controlled by autonomic functioning of the brain stem. This would leave completely inactive the frontal lobes of the brain where consciousness is supposed to reside. The brain of a philosophical zombie manages all the creature's behavior, including body language, speech acts and verbal interaction, by purely unconscious neural functioning. The outward appearance of a philosophical zombie is indistinguishable from that of a conscious psychological subject, but there is, so to speak, nobody home.

A philosophical zombie is an automaton. All its movements function autonomically without any accompanying conscious mental states. The philosopher's zombie is so fluid in its movements, and sufficiently natural-appearing in facial expression and what to it is meaningless verbal exchange in conversation, that it blends in perfectly in all walks of life in human society. No one can tell philosophical zombies apart from what I will call "conscios": that is, those of us with conscious inner mental lives. Philosophical zombies are capable of articulate speech that cannot be told apart from that of normal conscious persons. They can write and publish books, including novels, scientific monographs and abstruse treatises in philosophy. They can be President of the United States, members and even chairpersons of the boards of directors of major corporations, television evan-

---

[2] See the *Journal of Consciousness Studies*, special issue on Zombies, Volume 2, No. 4, (1995), and for criticism, Edward Ingram, "The Mark of Zombie," *Philosophy Now* (December 2000–January 2001), pp. 32–33.

gelists, university administrators, and no one need ever be the wiser! One way to describe the difference between Hollywood zombies and philosophical zombies is that philosophical zombies are so well-behaved as a rule that you can invite them to dinner (contrast evangelists and administrators), whereas a Hollywood zombie, given half a chance and without benefit of cutlery, will have you for dinner.

A Plea for Zombie Gladiators

Let's now take this philosophical thought experiment a crucial step further. It would be useful to have a visible way of distinguishing between zombies and conscios. We cannot see into their souls, because zombies have no thoughts, just as we cannot know for certain in ordinary circumstances whether another person, even one of long acquaintance, is truly conscious. Similarly, we cannot tell from behavior or conversation with another individual whether or not he or she has any interior light or is a philosophical zombie, a living robot devoid of mental states.

Let us therefore suppose for the sake of argument that all and only zombies have a birthmark on the backs of their necks, shaped like the little round yellow smile or happy face we often find in advertising, but with a straight line for a mouth and x's for eyes—

x x

The birthmark implies that zombies are born, not made, and that they stay that way for life. How do we know that all and only persons with the birthmark are zombies? Conceivably, the correlation could be verified when a CAT-scan detects the abnormal neurophysiology by which zombie behavior is autonomically controlled through neural exchange in the brain-stem only, with no activity in the brain's frontal lobes as in normal conscious subjects.

If we can visually distinguish zombies from conscios, then the practical possibility arises of treating them discriminatorily. Zombies, lacking conscious mental states, cannot experience pain, nor are they capable of intentions, beliefs, or desires. If morality presupposes these specific kinds of thought, as many moral theorists have assumed, then it would appear that zombies are in every sense amoral. They are never morally responsible for what they do, and their behavior as a result can never be morally right or morally wrong. If we can tell who (or what) is a zombie and who (or what) is not, then we might suppose that we can use zombies with moral impunity in any way we like, just as we use inanimate objects. Zombies will rebel and behave with indignation if we try to abuse them, just as we would. They will weep, strike back, protest, organize resistance, print leaflets condemning their treatment, and give lectures to rouse public opinion in their support. They will argue that the bad reputation they have received from the depiction of Hollywood zombies has created prejudice against them on the part of the conscious citizenry. From a moral point of view, on the present hypothesis, if we can restrain them, it nevertheless appears that we might be able without acting immorally to use zombies just as we use wood and stone and plants and lower animals for our own purposes in whatever ways we please.

If zombies have no moral rights or responsibilities, then there should be nothing morally objectionable about organizing blood sports events involving zombie gladiators. Zombie gladiators can hack each other to death for our entertainment, just as conscious gladiators did in ancient times during the glorious days of the Roman Empire. Armed combat is exciting to watch, and we can think of zombie gladiatorial events as an extension of reality television and cinematic violence brought together as a live spectator sport. There are moral objections to pitting conscious persons against each other as gladiators, to be sure, since they are subject to sensations of pain, panic and the anticipation of death, and other kinds of psychological trauma. We would be wrong to allow such experiences to be inflicted on conscious subjects, even if they were to volunteer as gladiators.

Where zombies are concerned, however, we need not concern ourselves about their mental states, because we know in advance that, despite their physical actions and reactions, they do not have any. Zombies no more hurt one another or feel pain when they battle it out in the coliseum than cartoon characters do when they clobber each other with mallets or flatten each other with steam rollers. Morally, their bloody confrontations are no more immoral than the mechanical contests we see waged between Battlebots on TV.

It may take the public some getting used to. When zombies are cut with swords and hacked with halberds, they will not only gush blood, but exhibit the same pain behavior as conscious human beings. With enough advance publicity about the differences between zombies and conscios, however, there should eventually be no serious conscientious complaints about hosting zombie gladiatorial competitions in every major city, much as in Roman times.

We turn to Lucius Annaeus Seneca, in his *Epistulae Morales ad Lucilium*, with these disparaging words about the matinée gladiatorial contests in his day: "All the earlier contests were charity in comparison. The nonsense is dispensed with now: what we have now is murder pure and simple. The combatants have nothing to protect them; their whole bodies are exposed to the blows; every thrust they launch gets home."[3]

In contrast, zombies ought to make morally unobjectionable gladiators. They experience no pain when they are battered and stabbed, bludgeoned and mutilated, even though they bleed and behave exactly as if they were in agony. They also die in the biological sense just as we would, which adds to the pathos and drama of witnessing their combat. When zombies expire, however, there is no destruction of a person in the sense that there is no cessation of thought, no bringing down the curtain on what had been a more or less continuous stream of consciousness, no elimination of memories or expectations, no collapsing of intentions, and in particular no fear of impending death or anticipation or awareness, or any of the psychological trauma we may otherwise associate with violent death by sword and mace and trident in a gladiatorial confrontation.

Zombie gladiators can go at it full tilt. They can put on a splendid carnal spectacle that will instruct at the same time that it fascinates. It will teach martial values, as it did for the ancient Romans, providing daily emotional catharsis and illustrating valuable techniques of strategy and self-defense. It will offer its audience a sublime surrogate confrontation with death and dis-

---

[3] Translated as *Letters from a Stoic* by Robin Campbell (Harmondsworth: Penguin, 1969), Letter VII, pp. 41–42.

memberment that will help them to better appreciate the relative safety and comfort of their own lives. They will be glad that they are not gladiators, and, however irrationally, they will be glad that they are not zombies. At the same time, zombie gladiatorial events can be highly lucrative for everyone associated with the enterprise. Zombies themselves can be made to work (fight) for free, and the outlay for arenas, advertising and promotion, equipment and training, security and logistics should be minimal compared to the potential box office earnings from ticket sales, merchandizing, cable television franchising, and all the surrounding industry that is sure to grow up around the new sport.

There are other respects too in which we can hope to improve on Roman gladiatorial events. We have more interesting and devastating weapons that require special kinds of skills to wield and do visually more absorbing kinds of damage to a human body. Thus, we read in Max Brooks's manual, *The Zombie Survival Guide*,[4] a playbook for dealing with outbreaks of Hollywood zombies, the following advice:

> *The Flamethrower.* This device, perhaps more than any other, strikes people as the ultimate zombie eliminator. A jet of flame, two hundred feet long, composed of jellied gasoline, can turn an Undead crowd into a wailing funeral pyre. So why not acquire one?

Why not indeed? While we're at it, why not outfit entire teams of zombies with these curious devices and turn those suckers loose on each other? And this is just the beginning. There are chainsaws and spear-guns, nail-guns, napalm and mustard gas, automatic machine guns of many different calibers, samurai swords, and all kinds of things that it would be cool to see zombies put to use in fighting each other to the death.

There are likely to be some, perhaps even significant numbers of individuals, who choose not to attend gladiatorial battles, who will be offended or repulsed by the violence and bloodshed, or are afraid that they might be. There is, we must say at the outset, no accounting for taste in this or any other field. The same is true among a certain percentage of the citi-

---

[4] *The Zombie Survival Guide: Complete Protection from the Living Dead* (New York: Three Rivers Press, 2003), p. 54.

zens and visitors to such countries as Spain that continue to sponsor bull fighting, not as a sport, but, as Ernest Hemingway reminds us in *Death in the Afternoon*, the ritual killing of a bull.[5] With such a striking comparison in mind, we can conclude that while there is a sound moral basis for objecting to the sufferings of a bull besieged by picadors and the matador in a bull ring, there are no similar grounds for moral complaint against the maiming and slaughtering of zombie gladiators. The most ardent animal rights advocates can have no sound reason for objecting to zombie gladiatorial conflict. Zombie gladiators are meat robots, we might say, and nothing more. They are not persons with conscious feelings, beliefs and intentions; they do not hurt, and they do not intend to do what they do or have any beliefs or doubts, hopes, fears, expectations or disappointments. They are hollow shells, psychologically speaking, lacking all moral meaning and value.[6]

Amorality of Zombies and Moral Obligations of the Conscious

Or are they? Can there be good reasons after all for objecting on moral grounds to the institution of zombie gladiatorial competitions? There may still be questionable aspects of the proposal to use zombies as gladiators, even though they lack consciousness.

Zombies, birthmarks aside, look superficially just like you and me, sharing the same characteristic human DNA type. They are capable of the same complex repertoire of behavior, "intelligent" conversation (at least from an external point of view to which we as conscious subjects are also limited), and apparent displays of feelings and emotions as the rest of us. Conscios are likely, therefore, in at least some instances, to develop emotional attachments, friendships, and feel sympathy, even concern and love, for zombies. The fact that they are indistinguishable from

---

[5] New York: Scribner's, 1932, p. 16.

[6] A similar argument can be made about the questionable morality of "bum fights," in which homeless people are paid to fight one another in gladiator-like street combat. Bum fights have been denied broadcast time on television, but videotapes are available for sale on the Internet. (Thanks to Bill Irwin for this information.) The subcultural interest in bum-fights could transfer directly to zombie gladiatorial competitions without the moral stigma of inducing down-and-out conscious persons to attack one another for money.

living persons encourages the possibility that some conscios may genuinely come to care for and even love zombies. When zombies have the backs of their necks checked and are taken away in armored vans to serve as gladiators, their plight might cause pain, suffering, and distress to the conscios who have developed personal feelings for them. If this were to happen, then even on the assumptions we are considering, it could be morally wrong for indirect reasons to promote blood sport competitions among zombie gladiators.

The remedy is nevertheless quite simple. We need only keep zombies destined for gladiatorial combat isolated from the general population, raised by other zombies in zombie camps, and managed by zombies in every phase of their preparation for the sport. That way, no conscio could ever form an intimate emotional attachment to any zombie slated to become a gladiator. Similarly, we should probably suppose that zombies are never born to or raised by non-zombies once the gladiatorial games are instituted, so that there are no familial relations tying zombies to conscios. Zombies must be total strangers to those who are in attendance in the audience at a zombie gladiatorial event, if the moral probity of such events is to be maintained.

Having started in this direction, we must then ask whether even these sorts of extreme precautions can possibly be enough to uphold the amorality of zombie gladiatorial contests. We must also somehow try to guard against vicarious suffering on the part of conscios at zombie bloodbaths. This challenge to the amorality of zombie gladiatorial competitions reveals something interesting about our understanding of the interrelation between consciousness and morality. Now perhaps we must expect to screen the members of an audience attending zombie gladiatorial events carefully and reliably to exclude any individuals who might suffer more emotional pain, anxiety, or trauma than an average audience member at the cinema, theater, or any non-gladiatorial sport. Assuming that these more conventional activities are morally unobjectionable, we cannot blame zombie gladiatorial competitions on moral grounds if those in attendance do not vicariously suffer more mental anguish than at less violent non-lethal entertainments, such as hockey tournaments, certain inflammatorily confrontational talk shows, or compelling performances of Shakespeare's *Macbeth*.

There is still another moral consideration to be taken into account in contemplating zombie combat sports. We should try to judge the potential effect of witnessing socially approved massacres of creatures who, to all external ˙appearances, except for their birthmarks, look and behave exactly like conscios capable of feeling pleasure and pain. The issue of widespread desensitization to repetitive acts of violence in movies, video games and gangsta rap as a factor in personal crime has already gained scientific and media attention. Whether or not these influences contribute significantly to violent behavior is likely to remain an open question in social psychology. It is nevertheless hard to see how exposing large numbers of viewers to live-action armed bloody killings as a sports event can help to improve the social climate of good will and compassion among the general population, on whom our happiness and security, such as they are, vitally depend.

We must remember that the audience members pre-screened for admittance to zombie gladiatorial contests are precisely those who have demonstrated the least emotional distress in the presence of the sufferings of others. These of all persons are surely the greatest sociological risks to the population at large, after dosing on a steady diet of the most ferocious kinds of live action violence. Reflect also that we are imagining the whole entertainment industry apparatus organized behind zombie blood sports. There will be souvenirs, memorabilia, details of gladiatorial fights published in newspapers and broadcast on TV, documentaries, movies, T-shirts, coffee table books, and refrigerator magnets celebrating the most popular gladiators and the most dramatic maiming and killing. There will be everything, in short, that can contribute to the understanding that terrible violence has society's full blessing, provided that it involves only zombies.

For all intents and purposes, anyone attending a zombie gladiatorial event will nevertheless experience the carnage just as though it were perpetrated by and upon conscios. Officials can emphasize the fact that the gladiators are not conscious, that they are mere automata. What they cannot be expected to do is to fully dispel the impression that the combatants are thinking beings like ourselves, that they feel pain and know fear as they are crushed and ripped apart and do their best to crush and rip apart their opponents. The audience will know at a rational level that these Undead martial arts warriors have no interior mental life. At an emotional level, however, as they watch the violence unfold, they may find it impossible to draw what is supposed to be the crucial moral distinction between conscious subjects and zombie automata. They will see human beings killing human beings in what look to be the most painful ways possible, even if no pain is actually experienced by the participants, in a context of unqualified moral permissiveness. The audience members, many of them anyway, are certain to come away from the repeated experience with the ingrained sense that killing human beings as sport is socially acceptable.

It should be obvious upon reflection that none of this is a particularly good thing. Even if no audience member ever becomes a dangerous psychopath and goes on a murder spree killing innocent conscios, there is still something morally objectionable about the proposal. What is wrong with using zombies as gladiators is that it enacts the socially condoned slaughter of genetically fellow human beings who just happen not to be conscious, and who as a result just happen to be incapable of feeling pleasure or pain. Human beings, even if they are transformed demonically into howling Hollywood zombies, strangling and cannibalizing all whom they may devour, are still human beings, however posthumous, as we can readily verify by counting their chromosome pairs (twenty-three). To validate killing members of our own species solely for the sake of entertainment, curiosity, morbid fascination and blood lust evinces an ideal that deprives all human lives of dignity. Thus, Roland Auguet argues:

> A gladiator, with movements clumsy and stiff because of his armour, half kneels and raises his hooked visor, pierced by mysterious holes, towards an imaginary grandstand, menacing with his curved sword the man prostrate at his feet. . . . In one sense these pictures, a little morbid and shocking, teach us a lesson: that the life of a man has not always had the value that our own morality strives to give it. In the past it could be a mere episode, and death the instrument of a collective pleasure.[7]

Zombies have no moral rights. In the movies, Hollywood zombies are made morally acceptable targets of the worst acts of

---

[7] *Cruelty and Civilization: The Roman Games* (London: Allen and Unwin, 1972), p. 13.

desperate violence. We can blow them up with dynamite, toast them with flamethrowers, lop off their heads with machetes. They are, after all, already dead, slightly warmed over, and they threaten the rest of us unjustifiably with a most unpleasant end. We identify accordingly with the co-eds, deputy sheriffs, and shopkeepers pursued by roving gangrenous hordes of the Hollywood Undead.

The zombie gladiators thought experiment, in stark contrast, says of human beings generally that it is morally permissible to have them kill one another for the enjoyment of conscious viewers. It is this *symbolic* statement that is made about the dispensability of human life that we may come to regard as morally indecent, a reprehensible public statement of a value judgment for which we, unlike zombies, would be morally responsible. The same is true whenever such life-cheapening values are acted out on the field of mortal combat, as much in the zombie thought experiment as in ancient Rome when the gladiators were conscious thinking subjects like ourselves. The symbolic import of setting up an institution in which human zombie gladiators slice and dice and slash and bash each other's brains out as a form of popular entertainment is intrinsically morally objectionable. It is wrong, we might conclude, because of what it says about us and about our attitudes concerning the value of human life, even if the victims never feel pain and never suffer death throes when they are defeated, subdued, and delivered the final *coup de grâce.*

If we conclude that it is morally wrong for a society to make such a symbolic statement concerning its sense of the cheap value of human life, then why might we not say the same with respect to big screen depictions of the horrifying treatment of Hollywood zombies in films like *Dawn of the Dead* and *Night of the Living Dead* that are also produced for entertainment? In the recent *Land of the Dead*, the writers envisioned something very much like Hollywood zombie gladiatorial battles, using zombies for target practice, and pitting them against a living person in a cage for the crowd's amusement and political edification.

There are two important differences. First, patrons of the cinema, even children old enough to attend, know that they are watching actors in makeup with a dazzling array of special effects. The whole institution of filmmaking and of viewing projected images that are shown over and over again in many places, that can be owned in VHS or DVD format, is understood as a work of fiction. Zombie gladiator mutilations and slayings, by contrast, would be real, taking place in real time before the spectators' eyes. Secondly, in the movies there is always an opportunity amidst all the carnage to incorporate morally and socially redeeming values as a part of the entertainment. In the zombie gladiatorial arena, there is at most only the possibility for a false display of such virtues as courage, cunning, clemency, among others, in the struggle to survive, and the nobility, strength and determination of what might look to an audience to be force of will.

If these qualities happen to surface in a live gladiatorial performance, it can only be by sheer accident, as in real life, and not by artistic design. In the cinema, if moral values are to be communicated, they must be built into the choices that determine a film as a product of art. It is to the filmmaker's moral credit when such redeeming features are made part of a Hollywood zombie production. If virtues appear to be exemplified in a real-life zombie gladiatorial contest, they are not due to the combat organizers, who cannot plan for or direct the spontaneous behavior of zombie combatants, nor to the zombies themselves, who are utterly devoid of all conscious mental states, and hence of all moral intent or responsibility for their "actions" on the battlefield, as the audience also well knows.

Postmodern Postmortem

What can philosophy learn from the zombie gladiators thought experiment? As we take stock of our findings, it seems inescapable that being a person presupposes consciousness, which in turn is presupposed by morality. It follows, then, as we have emphasized, that zombies, as automata falling outside of moral judgment, are altogether amoral.

Zombies are never morally responsible for what they do or fail to do, never right or wrong in their behavior, never morally blameworthy or praiseworthy. These facts need not preclude the possibility that it may turn out to be causally effective in shaping their behavior to praise or blame, reward or punish zombies physically, even though they cannot be aware of what we are doing or saying, and even though they experience no pleasure or pain as a consequence of such actions. In this as in other respects, again, philosophical zombies are remarkably different from those wanton flesh-gnawing Hollywood zombies milling about the shopping mall after dark. What is not true, as demonstrated now by the zombie gladiators thought experiment, if we have correctly understood its implications, is that morally, therefore, we can do whatever we like to zombies.

There are good solid reasons for thinking that we should not use zombies as gladiators. To do so with no higher purpose than entertainment makes a morally objectionable symbolic statement about our (dis-)regard for human life, conscious or Undead. What this proves in turn is that consciousness or personhood is not both necessary and sufficient in deciding all questions of moral responsibility. We can act wrongly, in a sense, toward ourselves, in the way we treat zombies, even though we cannot hurt or in other ways psychologically traumatize them. The blame, if any, and moral responsibility, will always be entirely on our side, shouldered exclusively by those of us who are conscious thinkers with an understanding of the difference between moral right and wrong. Zombies get a moral pass for whatever they do; we conscious beings, with a sense of moral right and wrong, do not.[8]

---

[8] My fellow zombies, let us hope the conscios fall for this. By keeping up the propaganda machine we may at last avert their dastardly plans to organize the first zombie gladiatorial combats at Lincoln Mall later this year. We rally after this week's release of the new StarBright Pictures premiere of *Night of the Living Emeritus Professors.* We shall mix with conscios sympathetic to our cause and strengthen their numbers, while trying to get some international press coverage to call attention to our plight. We must appeal to their better moral judgments if we are to avoid the impending catastrophe by the Sports Planning Commission. Unite! What's so great about awareness? Cover up your birthmarks! Blend in with the crowd! Let the conscios watch themselves hacking each other to pieces if they like the idea so much! All power to the brain stem! No idea what I just said!

10

Should Vampires Be Held Accountable for Their Bloodthirsty Behavior?

JOHN DRAEGER

Vampires versus Zombies

Flesh-eating zombies have been known to feast on innocent people in a violent frenzy. Vampires often keep their victims alive only to kill them another day. Any human being performing such actions would be considered morally despicable and rightly so. But while human perpetrators should pay for their violence, it's unclear whether the Undead can be held to the same standard.

The zombies in George Romero's *Night of the Living Dead*, for example, lack the cognitive sophistication to be held accountable for their bloodthirsty behavior. Operating according to some set of (un)natural laws, they smash through doors and devour people in a kind of catatonic trance. They behave more like a plant drawn to sunlight than a rational creature aware of its surroundings. If a poisonous plant were to inadvertently take an innocent life, it wouldn't be subject to moral condemnation. The nuisance might reasonably be destroyed, but a plant cannot be held accountable because it is unaware of the damage it inflicts. Similarly, Romero's zombies should be stopped, but they shouldn't be blamed.

By contrast, Dracula meticulously plans his move to London. He secures the services of Jonathan Harker. He carefully considers which pieces of real estate to purchase. And he arranges passage aboard a cargo ship. Furthermore, he willingly makes short-term sacrifices for long-term gains. He isn't some mindless zombie lacking self-control. If he were, then he would have gorged himself on Harker before they reached his castle. Because Dracula understands the nature of his actions, he seems accountable in a way that Romero's zombies aren't.

Dracula: Amoral or Immoral?

Not everyone should be blamed for their harmful actions. Some people, such as those with severe mental deficiencies, cannot comprehend the nature of their actions and thus lack the where-withal to be held accountable. Romero's zombies fit this description. Other people, such as those with certain emotional deficiencies, lack an emotional connection with those around them. Psychiatrist Hervey Cleckley, for example, describes the puzzling behavior of a patient, named Milt, who seemed utterly indifferent to the needs of others.[1]

By way of illustration, Cleckley tells us that Milt once went to the hospital to pick up his mother. While driving her home, the car broke down and he set off to find the parts to fix it. On the way, however, he became engaged in one distraction after another. He watched football and talked to a friend. Cleckley suggests that Milt was not absentminded. He knew that his mother had just been released from the hospital and he knew that she was waiting by the roadside, but he couldn't see her condition as being "any big deal." When he returned hours later, Milt was annoyed to find the car empty. He could not under-stand why his mother would be unwilling to wait. This lack of empathy helps explain why he was indifferent to his mother's situation.[2] In the literature on moral responsibility, Milt's case is often taken to show that those incapable of a certain level of basic empathic concern should not be held responsible for their behavior and should be treated as amoral creatures.[3]

Romero's zombies lack both the cognitive and the emotional sophistication to be held responsible for their behavior and thus

---

[1] Hervey Cleckley, *The Mask of Sanity* (St. Louis: Mosby, 1964).

[2] Antonio Damasio's patient "Elliot" demonstrated similar behavior after a tumor dam-aged his frontal lobes. See Damasio's *Descartes' Error: Emotion, Reason, and the Human Brain* (New York: Avon, 1994), especially Chapter 3.

[3] For further discussion, see Jeffrie Murphy, "Moral Death: A Kantian Essay on Psychopathy," in *Ethics* 82 (1972), pp. 284–298; Antony Duff, "Psychopathy and Moral Understanding," in *American Philosophical Quarterly* 14 (1977), pp. 189–200; and Lloyd Fields, "Psychopathy, Other-regarding Moral Beliefs, and Responsibility," in *Philosophy, Psychiatry, and Psychology* 3 (1996), pp. 261–277.

they are amoral. Dracula's case, however, is less cut-and-dry. I've suggested that vampires have the cognitive sophistication necessary to be held responsible for their behavior, but it is unclear whether they are emotionally sophisticated enough to fully appreciate the gravity of their actions. It all depends upon how vampires are portrayed. If they can empathize with others, then they can know of the suffering they cause. And this would demonstrate that they are capable of moral reflection and thus accountable for serial murders. However, if they are like Cleckley's Milt and are incapable of appreciating the pains of others, then they should be considered amoral. They can be locked up, but they can't be blamed. A vampire's emotional capabilities are morally significant because they mark the differ-ence between an amoral and an immoral creature.

Bram Stoker's Dracula, for example, seems devoid of moral emotion. True, he is enraged when his brides feed on Harker, but this is because their actions might undermine his long-term plans and not because he is particularly interested in the man's well-being. Throughout the novel, he seems more interested in satisfying his own desires than worrying about the value of a human life. In a particularly callous moment, he tells Mina, "You may as well be quiet; it is not the first time, or the second, that your veins have appeased my thirst."[4] Shortly thereafter, he forces her to drink of his blood. The extreme narcissism exhib-ited by Stoker's Dracula suggests that he may be incapable of appreciating the needs of others. Thus, he seems akin to the amoral Milt.

Francis Ford Coppola's film adaptation of *Dracula* is faithful to the novel in many respects, but Mina's conversion is impor-tantly different. Before turning her into a vampire, Coppola's Dracula respectfully explains that everlasting love comes at the cost of her mortal life and hints that immortality cannot guaran-tee bliss. Unlike Stoker's Dracula who seems willing to use Mina for his own purposes, Coppola's Dracula asks Mina to give her informed consent to the life he has planned for them. As he slits his chest and Mina begins to drink, he cries out, "I cannot let this be. You'll be as cursed as I am to walk in the shadow of death for all eternity. I love you too much to condemn you."

---

[4] Bram Stoker, *Dracula* (New York: Bantam, 1981), pp. 303–04.

These words indicate that he is fully aware of the consequences of his actions. His love for Mina compels him to sympathize with her future misery and causes him to regret the pain he is about to inflict. These feelings are important because they demonstrate that he has a deep appreciation of the value of a human life. In the end, however, he relents and she drinks.

It is somewhat of a mystery why anyone would hurt those they love, but this kind of behavior is all too common. Like many human beings, Coppola's Dracula finds that he just can't help himself. He knows Mina will be hurt, but he gives into temptation anyway. Unlike Stoker's Dracula, Coppola's Dracula is capable of "feeling Mina's pain" and thus seems capable of appreciating the gravity of his actions. And, like most human beings, Coppola's Dracula seems capable of self-control and thus can be faulted for his immorality.

Noble Louis and Villainous Lestat

Neil Jordan's film version of Anne Rice's novel *Interview with the Vampire* provides us with another example of a vampire tormented by his feelings for others and offers perhaps the clearest example of an Undead creature responsible for his behavior. Not wanting human blood on his fangs, Louis prefers to feed on poodles, chickens, and rats. He does give in to temptation when he tastes the blood of the young Claudia. However, he quickly runs away in self-disgust and spends the rest of her life caring for her as a member of the family.

Despite being a vampire, Louis tries to live a moral life. Time and again, he exhibits a "lingering respect for life." He is not only aware of the consequences of his actions, but he makes the self-conscious effort to treat others as he believes they ought to be treated. He refuses to turn Daniel Malloy into a vampire because he knows the misery it will bring. The fact that he self-consciously rejects Armand's call to be "beautiful, powerful, and without regret" demonstrates that he is capable of both moral reflection and self-transformation. In short, Louis's guilt as well as his decision to live with it suggests that he holds himself accountable for his bloodthirsty behavior and perhaps we should too.

Romero's zombies might enjoy the taste of human flesh, but they cannot enjoy watching terrified human beings beg for their lives because they cannot appreciate the nature of human terror. As we've seen, zombies are amoral and not evil. Lestat, by contrast, takes fiendish delight in the suffering of others. Like the cruel torturer, he knows of the pain he inflicts and enjoys it for this reason. He especially likes tasting the blood of aristocrats because he likes seeing the mighty fall. He understands their arrogance and so takes added pleasure in watching them wither in fear. Achieving this level of immorality took some work: Lestat had to find ways of silencing his inner conscience. As he tells Louis, "The trick is not to think about it." He knows that if he were to think about it, he would feel guilty and that would spoil his fun.

Lestat's behavior resembles that of someone wanting to commit common acts of immorality (say, adultery). Deceiving oneself about the true nature of one's bad behavior certainly makes it possible to continue down that road. And once someone has made a habit of behaving badly, it becomes easy. However, an action doesn't become morally permissible because people trick themselves into believing that it is the right thing to do. Marital infidelity, for example, is wrong despite the fact that lots of people do it. Similarly, a life of murderous cruelty is still wrong even if some folks enjoy it and some subcultures find it acceptable.

Warped sensibilities might explain why people (including vampires) behave as they do. The fact that someone was a victim of childhood sexual abuse may explain why they become child predators as adults. However, the fact that someone has warped desires doesn't change the fact that we can (and should) hold them responsible. Similarly, the fact that vampires must drink blood to survive explains why they kill so frequently, but it doesn't mean that their actions should be excused. The fact that Lestat must engage in self-deception shows that he knows (at some level) that his actions are wrong. The fact that he has an insatiable thirst for human blood makes overcoming temptation difficult, but it doesn't mean that his actions are above moral scrutiny. Like the human sex offender, if Lestat is capable of appreciating the consequences of his actions, then he should. The fact that he doesn't engage in moral reflection merely shows that he is morally lazy. And the fact that he enjoys being cruel shows that he understands what he is doing and he is all the more despicable because of it.

In sum, Coppola's Dracula as well as Jordan's Louis and Lestat should be held accountable for their bloodthirsty behavior. Each acts with an awareness of the consequences of his actions. Each can distinguish right from wrong. Each is capable of sympathizing with the needs of others and acting on their behalf. And even if they sometimes fall victim to temptation (or have become hardened over time), each is capable of exercising self-control. In short, they should be held responsible for their crimes because they share all the characteristics of human perpetrators of violence. This suggests that vampires aren't so different from us. Stoker's Mina recognizes as much when she urges Harker to punish Dracula for his crimes, but not to lose sight of the fact that under the bloodthirsty exterior is a pitiable (almost human) creature.

Some Implications: Equal Rights for Vampires

There's no question that wrongdoers ought to be punished. We want them off the streets and we want them to pay for their crimes. But most civilized societies recognize that even the moral scum of the earth deserve certain basic protections. Legal systems, for example, demand fair trials and moral systems prohibit torture. Once we recognize that someone is capable of moral reflection and self-transformation, we must also recognize that he deserves to be treated as such. If, as I have argued, vampires are capable of moral reflection, then they deserve to have their rights respected.

Van Helsing, Morris, and Harker indulge in a form of vigilantism when they hunt down Dracula as if he were some animal. They don't attempt to capture him in order to bring him to justice. They don't provide him with adequate legal counsel capable of presenting his version of events. They don't allow him to be judged by a jury of his peers. Instead, they presume he is guilty or, worse, assume that he is incapable of being held to account for his crimes. They are justifiably afraid of his violent actions, but fear can't justify vigilantism.

Most civilized societies recognize that everyone deserves their day in court. If vampires deserve equal rights, then they deserve this legal protection as well. Of course, justice isn't always done. History is full of mobs taking the law into their own hands. However, we should not confuse the treatment that some people actually receive with the treatment that they actually deserve. If vampires deserve equal rights, then they should not be victims of vigilante justice.

Vampires may be difficult to capture and even more difficult to incarcerate. However, we should not suspend our system of justice simply because it is easier. After all, executing shoplifters would effectively prevent theft, but surely delinquent children deserve a chance to learn from their mistakes. Despite their ease and effectiveness, some punishments are unjust. Moreover, if Louis is any indication, then it seems reasonable to suppose that vampires can be rehabilitated. But even if they must be executed, we should at least feel bad about it. Any creature capable of moral reflection and self-transformation should be regarded as a thing of value. It is at least regrettable when this is not or cannot be done.

Criminals aren't typically allowed to participate in civil government because they are thought to forfeit such rights as soon as they commit a crime. But suppose Louis were to survive on a strict diet of chicken, lamb, and cow blood. If he were to behave like any other decent citizen, then why shouldn't he be allowed to vote or run for public office? There are legitimate worries about the feasibility of this new form of government. Should legislative assemblies meet at night or during the day? What kind of meals should be served at state functions? Even so, practical concerns should not be confused with the question of whether vampires deserve the right of civic participation.

Recognizing equal rights for vampires has an even more startling implication. If my sister were to announce her upcoming nuptials (or civil union) with a vampire, there may be little that can be said. This arrangement would be undoubtedly odd. But if the Undead are capable of rational action and capable of a full range of emotions, then they seem capable of forming meaningful bonds. This suggests that a vampire could be as good as any other suitor.

There are many reasons she might choose not to marry a vampire. Vampires can't procreate and she might want biological children. Vampires are immortal and she is not. These might be legitimate reasons not to marry someone, but they have nothing uniquely to do with the fact that her suitor happens to be a vampire. If biological children and a similar life expectancy are truly important to her, then my sister will reject any human suitor who does not fit the bill. And if she does not value these things, then there is no reason she shouldn't marry a vampire (at least not on these grounds).

Of course, there's the obvious worry that my sister will fall victim to the vampire's violent desires. But the fact that someone can be victimized by those they love is nothing new. As with humans, spousal abuse is reason to call the authorities. But the fact that someone happens to be a vampire is irrelevant. Violence and not Undeath is the problem. Similarly, if a vampire waited until his wedding night (or tenth wedding anniversary) to disclose his true identity, then this deception provides a reason to call things off. In this case, however, deception and not Undeath is the problem. I may not like the fact that my sister plans to marry a vampire, but I can only legitimately object if he gives me a reason (say, violence or deception). It seems reasonable to suppose that a well-behaved vampire may never provide such a reason. If so, then perhaps I should rather see her marry a non-violent vampire than a violent human being.

Current debates over same-sex marriage suggest that many people will reject arrangements that seem unfamiliar, unconventional, or unnatural. Marrying a vampire would surely be all of those things. As with the case of same-sex marriage, however, we shouldn't confuse discomfort with a principled objection. If vampires are capable of entering into meaningful relationships, then they ought to be considered as prospective life-partners. If they aren't, then they should be rejected because they make terrible lovers and not because they happen to be Undead.

Universal Rights: Vampires, Space Aliens, Robots, and Humans

All of this may seem absurd, but the argument is simple. In the human case, it is wrong to discriminate on the basis of race, class, gender, or sexual orientation. All those capable of understanding their environment well enough to engage in self-conscious moral reflection ought to be considered moral agents. If they behave badly, they should be held responsible. Indeed, holding people accountable for their wrongdoing demonstrates that we respect their ability to behave better.

Extending this well-established principle, I'm suggesting that all those capable of self-conscious moral reflection should be held accountable for their choices even if they are aliens from outer space, artificially created humanoids, or Undead creatures of the night.[5] If they behave badly, then we should respect their ability to behave better by holding them responsible. It would be wrong to hold them to a lower standard simply because they are old, ugly, and eat strange foods. Since at least three vampires exhibit the capacity for self-conscious moral reflection, we can reasonably conclude that some Undead creatures can be held responsible for their bloodthirsty behavior. And if being a full moral creature demands being treated with dignity, then vampires deserve equal rights as well.

---

[5] For a more detailed argument for the moral capacity of artificially created humanoids, see William Lycan's *Consciousness* (Cambridge, Massachusetts: MIT Press, 1987), especially pp. 123–130

11

The Bloody Connection Between Vampires and Vegetarians

WAYNE YUEN

> DR SEWARD: Your diet, Mr. Renfield, is disgusting.
> RENFIELD: Actually, they [flies] are perfectly nutritious. You see, each life that I ingest gives back life to me.
>
> —Francis Ford Coppola's film *Bram Stoker's Dracula*

Vampires should not drink human blood. This is not a terribly controversial statement, but asking ourselves why this is so leads to the underlying moral principles that govern how we make decisions about what is right and wrong. It's our job as moral individuals to investigate these principles and try to live a life that is consistent with them. If we look at the situation of vampires and come to understand why it is that we evaluate their particular eating habits as immoral, we will discover the moral principles that can help us gauge whether or not our own eating habits are consistent with our belief that vampires should not eat people.

We get plenty of examples of the eating habits of vampires from *Bram Stoker's Dracula* and *Buffy the Vampire Slayer*, but we actually see a vampire learning to become a vampire in the film *Interview with the Vampire*. So this chapter will concentrate, for the most part, on that particular film.

Reasoning with Vampires

Before we look at the principles governing vampires' eating habits, we should examine what it takes for something to have moral responsibility. Moral agency, the ability to have moral responsibilities, at minimum requires two conditions: sufficiently developed rationality and free will. For example, I wouldn't say that my cat, Fizzgig, has a moral responsibility not to kill birds in the backyard, even if the birds are endangered species. I would like it if she would not kill the birds in our backyard, especially the endangered ones, but she does not have what it takes to be a moral agent. She lacks moral agency because she does not have the rationality necessary to think about the world in moral terms.

Are vampires rational creatures? The answer is an unequivocal yes. Aristotle believed that if an agent can envision the best outcome of a situation, and can successfully bring that outcome about through acting in a way that best and most consistently promotes the desired outcome, then he or she holds practical wisdom, a high form of rationality. The ability to deliberate well is difficult to obtain, but vampires can clearly envision a goal, such as kidnapping or seducing a woman, and produce fairly intricate plans to achieve the goal. Although Aristotle would disapprove of most of the goals envisioned by vampires as the "best outcome," vampires match all of the other criteria set forth by Aristotle to be a rational deliberator.

By this standard of rationality, vampires are rational creatures. In *Interview* Lestat is intelligent enough to make financial investments for the future so that he can live a comfortably luxurious lifestyle. Vampires can reflect intellectually (if not in mirrors) about the world and, more importantly, upon their own actions. They are aware of the consequences of their actions. They even make moral judgments. Lestat believes that "evildoers are easier and they taste better," referring to Widow St. Clair, who blamed a slave for the murder of her husband. Lestat's claim is an aesthetic judgment about the tastiness of evil people, but to make this judgment at all, one must be able to morally judge people to be good or evil.

The second quality, free will, is much more problematic. Some philosophers believe that free will does not exist, and that all actions are fully determined. However, since we are concerned about ethical behavior here, we may rightfully assume that free will is possible. If there is no free will, then it makes little sense to talk about ethical behavior at all. It's beyond the scope of this chapter to offer a defense of free will;[1] the question at hand is whether vampires *have* free will. Just because free will exists, it does not follow that vampires have it.

Free will is the capacity to act in a way of our own choosing, without being forced by something external to ourselves. Imagine if someone were to hold my family hostage and ordered me to rob a bank or they would kill my family. In this case an external force would be compelling me to commit an act that I know was wrong. My free will has been compromised. If I am in a straitjacket, I do not have the freedom to pet my cat.

To say that somebody *ought* to do something, in the moral sense, implies that they *could* do it. Imagine this scenario: a woman dies during childbirth. It would make little sense to say that the baby is morally responsible for killing his or her mother. The baby is the cause of the mother's death, but is not responsible for her death because the baby could not do otherwise. Similarly it wouldn't make sense to say that vampires should not drink human blood if they did not have an alternative. If the blood of humans was the *only* thing that could sustain them, then we couldn't say that vampires should not drink human blood. I believe that vampires in popular culture have an alternative to drinking human blood.

In *Interview* we get an intimate look at the life of a particular vampire, Louis de Pointe du Lac. After Louis is turned into a vampire by Lestat, he confronts the nature of the vampire, feeding on human beings, and is disturbed by it. He struggles with the morality of his previous life as a human being and his existence now, dependent upon blood. But when Lestat reveals to Louis that he could live off animal blood, he tries living off rats, but eventually drinks human blood. Other examples of vampires living off of non-human blood can be found in the *Buffy the Vampire Slayer* and *Angel* television series: Angel, and later Spike, survive by drinking the blood of animals.

Damned if You Do, Damned if You Don't

The freedom of vampires is closely connected to the nature of what vampires are. Vampires at the most basic level are human

---

[1] An excellent treatment of free will can be found in Timothy O'Connor's *Persons and Causes: the Metaphysics of Free Will* (Oxford: Oxford University Press, 2002).

beings who have been condemned to an eternal life. Most people would see eternal life as a gift, or a blessing. But the vampire is damned because of this "gift." Vampires are left to live their lives with an eternal hunger. Dracula hungers not only for human blood, but for love. He is only released from his curse when Mina finally is able to satisfy that craving. With such a craving driving the vampire's action, can a vampire exhibit free will? Again this is a difficult question to answer, but let's imagine that it does annihilate the vampire's free will. If this is so then any case of extreme craving would remove a person's free will. A heroin addict, who because of her compulsion for the drug robs a store in order to get money to get more drugs, would not be considered morally responsible for her action. If we cannot accept this conclusion, we must reject the initial assumption that leads to this conclusion, that the craving for blood annihilates a vampire's free will. This leads one to believe that vampires have free will over themselves when choosing to drink human blood.

To make matters worse, there seem to be important differences between the heroin addict and the vampire. Firstly, vampires seem to be in full control of their faculties even while they crave human blood, whereas drug addicts typically cannot control themselves. They are compelled, depending upon the degree of addiction, to seek the drug. Consider another example of compulsion: people who are lost at sea have been known to drink ocean water, even when they rationally know that they should not drink the water. Their thirst is so great that it overwhelms any kind of rational ability. Dracula, Louis, and Lestat all exhibit restraint even when they are in densely populated cities. This suggests a difference between a craving and a compulsion: a compulsion cannot be resisted. A drug addict is under a compulsion to seek drugs. A craving is a strong preference. When I crave vanilla ice cream, I have a strong preference, but I would not rob the grocery store to satisfy it.

A second problem that is unique to the vampire is a question of character. If a vampire is damned, then perhaps nothing that the vampire can do is good, because the character of the being prohibits any good from being done. Being damned then does not compel a being towards evil acts, but rather it taints all their acts with evil. This idea is rooted in a model of virtue ethics associated with Aristotle. Developing a good character is primary. From a virtuous character, virtuous acts follow, and from a vicious character, vicious acts follow. Hitler is the typical example of a person who has a stained character. No good that Hitler has done can change the fact that he is a morally vicious character. Vampires are stained with evil, someone might claim, and so consequently nothing that they do can ever make them good moral agents. When it comes to new vampires like Louis, however, there are few if any character traits that we can point to when trying to evaluate his moral character. Louis is a different person after he becomes a vampire. Perhaps more importantly, we can evaluate an agent's character separately from his or her actions. For example, if Hitler decided to give a large donation to famine relief in the world, the act of donating can be evaluated as good, even though the person's character (Hitler) is vicious. In this chapter, we're mostly concerned about a particular action of vampires: their feeding habits.

A third and final problem that is unique to the vampire is rooted in a different conceptual model of the vampire. If the vampire is not merely an Undead human cursed with a craving, but rather a demonically possessed body whose human soul has left,[2] then do vampires simply have different moral values? This might be true in a cultural sense of the word. In America most people believe that it is wrong to eat dogs, but acceptable to eat cows; in other parts of the world, it is acceptable to eat dogs; and in still others, wrong to eat cows. However, all things being equal, there are principles that appear to be universal. For example, a world with more unnecessary suffering is worse than a world with less unnecessary suffering. Even our model vampire Lestat tells Louis that vampirism is a gift that helps him escape a painful world. It is precisely this principle that motivates Louis to live off rats instead of human beings. Ironically, Lestat appeals to the same principle, in a short-sighted way, to justify drinking human blood, to spare himself from the unnecessary discomfort of not drinking human blood. It's shortsighted in that Lestat does not consider the unnecessary suffering that is brought about for the victims.

---

[2] This model is seen in Joss Whedon's vampire series *Buffy the Vampire Slayer* and *Angel.*

It's a Matter of Taste

The obvious "justification" for vampires eating people is that, for vampires, humans are really tasty. If humans taste better than rats, then that may be enough reason to choose to eat them. Louis describes Lestat's killings as if describing a gourmet dinner: "A fresh young girl, that was his favorite for the first of the evening. For seconds, he preferred a gilded beautiful youth. But the snob in him loved to hunt in society, and the blood of the aristocrat thrilled him best of all." Compared to rats, humans are a marvelous delicacy. But the pleasures of the palate do not excuse the immorality of drinking human blood either. Given the choice between killing a person and killing a rat, killing the rat is the lesser of the two evils. Saying that killing the human is the better choice, because they taste better, does not make the act any less evil.

All of this, of course, presupposes that human beings do have some kind of value that is of greater worth than that of a rat. All kinds of justifications have been offered for the greater worth of humans, but many of them fall flat: that human beings have souls, and animals do not, for example. It's hard to prove either way that humans have souls and animals do not, without appealing to the authority of a religious text, which draws its authority from faith, not reason. However, since we are discussing vampires as possibly humans who have lost their souls, we should entertain the notion. The intrinsic value of a soul might provide a reason to choose animals over humans. Something is intrinsically valuable if we value it for no other reason other than for what it is. Money has instrumental value because it can get us stuff. Happiness has intrinsic value, because we value it for what it is. The Judeo-Christian tradition is pretty clear on the non-soul status of animals, but this does not mean that animals should receive no consideration when we make decisions that concern their well-being.

Another quality that should be considered is human rationality. Although it's safe to say that humans reason, since we are aware of our own internal mental states and operations, we cannot say with any kind of authority that animals cannot reason in any manner. On the contrary there are many animals that seem to have an intellect that is at least equivalent to a human child's.[3]

---

[3] Koko, the gorilla who uses sign language, has an IQ between 70 and 95. Twenty-five percent of children have an IQ within the same range.

Finally, consider that both humans and animals can feel pain and suffering.

What separates humans from animals may not be any particular quality, but more precisely, the degree to which humans possess the quality. Humans clearly have a greater capacity for reason than animals do, and this extends our capacity for suffering in unique ways. We as humans can worry about our futures. We can be actively aware of the things we have not acquired yet and be aware of our lost *capacity* for acquiring those things. When I see my lemon tree slowly withering from disease, I realize that I have lost all the future fruit that the tree will bear, which makes the loss of the tree that much more unfortunate. When my life is put into danger, I realize not only that I may lose my life, but also that my wife may lose her husband. Choosing to kill a human over a rat is choosing to bring more unnecessary pain and suffering into the world, which is universally undesirable, something that even some vampires try to avoid.

Perhaps vampires don't need human blood to survive, but to thrive. To reach their full potentials, they need to eat humans. Vampire popular culture is a mixed bag on this point. Vampires in *Buffy the Vampire Slayer*, notably Angel and Spike, can thrive on butcher's blood fighting off a litany of demons and gods.[4] However, when Lestat survives and grows stronger "on the diet of the blood of snakes, toads, and all the putrid life of the Mississippi" he still looks likes a corpse. Without human blood Lestat is weak and putrid; with human blood, Lestat can read people's minds and is handsome and vital.

There are two problems with this position. First is the problem of what is meant by full potential. Peak physical condition is not always necessary for a person to reach his or her fullest potential. Steven Hawking is an excellent example of a person who has been hampered in reaching his fullest potential, yet still greatly excels in life. Or perhaps Hawking has reached *his* own individual physical potential. In either case, the condition of his physical body is irrelevant to whether or not Hawking is excelling in life. Few would argue that Lou Gehrig's disease has

---

[4] Perhaps the only exception to this was when Angel was infected with a mystical disease by Faith. The only cure was to drink the blood of a Slayer.

made Hawking less of a physicist. The second problem with this position is to assume that there is only a singular maximum that people can reach. Imagine Louis swearing off humans, and surviving solely on rats. He could have a lucrative career as an exterminator. What makes this choice better or worse than his eating human beings and developing mystical empowerments? Any answer that could be given to this would rely on either an arbitrary social standard (being an actual mind reader is better than being an excellent exterminator), or on some moral standard. It's almost not worth stating that being an excellent rat exterminator is better, morally speaking, than being a serial killer.

In *Interview* Louis says, "I knew peace only when I killed. When I heard her heart in that terrible rhythm, I knew again what peace could be." So, another reason that vampires drink human blood is because it brings them a spiritual peace of sorts. But this doesn't give us the kind of justification Louis might hope for as to whether it is right for vampires to eat people. For example, a cult that derives spiritual satisfaction from human sacrifice would not be morally justified in their practice, especially if the people being sacrificed were unwilling, like the victims of vampires. David Berkowitz claimed a great feeling of peace after his killings as well. Robbing a person of their life for an individual's temporary spiritual gain fails the simplest moral litmus tests like reversibility, equality, and fairness.

When Louis is first turned into a vampire, Lestat has to teach him to overcome his feelings of guilt and anguish. "You'll get used to killing. . . . You'll become accustomed to things all too quickly." No doubt, a person can become accustomed to many things, even killing, but Louis feels the guilt that comes with it. Louis gets no spiritual peace from killing people at first. Perhaps the spiritual peace that comes with killing humans is a feeling that comes only through habituation. Only through his love of Claudia, who is arguably more psychotic than Lestat, does Louis ironically lose his humanity and begin to drink human blood. Louis's love for Claudia encourages him to engage in the habit of drinking human blood, much as the love for a child may encourage a parent to engage in the habit of exercise. In both cases they aid in the improvement of the self for the sake of another, but of course the analogy breaks down when we compare the two morally, which is the question at hand.

Thus far, we have seen that vampires are moral agents, because they possess both reason and free will; that vampires have a viable alternative to eating humans, namely animals; and that we cannot morally justify drinking human blood over animals via a preference of taste, a fulfillment of maximum potential, or because of a spiritual peace that is derived from it.

Cold Clammy Consistency

There is much to be learned from beasts.

—Dracula in *Bram Stoker's Dracula*

If vampires have a moral obligation not to drink human blood, what does that mean for us as humans? On the surface it may allow us simply to say that vampires who kill humans are morally corrupt, which can give us justification for slaying them. More importantly, however, it offers us an opportunity to evaluate our own actions to see if our actions are consistent with what we would demand of vampires. Consistency can be conceived of in a few related but different ways. Consistency may mean a lack of contradiction; that is, it is not possible for both claims to be true at the same time. We cannot within our moral beliefs hold that it is acceptable to stab innocent people in the heart with a stake, and that murder is wrong. Consistency also means that we should apply rules and justifications in a consistent manner. If I use an argument in one case, I must apply that same argument in every similar case, unless there are relevant differences. Consistency in our moral beliefs is imperative. Barring relevant differences, we assign rights and freedoms to everyone consistently. The Golden Rule demands that we treat other people according to the standard by which we would like to be treated, and we expect consistent application of the law. If I were to get ten years in jail for murder and someone else were to get only a fine for the same crime, it would be a gross miscarriage of justice, precisely because the law would not be treating two similar cases equally.

We have examined and rejected a number of arguments for why it is acceptable for vampires to drink human blood. Vampires get a spiritual peace from eating humans. Vampires need human blood to reach their full potential. Humans are pleasing to the palate of vampires. We've also found a reason why vampires should drink the blood of rats rather than humans: More unnecessary suffering is caused when a human dies at the hands of a vampire than when a rat does. If we are to be consistent in our condemnation of vampires for eating humans, then we must examine our human eating habits in a similar fashion. Clearly, cannibalism, a type of human-eating, is wrong under normal circumstances.[5] But most people don't eat other people on a daily basis; instead we eat chicken, pork, or beef, with a generous helping of potatoes. If we are to be consistent in our condemnation of vampires, can we continue eating like this?

We are in a very similar position to the vampire's to begin with. We are rational creatures who can reflect upon the morality of our actions. We also have options before us. It's not absolutely necessary for us to eat meat to survive. There are eight essential amino acids that people need to ingest to survive (ten for children), and they can all be found in plant sources. All vitamins and minerals that are necessary to avoid deficiency diseases like scurvy, pellagra, and rickets can either be manufactured by the body or readily found in fruits and vegetables.[6] Vegetarianism is the alternative to the human diet, just as rats are the alternative to the diet of vampires.

So why do we eat animals? Few would argue that they get some kind of spiritual peace from eating chicken, beef, or pork. But even if they did, it seems like there is a more important concern that we must take into consideration: the pain and suffering inflicted upon animals. To meet the demand of human consumption, animals are often raised in what are known as "factory farms" that aim to produce the greatest amount of meat with the least amount of input in the shortest amount of time. Little concern is given to the animals' welfare at these farms. Chickens' beaks are cut off and talons are removed, so they do not peck or scratch each other to death in overcrowded condi-

---

[5] Even under extreme conditions killing another person to eat them seems to be wrong. It may be justified to eat people who have died from other causes like dehydration or exposure given extreme circumstances.

[6] There is some concern that vegans (people who do not eat dairy and egg products as well as meat) may become deficient in vitamin B-12 which could lead to anemia, but because the body can reabsorb utilized B-12, even amongst vegans this deficiency is very rare.

tions. Pigs' tails are cut off to prevent them from being chewed on by other pigs. Slaughterhouses (which almost all animals go to before they reach the supermarket) sometimes skin or boil animals alive because their conveyer system runs too quickly for the animal to bleed to death.[7] Reducing these creatures' pain and suffering is much more important than achieving some kind of spiritual peace from eating them. Indeed, it may be rather difficult to attain spiritual peace knowing that the animal you are eating lived a life of painful misery, solely to provide meat at $4.50 a pound instead of $6.00 a pound. The efficiency of the factory farm keeps prices low, but the cost savings is at the expense of the quality of animals' lives.

Perhaps humans need to eat meat to reach their fullest potential. Again the question arises: what do we mean by fullest potential? But even if we push that argument aside for the moment, we are faced with yet another problem: the world-class vegetarian athlete. Athletes that win gold medals at the Olympics and hold world records are generally considered the pinnacle of human physical potential. Dave Scott is a six-time Hawaii Iron Man Champion (a triathlon competitor) and a vegetarian. Andreas Cahling won the Olympic gold medal in the ski jump in 1980. Bill Pickering swam from England to France in 14 hours, 6 minutes—a world record time—and is a vegetarian. Bill Pearl won the Mr. Universe Bodybuilding title in 1971, without steroids, on a vegetarian diet.[8] These are just a few examples of people who have reached the pinnacle of physical human performance, and are vegetarians. Peter Singer (a philosopher who holds the chair of the University Center for Human Values at Princeton University), Ralph Waldo Emerson, and the Dalai Lama (Tenzin Gyatso) are all vegetarians who have arguably reached the pinnacle of mental human performance. If fear of not reaching one's own fullest potential is keeping a person from being a vegetarian, then these examples show that it can be done. It may not be easy, but reaching one's full physical or mental potential is not an easy task, vegetarian or not.

---

[7] For more information on this read Joby Warrick's Article "They Die Piece by Piece," *Washington Post* (10th April, 2001). Online try www.meetyourmeat.com and www.the-meatrix.com

[8] See John Robbins, *The Food Revolution* (Berkeley: Conari Press, 2001) for a very impressive list of vegetarian athletes.

Finally, we reach the last argument: that animals are pleasing to the taste of human beings. Just as vampires prefer the taste of human blood, many people prefer the taste of animals. But for the same reasons, this provides little justification for the eating of animals. Morality is not about satisfying our preferences, but rather evaluating our actions and choices to make the best one. I may have an intense desire to bite Kirsten Dunst in the neck, but it would be wrong for me to do so, at least without her (and my wife's) permission. The wrongness in eating animals stems from the pain and suffering that is caused not only from raising them, but from their unnecessary slaughter. It is unnecessary because we have a viable option to do otherwise—vegetarianism.

There are many opponents of vegetarianism. Some may argue that animals in the wild will kill each other, so what makes it wrong for us to kill them? The difference is that animals, for the most part, are not moral agents. They cannot think and reflect about their actions in a moral fashion, so they cannot be held morally accountable for their actions. It would be wrong for me to relieve myself on the lawn of a neighbor—in fact I could be arrested for such an act—but my cat would not be arrested for such an act since she doesn't know any better and cannot do otherwise.

Some might wonder why vampires should be allowed to eat animals, while humans should not. If vampires could exist without drinking blood of any kind, then perhaps they would have a moral duty to do so as well. But by most accounts vampires need some kind of blood to continue in a minimal way. Usually insanity is the result of a lack of blood for a vampire. When a vampire is insane, he or she cannot reason, and would be free of moral responsibilities not to drink human blood. Much like a person who is so drunk that they are not aware of what they are doing, they technically have no moral responsibilities. However, this is not to say they are off the hook entirely, since they have the ability not to get that drunk in the first place. Similarly if vampires simply refuse blood until they go insane, they can still be held accountable for that action. This accounts for a need to drink blood. Without blood, they cannot be moral agents. So between the lesser of two evils, they should choose to drink animal blood in the most humane way, rather than human blood. When vampires choose to drink human blood they cause unnecessary suffering to the victim and to the victim's loved ones. Since it is necessary for vampires to eat, choosing to eat a less intelligent animal would cause less suffering. Similarly, we as humans must choose between killing vegetables or animals. Since vegetables cannot feel in any sense of the word, because feeling would require a nervous system of some sort, there would be less pain and suffering generated by eating the plant than the animal.

The connection between vampires and vegetarians is a simple one: we as human beings are vampiric. We need to ingest life for us to live, just like vampires. But how we choose the life that we ingest determines whether or not we are monstrous like vampires, or virtuous.

12

Damned if You Do, Damned if You Don't: Vampires and the Hedonistic Paradox

ROBERT ARP

The Vampire's Plight

How long have I shunned the caress of soft light upon my cheek, how long have I longed to feel the gentle wind in my hair, love in my heart, and hate? Yet, my soul is dead; I cannot feel, cannot see the light of day. Still, my curse is the greatest of gifts. The taste of blood is sweet as the sweetest honey to me. I embrace each passing night of my unlife, and the call of blood is my blessing.

This anonymous quotation from the Internet captures the plight of the vampire. Imagine having the capacity to live for several lifetimes driven by a thirst for blood, while not really being able to feel or experience what you are going through in those lifetimes. At best, there is some sort of relief when you have had your fill of blood. The hollowed-out life of a junkie might be the closest thing to a vampire's life we could imagine, with the desire for the next "fix" consuming all of one's existence.

Think of Jason Patric's vampire character, Michael, in Joel Schumacher's 1987 film *The Lost Boys*, or Brad Pitt's vampire character, Louis, in Neil Jordan's 1994 *Interview with the Vampire*. When they try to resist their urges for blood, they become wild-eyed, frantic, and driven to "feed their need." Add to this picture the fact that the vampire is *aware of* the inability to feel, then one can see how the vampire's situation kind of sucks (pun intended)! Again, talk to ex-junkies, and they will tell you that they knew their lives were hollowed-out, devoid of anything other than the desire for the next fix.

Such is the plight of a vampire's *un*life, in a nutshell. I do not
mean to say that all vampires in every vampire story have such
an unlife. There are vampires who seem to be content with who
and what they are, as appears to be the case with the vampire
community in the movie *Underworld.*[1] But, there are a great
number of vampires in a great number of stories whose unlives
really do suck. And a vampire's unlife can teach us valuable
lessons about our own real lives. After all, vampire lore emerges
from our innermost desires, not only to live forever, indulge in
our basest passions, and be subversive, but to embrace our mortality, control the animal within, and blot out evil wherever it
may lurk.[2] There are many different vampire stories as well as
many different kinds of vampires. As one might expect, the personalities of vampires and the stories told about them are as varied as the authors who tell us the tales.[3]

I Am Neither Living nor Dead—I Am Undead

What is the fundamental nature of a vampire? How and in what
form exactly does a vampire exist? These questions are metaphysical in nature. *Metaphysics* is the area of philosophy that
investigates the nature and principles of things that exist.
Metaphysicians want to know what really exists in reality, what
kinds of things make up reality, and how things are related to
one another. If vampires really did exist, then we would see
that, as members of the Undead community who make their
way around the planet earth, vampires seem to be a composite
of a dead material body and an immaterial soul/spirit/mind. This
view is akin to a version of *metaphysical dualism* in the philosophical subdiscipline of metaphysics known as philosophy of
mind. According to metaphysical dualism in philosophy of
mind, a person is made up of a material body and an immaterial mind.

---

[1] Directed by Len Wiseman, 2003.
[2] See Nina Auerbach, *Our Vampires, Ourselves* (Chicago: University of Chicago Press,
1995); Bob Madison, ed., *Dracula: The First Hundred Years* (Baltimore: Midnight
Marquee, 1997); and Andrew MacKenzie, *Dracula Country: Travels and Folk Beliefs in
Romania* (London: Arthur Baker, 1977).
[3] See J. Gordon Melton, *The Vampire Book: The Encyclopedia of the Undead* (Farmington
Hills: Visible Ink Press, 1999).

Let's consider two versions of metaphysical dualism, *substance dualism* and *property dualism*. According to substance dualism a person is made up of two wholly distinct substances, a mind and a body, that can exist apart from one another. Those who believe in the immortality of the soul are substance dualists because they think that the death of the body does not mean the death of the soul. The soul lives on after the death of the body. According to property dualism a person is one substance that is made up of two wholly distinct properties, an immaterial mental property (the mind and mental states) and a material bodily property (the brain and neurophysiological states). On this view, the mind and brain are distinct properties of some one person similar to the way "roundness" and "blackness" are distinct properties found in the one period at the end of this sentence. Just as we can distinguish the property of roundness from the property of blackness in some one period, so too, we can distinguish an immaterial mental property from a material bodily property in some one person. However, just as the roundness and blackness of that particular period can exist only while that particular period exists, so too, according to property dualists the mental and bodily properties of a person can exist only while that person is alive. So when we delete the period, the properties of roundness and blackness in that particular period cease to exist along with the period. Likewise, when a person dies, both that person's body and mind cease to exist. Such a view of mind in relation to body seems to be consistent with scientific data, and is appealing to those who do not believe in the immortality of the soul.[4]

According to some vampire stories, the vampire's cursed soul will continue to live on in hell or some other non-worldly realm after its dead body has been destroyed, indicating a substance form of dualism. This seems to be the case for Lestat, Louis, and the other vampires in Anne Rice's stories; also, Bram Stoker undoubtedly had this conception in *Dracula*. In other stories, the vampire's soul ceases to exist when its dead body is destroyed by sunlight or a stake through the heart, indicating a property form of dualism. This seems to be the case in Marv

---

[4] See the sections on substance dualism and property dualism in K.T. Maslin, *An Introduction to the Philosophy of Mind* (Oxford: Polity Press, 2000).

Wolfman's *Blade the Vampire Slayer* comic book series as well as with Carol Jones Daly's 1947 vampire novel, *The Legion of the Living Dead*.[5] In either form of dualism the dead body, in some form, seems to be necessary in order to maintain the vampire's existence as it makes its way around in this world. At the same time, in both substance dualism and property dualism a distinction can be made between characteristics or properties of one's bodily life, and characteristics or properties of one's mental life. In other words, both substance dualists and property dualists think that there is something about the mental realm that makes it distinct from the bodily realm—again, either in *substance* or in *property*. In a moment, we will see why this distinction is important for understanding how it is that a vampire might be able to experience a certain form of pleasure and pain.

Many vampires are portrayed as unable to experience the pleasures and pains associated with things like love, food, and drink or, like the vampire in the opening quotation, the pleasure of the wind in one's hair or the pain of hatred. Not only do Lestat and Louis have this problem in the Anne Rice stories, but the vampires in Jeff Rice's *The Night Stalker*,[6] Jacques Cazotte's *The Devil in Love*,[7] and James Gunn's *The Immortals*[8] as well. The vampire Strahd bemoans his lack of feeling in *I Strahd: The Memoirs of a Vampire*,[9] and even Dracula himself, the original bloodsucker, can't seem to get any satisfaction. These portrayals should strike us as strange because the vampires usually appear to be in some state of anger, pain, or anguish when describing their state, indicating that they can, in fact, feel something . . . pain! Consider the movie *Van Helsing* when, during a conversation with his two female vampire minions, Dracula screams in anguish that he feels nothing, but longs to feel nonetheless.[10] Or consider what George Hamilton's vampire character says to Renfield in *Love at First Bite* when Renfield asks the vampire if he is happy: "Happy? How would you like to dine on nothing but a warm liquid protein diet while all around you, people are eating lamb chops, potato chips, Mallomars . . . Chivas Regal on

---

[5] London: Popular Press.
[6] New York: Pocket Books, 1974.
[7] Cambridge: Dedalus Press, 1991.
[8] New York: Ballantine, 1958.
[9] By P.N. Elrod (Geneva: TSR, 1993).
[10] Directed by Stephen Sommers, 2004.

the rocks with a twist?"[11] Maybe it is just that, because they are cursed in some way or damned by a god, vampires can experience only pain and will never be able to experience pleasure as part of their continual cursedness or punishment. If the idea of vampires experiencing some form of pain seems unconvincing, there are plenty of instances where vampires seem to be experiencing pleasure while sucking blood, deceiving, wooing women (or men), or engaging in sexual intercourse.

The most straightforward reason usually given as to why vampires cannot feel pleasure or pain is their bodies are dead, or no longer functioning. Since pleasure and pain are feelings requiring a functioning body to experience them, it makes sense that vampires cannot have these feelings. Yet, Dracula's frustration in *Van Helsing* is a common theme among vampire personalities and their stories. So, it seems that vampires both do and do not have experiences of pleasure and pain. What accounts for this contradiction?

A way to clear up this problem might be to distinguish between two different senses of pleasure and pain, the way that the moral philosopher, John Stuart Mill (1806–1873), does in his famous work *Utilitarianism*. There are those "lower" pleasures or pains that are most appropriately understood as *feelings associated with a body*. Examples of these pleasures and pains would be aches, pains, and "butterflies in the stomach" as well as euphoric surges and adrenaline rushes. Normally when we think of pleasure and pain, we think of them in this bodily way, associated with the neurophysiological processes of a living animal with an intact nervous system. Then there are "higher" pleasures and pains understood as *qualitative experiences associated with a mind*. Examples of these would include the pleasure of discovering the solution to a complex math problem, the pain of having made an immoral decision that cannot be undone, or the pleasure of knowing one is loved by a friend. Here, the pleasures and pains are less bodily and more mental, and have names like *joy, contentment, satisfaction, regret*, and *sorrow*.

Armed with this distinction between lower and higher pleasures and pains, we might be able to clear up some of the confusion concerning a vampire's experience of pleasure and pain.

---

[11] Directed by Stan Dragoti, 1979.

We can make sense of the quotation at the beginning of this chapter by noting that the cursed soul or spirit or mind of the vampire, its immaterial, mental part, is expressing regret or sorrow (qualitative experiences associated with the mind) at being unable to be pleased by wind in its hair or the taste of fine wine (feelings associated with the body). The vampire is expressing a higher, mental pain about a lack of a lower, bodily pleasure.

Either Way, I'm Damned if I Do

Even though we hear vampires lament the fact that they cannot experience pleasure and pain, we have to question their sincerity. They seem to be in some kind of pain while lamenting and seem greatly to enjoy sucking blood from their victims. The distinction between higher and lower pleasures may help us out here. Vampires may be cursed with a higher, mental pain while lamenting their lack of feelings in their bodies. Similarly, they may gain a higher, mental pleasure from satisfying their need for blood. (By the way, it is a curious thing that vampires should need blood in the first place. What do they need it for? On most vampire accounts, their bodies are dead, so the blood does not act like a food product.) However, on several accounts, it appears that the vampire is deriving a kind of base, physical, bodily pleasure from its evil pursuits of blood-sucking, deception, and "turning." Recall that the taste of blood is "sweet honey" and a "blessing" for the vampire in the opening quotation. And consider what Louis says about Lestat in *Interview with the Vampire*:

> Lestat killed two, sometimes three a night. A fresh young girl, that was his favorite for the first of the evening. For seconds, he preferred a gilded beautiful youth. But the snob in him loved to hunt in society, and the blood of the aristocrat thrilled him best of all. (p. 46)

If we put aside the obvious problem that a vampire's body is dead, and we imagine that there is some connection between its bodily desires and its own cursed mental satisfaction, then there is another way in which we can make sense of the vampire's plight. It may be that the vampire "can't get no satisfaction" because of its inappropriate focus on the pursuit of "bodily" pleasure. One of the reasons why the vampire Lestat is so fascinating in the Anne Rice stories is that he is somewhat of a pleasure-seeker who continually searches for, but never really finds, satisfaction or contentment in his cursed life. His cursed, fictitious life reminds us of our own real lives. As we shall see, there are problems that arise from focusing either on pleasure itself, or the wrong pleasures in life.

Both vampires and mortals must confront the *hedonistic paradox*.[12] The basic idea behind the hedonistic paradox is that whenever pleasure itself is the object sought, either it is not found or it is found. If pleasure is not found, the result is the pain associated with not finding the pleasure one seeks. In an episode of *Buffy the Vampire Slayer* that I watched recently, one of the vampire characters says to another vampire that he "hates not getting what he wants," in reference to having to suck the blood from a less-than-desirable woman.

On the other hand, if pleasure is found, especially on a consistent basis, the result is still pain. The pain results from either finding pains that are *mistaken for* pleasures in the long or short term, or from the boredom of always getting the pleasures one wants. Think of the way that Louis fools Lestat into sucking the blood from the already dead twin girls in *Interview with the Vampire*, and how Lestat mistakes this painful experience for a great pleasure; albeit it was a mistake, in part, prompted by Louis's deception. Or think of the vampires who are destroyed by Blade (presumably, a great pain) at the "rave" in the beginning of the movie *Blade*, and how they mistakenly think that they have come to a bloodfest featuring fresh young human meat (presumably, a great pleasure).[13] Concerning the issue of boredom, consider Lestat's complaint of virtually "seeing it all" and being bored in *The Vampire Lestat*, or a deluded man who thinks he's a vampire in Katherine Ramsland's *Piercing the Darkness: Undercover with Vampires in America Today* claiming that "it's somewhat boring, living forever."[14]

Either way, whether pleasure is found or not, the result *paradoxically* is still pain. The hedonistic paradox is "hedonistic"

---

[12] The term first was introduced by Henry Sidgwick, *The Methods of Ethics* (London: Macmillan, 1874); see also Fred Feldman, "Hedonism," in Lawrence Becker and Charlotte Becker, eds., *Encyclopedia of Ethics* (London: Routledge, 2001), pp. 100–113.

[13] Directed by Stephen Norrington, 1998.

[14] New York: Harper Collins, 1999, p. 501.

because of the focus on the pleasure being sought (*hedon* is Greek for pleasure). It is a paradox because one consistently finds the exact opposite (pain) of what one set out to find in the beginning (pleasure).

Is there any way out of the hedonistic paradox for a vampire who wants to continue pursuing pleasure for the sake of pleasure itself? Vampires may not fall victim to the hedonistic paradox for a couple of reasons. One of the problems with pursuing pleasure is the boredom associated with always getting what one wants. A central question that needs to be answered is whether there could be innumerable pleasures to be had at one's disposal. Put another way, given the number of possible activities imaginable, and the pleasures associated with those activities, is it possible to exhaust all of those activities, gain the pleasures, and become bored with the pleasures attained? If there could be innumerable pleasures out there to be had, then it seems as though it would not be possible, even for a vampire with many lifetimes at its disposal, to achieve all of them—in which case, boredom would never ensue.

Now it would seem that a vampire, who has the capacity to live several lifetimes, surely would become bored after a certain amount of time. But this would depend upon whether that vampire had experienced each and every possible pleasure to be experienced. If one is inclined to think that the amount and range of possible pleasurable experiences are limited or finite, then it is more likely that boredom would result for a vampire who lives several lifetimes. On the other hand, if one is inclined to think that the amount and rage of possible pleasurable experiences are unlimited or infinite, then it is more likely that boredom would not result. Again, the primary question that needs to be answered is whether there could be innumerable pleasures to be had at one's disposal. If the answer to this question is yes, and one never gets bored or experiences pain, it would seem that one horn of the paradox can be avoided. If the answer is no, and one does get bored or experience pain, it would seem that it cannot.

Further, the distinction between lower bodily pleasures and higher mental pleasures may help us out once again. Within the bodily realm, there seem to be a variety of different pleasures associated with a variety of different bodily activities. In fact, any pleasure or pain is only a pleasure or pain as it is associated with some form of bodily or mental activity for a human. There are no lower or higher pleasures or pains without bodily or mental activities. This being the case, pleasures are aligned with activities that run the gamut from hurting us in the short term and hurting us in the long term to helping us in the short term and helping us in the long term. For example, there's a difference between the pleasures to be had from smoking crack and from pursuing a variety of extreme sports. All things considered, the likelihood of the crack harming you regardless of the precautions you take is much higher than the likelihood of being harmed while consciously and cautiously pursuing an extreme sport.

Is it possible to pursue pleasure and avoid the paradox? It's easy to see how a life of pursuing lower, bodily pleasures leads one into the pains of not finding what one seeks, mistaking pain for pleasure, or even boredom. This becomes all the more obvious in the case of a vampire that can live several lifetimes. But could one fall victim to the hedonistic paradox in the pursuit of higher, mental pleasures? Consider the distinction between pleasures that result from *ongoing activities* and pleasures that result from *the knowledge of being in certain completed states.* Recall the earlier examples of solving a math problem and being loved by a friend. These are not ongoing activities, but completed states of being, where one has knowledge of these states. The knowledge of these states brings with it a sustaining, almost satiating, form of mental pleasure.

Aristotle has something like this in mind when he investigates various forms of pleasure in Book Ten of his *Nicomachean Ethics.* It may be that bodily pleasures are more the result of ongoing activities, while mental pleasures are more the result of being in a certain state. With this distinction in mind, we may be able better to understand how hardcore mathematicians or true friends achieve satisfaction, contentment, or joy associated with these states. If math equations don't do it for you, think of some tough project, assignment, or task that you completed and are happy about having completed. Or, think of the runner who trained all of her life for and actually finished the big marathon, the father of three who finally got his Masters in Business Administration through night school, or the hero who saved the child from drowning. Now think of these folks reflecting upon their accomplishments with joy. Such joys would seem to be of the kind that, when reflected upon, last a lifetime. A stronger case might be made for one falling victim to the hedonistic paradox in the *pursuit* of either the solution to a math equation, a lasting friendship, a marathon race, or an MBA *prior to* achieving a completed state, in that one may never find what one seeks. However, once in a certain completed state it would seem that the pleasure is continuous with the knowledge of the completed state.

Good Guy Vampires?

If a vampire engages in physical pleasure-seeking for its own sake, then we can see how such a lifestyle would lead to a kind of hollowed-out existence, not unlike that of a junkie. A junkie gets to the point where he or she physically must have the drug in order to survive, at least in the short term. Most junkies choose, at first, to use drugs and can change their ways. Maybe vampires should be pitied for their blood-sucking ways. After all, it seems that they are unlike junkies in that they are just built to suck blood. In fact, for most vampires, human blood is a necessary food source.

As Angie says to Joel, the serial killer who is becoming a vampire in the movie *Addicted to Murder:* "You can't change your nature. You can't contain it, you can't shift it. You can only be what you are meant to be."[15] But even those members of our community who cannot control themselves, like pedophiles, must regulate their desires or have their desires and actions regulated for them. Vampires could ask members of the human community to donate enough blood to their cause so that they need not take it forcibly, and I am sure that there would be kind-hearted souls willing to oblige. In Barbara Hambly's book *Those Who Hunt the Night*, we are told that vampires "can—and do, at need—live upon the blood of animals, or blood taken from the living without need of their death."[16]

Starting in the 1960s with vampires like Barnabas Collins in the television series *Dark Shadows* and Forrest J. Ackerman's comic book character Vampirella, and continuing through the

---

[15] Directed by Kevin J. Lindemuth, 1995.
[16] New York: Del Rey, 1990, p. 123.

1980s and 1990s with Chelsea Quinn Yarbro's vampire hero, St. Germain, and Nick Knight in the series *Forever Knight*, there have been "good guy vampires." These vampires actually recognize that, although they must feed upon blood to survive, they can do so without either giving in to their basest needs or harming people in the process. Further, they have been able to generate moral codes, establish vampire cultures, create strong bonds with mortals, pursue "loftier" activities such as are found in academia and the arts, and find contentment in using their "dark" powers for the good of their own kind as well as humankind.[17] In other words, these vampires have been able to skirt the hedonistic paradox altogether either by pursuing higher mental pleasures or by engaging in activities for the sake of the activities themselves, rather than for the pleasure to be gained from the activities.

Vampires, like the humans who invented them, have varying degrees of desires for different kinds of things. Consequently, certain vampires will fall victim to the hedonistic paradox. If one's focus is consistently the pursuit of bodily pleasure itself, then we can see how pain will result, especially if one is a vampire with the capacity to live several lifetimes. More banal vampires could live lives that are both blessed and cursed. They could be "blessed" in that they have the potential to live forever, indulge in their every physical desire, and do what they want irrespective of any moral code. Yet, these are the very things that ultimately become "cursed" for them. Living several lifetimes gets boring because they have "seen and done it all." Indulging their physical desires becomes either painful or boring, and doing what they want makes them targets of evil and corruption to be hunted down and destroyed.

One need not be a vampire, nor live several lifetimes, to see that the pursuit of pleasure *solely*, especially bodily pleasure, offers few blessings. There is wisdom in the famous moral philosopher John Stuart Mill's claim that happiness in life is

---

[17] See Elizabeth Miller and Margaret Carter, "Has Dracula Lost His Fangs?" in Elizabeth Miller, ed., *Reflections on Dracula: Ten Essays* (White Rock: Transylvania Press, 1997), pp. 25–46.

[18] *Autobiography*, in Charles Eliot Norton's Hardvard Classics edition (New York): P.F. Collier and Son, 1909), Volume 25, p. 94.

attained by not making pleasure one's focus: "Those only are happy who have their minds fixed on some object other than their own pleasure. . . . Aiming thus at something else, they find happiness along the way. . . . Ask yourself if you are happy, and you cease to be so."

13

Deserving to Be a Vampire: The Ethical and Existential Elements of Vampirism

TED M. PRESTON

I was once paid an extraordinary compliment: "Ted, I can't say this about many people, but I think you would make a great vampire." I swelled with pride. Vampires are powerful, mysterious, immortal, and sexy (just review the vampire "headquarters" in the film, *Underworld*, if you have any doubts). I have sometimes found myself daydreaming about what it would be like to be a vampire. In my daydreams, it's always good (though I'd have to teach only evening classes if I wanted to continue in my current profession). But (and here the "professional philosopher" bares *his* fangs), upon reflection, I have to wonder, would it truly be *good* to be a vampire? Morally good? Desirable?

If there's something immoral about vampirism, and if being a good person is of some importance to me—shouldn't that give me an overriding reason to reject vampirism (in the fantastic and fictional scenario in which it's offered), no matter how supernaturally sexy I might become?

It's often assumed that vampires are evil by their very nature. There's a strong and immediate objection to vampirism from within a Christian perspective. If Jesus of Nazareth is "the Way, the Truth, and the Life," and the only legitimate source of eternal life, then any alternative route to immortality could easily be regarded as rebellion against God. Indeed, many of the stereotypical weaknesses of vampires depend upon this perception that they have somehow rebelled against God. Consider their aversion to crosses, their "allergy" to holy water, and so on. Indeed, in the film *Dracula 2000*, this notion of rebellion is expressed by making Dracula's true identity none other than Judas Iscariot (the betrayer of Jesus) himself.

But not everyone agrees with the explicit and implicit claims and assumptions of Christianity. If our sole concern with respect to vampirism is that it's "sinful," then anyone who can't appreciate or take seriously the notion of sin (or at least sin within that particular religious context) will already be alienated from our investigation. Accordingly, I will focus on the concerns potentially arising from vampirism in a way that doesn't rely on any overt theological assumptions.

Got Blood?

Perhaps Vampirism is both immoral and undesirable due to the unquenchable thirst for blood it causes. If vampirism is akin to addiction, then perhaps we have available a secular interpretation of being "cursed"—especially if a vampire's thirst causes irresistible compulsions to feed. In the tragic television series finale of *Forever Knight*, vampire-cop "Nick" loses control of his hunger and drains to death the mortal woman he loves. So distraught is he when he realizes what he has done, that he begs for his maker ("Lacroix") to stake him out of his misery.

Either vampires can control their feeding, and exercise discretion, or can't. If they lack the ability to exercise restraint or judgment, wouldn't we be inclined not to hold them morally responsible for their actions anyway? This doesn't mean, of course, that we wouldn't defend ourselves against them—much as we do against dangerous (but deranged) mortals. What's important, though, is that we don't hold responsible (morally or legally) those who literally could not help but do as they did— with one important qualification: we often do hold persons responsible if it is their own free choice that leads them to the point of compulsion. As Aristotle claimed long ago, we are responsible for *becoming* the sorts of persons we are. If someone knows the consequences of certain choices and behavior, they are, in some sense at least, responsible for those consequences even if they lose the power of free choice later on.[1] We might have compassion for an alcoholic, but nevertheless

---

[1] See Aristotle's *Nicomachean Ethics*, Book III, Chapter 5, lines 1114a5–13.

hold him responsible for drinking himself to the point of addiction. Accordingly, we might have pity (rather than moral condemnation) for unwilling ("infected") vampire spawn, but regard with contempt those like me who might actively seek it out.

Alternatively, vampires *can* control their hunger. Note that it doesn't matter that their hunger is never fully satiated. Neither is ours! Mere mortals must feed again and again, or else grow increasingly weak and die. So, if vampires *can* exhibit self-control, despite their hunger, they're no worse off than mortals are, and the only concern is *how* they feed.

Vampires, like the rest of us, must feed to survive. It just so happens that (with a few questionable exceptions) the only food that (apparently) serves to sustain them is human blood.

If feeding on the living in order to survive is, in itself, morally unacceptable, then predatory behavior itself is evil, and at least those of us who have a choice with respect to what we eat are in a lot of moral trouble. After all, this is something we all do, with the possible exception of fruitarians (who consume only fruits, nuts, and seeds so as to avoid killing anything whatsoever). If consuming other living things is morally wrong, then vampires have a lot of similarly immoral company, since billions of mortal humans consume other living things every day. What's more, when we mortals consume a hamburger, that cow is dead, regardless of how little of it we personally consume. On the other hand, typically it's not necessary for a vampire to drain his or her victim of *all* blood. Accordingly, feeding only results in death if the vampire *chooses* to make it result in death. Then it's just good old fashioned murder, and the fact that the murderer is a vampire has little, if anything, to do with the moral condemnation.

It stands to reason, then, that the typical feeding pattern of mortals is far more destructive and lethal, on average, than that of vampires. If they are in the wrong, how much more so are most of us?

In summary, vampires can either control their feeding habits, or not. If they can't, we have a reason to find vampirism undesirable, and we might well be culpable if we seek it out anyway. If self-control is possible, however, we've not yet arrived at a reason to find vampirism either immoral, or undesirable.

Does It Hurt?

We must acknowledge that it's entirely possible that mortals and vampires alike *are* doing something morally wrong when they consume other living things, on the assumption that simply inflicting pain on something capable of experiencing it is morally suspect. A basic (and overly simplified) utilitarian assumption, for example, is that pain and unhappiness are morally bad to inflict, and pleasure and happiness are morally good to "inflict." If our mental image of a vampire feeding is that of a hungry monster leaping from the shadows to wound and drain a helpless and shrieking victim (as is the case, for example, in the "feeding" scenes of the film *The Lost Boys*), such activity *does* appear to be morally wrong, and if vampirism requires such activity, it appears to be morally wrong as well.

At the least, getting bitten by a vampire probably hurts! But, the "pain," the harm inflicted, is not merely the physical trauma of the bite. Unwilling victims are harmed in a way analogous to being sexually assaulted.

The sexual associations and imagery long associated with vampire lore are apt. The experience of penetration, unwelcome intimacy, and commingling is applicable to the vampire's "embrace." We can easily imagine how terrifying it would be to be attacked from the shadows by someone with the power to do with us whatever they desire. Beyond the fear, we can imagine the humiliation as our personhood is violated even as our veins are. It just seems intuitively obvious that, if anything is morally wrong, grabbing someone against their will, wounding them, weakening them through loss of blood (and maybe even killing them in the process), is wrong. However, it should be clear that the moral problems arising here are not unique to vampires. It's not the fact that a *vampire* is doing such things that makes them wrong; it's something about the actions themselves.

Certainly, not all pain-infliction is unjustifiable. We can imagine all sorts of contexts in which even an intentional, premeditated infliction of pain is not regarded as morally wrong. Going to the dentist often hurts, but we recognize that the normally morally-questionable infliction of pain is overridden by the greater good of preventing even more pain due to tooth decay. Moreover, when we're taking *ourselves* to the dentist, we introduce another (important) mitigating factor: *consent* to being "harmed." Why should we assume that a vampire's "meal" must be a victim rather than a willing partner? We could easily imagine an entrepreneurial vampire establishing a blood bank and soliciting voluntary donations (presumably for pay). Indeed, the main character of *Blade* (the series' namesake, and another conscientious vampire—morally conflicted to the core) relies on stored blood preserved in his refrigerator for sustenance, rather than going out for something more "fresh."

If vampires sucking up vials of blood isn't romantic enough, we can instead easily imagine vampires seeking out, and finding, any number of people who would willingly, and perhaps even happily, submit themselves to a non-lethal "embrace." In the first *Blade* film, the character Dr. Karen Jenson altruistically offers her blood to Blade in order to restore his depleted vitality. In Anne Rice's *Interview with the Vampire*, Madeleine offers herself to Louis in hopes of becoming a vampire mother-figure to "Claudia." Accordingly, while pain might be experienced due to the bite, the infliction of pain might be justifiable—particularly if we consider the stories in which vampire "victims" experience a state of ecstasy akin to orgasm.

Vampire feedings could be violent and unwanted, just as sex can be. But, in neither case is violence or coercion a *necessary* feature of the act. Once again, we come to a common-sense conclusion. It's not the fact that a vampire is performing a certain act that renders it morally problematic; it's the nature of the act itself. Acts of violence against unwilling victims are typically regarded as morally wrong whether it's Dracula doing the deed, or you, or me. It would seem to follow, then, that if a vampire is morally "bad," it's because of his or her choices and actions, and not simply by virtue of being a vampire.

Undeath Sure Beats the Alternative

Perhaps the greatest appeal of vampirism is the immortality it promises. One never grows old, never grows weak, never suffers the inevitable decline of body and mind due to age, and never experiences death (unless slain by another, or too long deprived of blood). David, in *The Lost Boys*, encourages the newly-embraced vampire Michael, "You'll never grow old, Michael, and you'll never die."

Contrast this with the lives we all know, recognize, and expect for ourselves and our loved ones, and the appeal of vampirism is obvious. Who wouldn't be tempted to evade becoming infirm or senile, to be spared from cancer, Parkinson's disease, arthritis, and the fear of what awaits us when our bodies are all worn out? Vampirism promises an escape from all such things, and the *time* to pursue any project we might imagine, do anything we might wish to do. And at what expense (excluding religious concerns)? Daylight? Garlic? As much as I love garlic, and can appreciate a good nap in a sunbeam (a treat taught me by my cat, Morgana), they seem like small prices to pay for an eternal life of strength, vitality, and precious time.

Are we misguided, though, when we try to prolong our lives and avoid death? The ancient Greek philosopher Epicurus (341–271 B.C.E.) famously argues that death is not a bad thing (for anyone, mortal or vampire, we might suppose). Assuming that there is no afterlife, he claims that death is "nothing" to us "since when we exist, death is not yet present, and when death is present, then we do not exist. Therefore, it is relevant neither to the living nor to the dead, since it does not affect the former, and the latter do not exist."[2] In other words, when we're alive, we're not yet dead (and so we don't experience death). And, when we're dead, since we don't exist, we don't experience anything at all (including death).

Even if we grant Epicurus his assumption that nothing persists that would actually experience what it is like to be dead, we can nevertheless find ourselves losing sleep about the anticipated pain of the dying process. Maybe death is "nothing," but getting there might hurt a lot! Even if my loved ones cease to exist at death, I'm still around to grieve their passing. Their death is certainly something to me even if it's "nothing" to them. Before Rice's Louis is made immortal, he reports: "I had lost my wife in childbirth. She and the infant had been buried less than half a year; I would have been happy to join them. I couldn't bear the pain of their loss: I longed to be released from it."[3] So deep was his pain from their death, he longed for death himself.

---

[2] "Letter to Menoeceus," in *The Extant Remains*, translated by Cyril Bailey (Oxford: Clarendon, 1926), Sections 124–25.

[3] All my references to *Interview With the Vampire* are to the film version.

Moreover, some have argued that there are ways in which it makes sense for us to say that even nonexistent people (that is, the dead, if they truly cease to exist) can be "harmed" by their death, even if they aren't around to actually experience it. Contemporary philosopher David Furley puts it in this way: death is bad for the one who dies because it renders empty and vain the plans, hopes, and desires that a person has during life.[4] As an example, imagine that (unbeknownst to you), you have a terminal disease, and have very little time left to live. Of course, you're unaware of this fact, so you continue to make plans, assuming that you'll be alive to pursue them. Also unbeknownst to you, your friends and family know of your true condition, and know all too well that you'll soon be dead. From the perspective of your better-informed friends and family members, your hopes and plans for the future seem (presently, to them) vain, futile— even perhaps pathetic—since your goals are doomed to incompleteness. How sad that you're planning a vacation that you'll never take! Moreover, the futility is not removed by removing the knowing spectators. Furley claims that any death that frustrates hopes and plans is bad for the person who dies since it reflects, retrospectively, on that life, and shows that the hopes and projects the person entertained have been, at the very time the person was forming them, empty and meaningless.

Another contemporary philosopher, Martha C. Nussbaum, appreciates this argument because it shows how death reflects back on an actual life, and how our intuitions about the "badness" of death don't depend on "the irrational fiction of a surviving subject."[5] This has the advantage of sidestepping Epicurus's claim that death is "nothing" because we don't exist to experience it. After all, it's not a non-existing (dead) person who is being harmed by death, but an actual living person (like you or me) that is being threatened *right now* by the power that death has to ruin all our plans and make us look like fools for assuming we had a future in the first place.

In an impressive (and depressing) move, Nussbaum adds to Furley's argument by appealing to the apparent fact that the

---

[4] "Nothing to Us?" in Schofield and Striker, eds., *The Norms of Nature* (Cambridge: Cambridge University Press, 1986), pp. 75–91.
[5] Nussbaum, *The Therapy of Desire: Theory and Practice in Hellenistic Ethics* (Princeton: Princeton University Press, 1994), pp. 208–09.

relationships and activities we tend to cherish all take place over some span of time, and by showing how death threatens them by threatening that span. Our relationships have a structure that evolves and deepens over time; they project into the future and involve planning and hoping. Our projects and activities, too, develop over time.

The sorts of "projects" referred to are not necessarily discrete activities, but can also be complex projects involving plans to do something, or certain sorts of things, repeatedly over the course of a complete life. Projects such as having a good marriage, or being a good philosopher, or a wine enthusiast, are subject to frustration by death not because some particular activity is inter-rupted. That is, the threat doesn't arise because death interrupts a honeymoon, or the completion of an essay for *The Undead and Philosophy*, or finishing a glass of Vampire Merlot (not a joke—this wine label really exists!), but because of the inter-ruption of "a pattern of daily acting and interacting, extended over time, in which the temporal extension, including the for-mation of patterns and habits, is a major source of its value and depth"[6] Death threatens to bring to an abrupt halt the project of my marriage, and any sort of project whatsoever. In fact, death interrupts the most basic (but perhaps most profound and important) project of all: living a complete human life.

The appeal of vampirism should now be obvious, if it was-n't already. Being a vampire allows us to defy death. In so doing, our projects remain open. We always retain hope that our goals can be accomplished, whatever they might happen to be. Thus, the avoidance of death alone makes it a good (desirable) thing to be a vampire. So long as vampires don't abuse others (for example, by feeding on unwilling victims), that is, so long as they are not *bad* vampires, then there is nothing bad about *being* a vampire.

Undeath: Ultimately Uninteresting?

Even if we can agree that being a vampire isn't itself morally objectionable, it might yet remain *undesirable*. What on Earth could make a potentially eternal life undesirable? Eternality.

---

[6] *Therapy of Desire*, p. 210.

A common theme in vampire stories, especially the contemporary variety, is the ever-present threat of boredom. The idea is this: once you've had a few centuries of life, let alone a couple millennia, you've "seen and done it all." Novelist Susan Ertz writes, in *Anger in the Sky*, "Millions long for immortality who do not know what to do with themselves on a rainy Sunday afternoon."

If your life is boring, death eventually becomes an attractive and preferable alternative. Rice's "Armand" says, "the world changes, we do not, there lies the irony that finally kills us." One can then imagine vampires, suffering from *ennui*, intentionally hurling themselves chest-first onto stakes or venturing too far from their coffins to make it back before sunrise.

I suspect that many of you, like myself, have little sympathy for this concern. The solution that presents itself seems obvious enough: don't let your life be boring!

This criticism of the value of immortality assumes that existence *necessarily* becomes wearisome, given enough time.[7] To combat this line of reasoning we need only believe that there are "repeatable" pleasures—pleasures that are satisfying when experienced, but such that one would desire to repeat the experience in the future (though not necessarily right away). Candidates for such pleasures are the delights of sex and food and drink, experiencing fine art, pleasant conversation, and so on.[8]

I doubt that I'll ever get tired of really excellent food. There are so many different types of cuisine and dishes, after all. On the very plausible assumption that there are a great many repeatable pleasures (admittedly relative to each person), does it really seem plausible that vampires would necessarily be overwhelmed by boredom? Why couldn't "the simple things" continue to entertain them? As "Kraven" from the film *Underworld* poses (rhetorically): "What's the point of being immortal if you deny yourself the simple pleasures in life?"

Billions of humans (with new ones born every day) offer seemingly limitless potential for interaction. Ever-evolving

---

[7] Those interested in this argument should consult Bernard Williams, "The Makropulos Case," in Williams, *Problems of the Self: Philosophical Papers 1956–1972* (Cambridge: Cambridge University Press, 1973), pp. 82–100.

[8] John Martin Fischer, "Why Immortality Is Not So Bad," in David Denatar, ed., *Life, Death, and Meaning* (Lanham: Rowman and Littlefield, 2004), p. 355.

human creativity and invention means vampires will enjoy new technologies and art forms. Imagine the possibilities opened by cyberspace for an ancient vampire! Is it really plausible that vampires would necessarily be doomed to boredom? I don't think so. Having "done it all" only seems possible in a static world, but our world *changes*. Even if I'm wrong, sunlight always remains as a release from the alleged tedium of Undeath.

Although I remain convinced that vampirism is awfully appealing, I will consider one final (though related) concern. Despite arguing that death is, indeed, a "bad thing," Nussbaum also claims that the intensity and dedication with which we pursue certain of our tasks is necessarily related to the awareness we have of our mortality. We don't have the luxury of an eternity ahead of us. "In raising a child, in cherishing a lover, in performing a demanding task of work or thought or artistic creation, we are aware, at some level, of the thought that each of these efforts is structured and constrained by finite time."[9]

If I had (literally) "forever" ahead of me, would I ever get around to pursuing my goals? Couldn't I always put them off, knowing that I could always come back to them? It was a recognition that I'm getting older, and that I don't have too many decades left (at best!), that inspired me recently to return to my martial arts training in preparation for opening my own dojo when I'm ready to retire from academia. Without the limits set by mortality and declining health and vigor, would I have seen any pressing need to resume training?

The answer is a resounding, "I don't know." What I do know is that an awareness, even a keen awareness, of mortality, is certainly no guarantee that one will "seize the day." Thoreau's words in *Walden* are beautiful: he "wanted to live deep and suck out all the marrow of life . . . to put to rout all that was not life; and not, when I came to die, discover that I had not lived." However romantic it might sound, how many of us actually live like *that* despite our mortality staring us in our face? Mortal that I am, I know that I value the present moment far less frequently, and far less intensely, than I should. I doubt I'm alone in this. The point is that mortality is no more a guarantee of a life lived to the fullest than immortality is a guarantee of boredom and

---

[9] *Therapy of Desire*, p. 229.

value lost. The determining factor is our own idiosyncratic contribution to our own lives.

So, having shown that vampirism needn't be intrinsically immoral, and that there are certainly reasons to desire it for oneself, we're left with an uncomfortable but uncompromising fact: neither I, nor you, however much we might desire otherwise, is going to become a vampire. So what's the point of musing about it at all?

Deserving to Be a Vampire

In the end, the thought-experiment of Unlife serves us as a means of understanding the mortal life we actually know and experience, and allows us to focus on just what it is that makes life valuable in the first place. A life that wouldn't be much good over a span as long as eternity might not be terribly worthwhile for a mere eighty years either. On the other hand, a life overflowing with joy and stimulation, with healthy and thriving relationships, with the satisfaction that comes from dreams pursued and goals accomplished—who wouldn't want that to last forever? And wouldn't it be wonderful if it could?

Vampires can be immoral just like we can. It all depends on choices made. A vampire's eternal life might be as unbearably unsatisfying as our own can be. It all depends on choices made. Since it's unlikely any of us will find ourselves vampires some day, why not do the next best thing? Try to live a life that would be worthy of eternity.

PART IV

Digging Up the
Body Politic

14

The Political Economy of Non-Coercive Vampire Lifestyles

DOUGLAS GLEN WHITMAN

In a Season 5 episode of *Buffy the Vampire Slayer*, Buffy discovers the existence of a vampire brothel, where thrill-seeking humans pay vampires to suck their blood.[1] The vampires benefit from the arrangement because, as Buffy's friend Anya observes, "they get cash, hot-and-cold running blood, and they don't leave any corpses behind, so they don't get hunted." An angry Buffy eventually burns down the brothel. But her Watcher, Rupert Giles, adopts a more accommodating attitude, noting that all the brothel's customers are "willing victims" and suggesting that Buffy's efforts might be better spent combating a "less ambiguous evil."

In the movie *Blade*, occasional reference is made to blood banks that take deposits from humans and allow withdrawals by vampires.[2] Although the movie does not state clearly whether the donations are mandatory or voluntary in nature, the strong implication is that the human government requires humans to contribute blood in order to placate the vampires, thereby forestalling a war between the two groups.[3]

The *Buffy* and *Blade* scenarios present radically different templates for interaction between humans and vampires. The

---

[1] Marti Noxon, "Into the Woods" (2000). The script refers to the vampires' nest as a "drug den," not a brothel.

[2] *Blade*, directed by Stephen Norrington, 1998.

[3] This is only my interpretation of the situation in *Blade*, as the script only hints at the nature of the arrangement. Another possibility is that humans are duped into contributing blood, believing it will be given to other humans. Even if my interpretation is off, the hypothetical case of mandatory blood contributions is a useful one.

former "brothel" model shows the potential for peaceful and non-coercive coexistence, sustained by the possibility of voluntary exchange. The latter "blood bank" model reveals a quasi-peaceful but coercive coexistence, enabled by forced transfers from humans to vampires.

In this chapter, I will use these two models of vampire-human interaction to explore the conflict between two popular perspectives in political philosophy, which I will refer to as "libertarian" and "welfarist." In the libertarian perspective, represented by such thinkers as Robert Nozick,[4] Loren Lomasky,[5] and David Schmidtz,[6] people have individual rights the violation or curtailment of which cannot be justified by the needs of other beings, except perhaps under very unusual circumstances. Ideally, interactions between rights-bearing persons should be voluntary in nature, and social cooperation is sustained by the possibility of many such voluntary interactions. In the welfarist perspective, represented by such thinkers as Peter Singer,[7] Peter Unger,[8] and G.A. Cohen,[9] society should be structured to ensure that the basic needs of all people are met, even when it entails sacrifices by others. Social co-operation for this purpose may properly be mandated if it does not occur voluntarily.

Either perspective must specify what kind of beings should be included in the moral calculus. Do only fully developed humans have rights or interests worthy of consideration? Or does moral consideration extend to other types of beings, such as animals, fetuses, and the Undead? I will argue that, on almost *any* plausible definition of moral personhood, vampires ought to be included. Yet humanity does not seem inclined to adopt such an inclusive definition. On the contrary, most humans believe vampires' interests ought to be actively opposed. I will

[4] Robert Nozick, *Anarchy, State, and Utopia* (New York: Basic Books, 1974).

[5] Loren Lomasky, *Persons, Rights, and the Moral Community* (Oxford: Oxford University Press, 1987).

[6] David Schmidtz and Robert E. Goodin, *Social Welfare and Individual Responsibility* (Cambridge: Cambridge University Press, 1998). In this book, Schmidtz and Goodin take opposite sides of a debate; Goodin is another good representative of the welfarist point of view.

[7] Peter Singer, *Practical Ethics* (Cambridge: Cambridge University Press, 1979).

[8] Peter Unger, *Living High and Letting Die: Our Illusion of Innocence* (Oxford: Oxford University Press, 1996).

[9] G.A. Cohen, *Self-Ownership, Freedom, and Equality* (Cambridge: Cambridge University Press, 1995).

suggest, however, that intolerant human attitudes toward vampires are neither fixed in stone nor fully malleable, but instead are influenced by political and economic institutions. People will be most willing to recognize vampire personhood under a more libertarian system (the brothel model), which emphasizes voluntarism and gains from cooperation. On the other hand, a more welfarist system (the mandatory blood bank model) will motivate humans to adopt more restrictive notions of personhood in order to avoid the burdens—in blood and money—of supporting the vampire population.

Libertarianism and Welfarism Defined

I Have Learned Not to Think Little of Any One's Belief, No Matter How Strange It Be.[10]

Libertarian philosophers are united by their support for limited government and individual rights of person and property. They envision a social world in which people interact, for the most part, on the basis of consent and contract. Individuals are regarded as self-owners: they have the moral and legal right to determine the use of their own bodies as they see fit. They may also own parts of the world outside their bodies, usually in the form of private property. In the libertarian vision, people strive to meet their needs and wants through voluntary cooperation and trade with others. Although most libertarians agree with these general conclusions, they arrive at them by various routes. Some, like Robert Nozick, rely on a Lockean notion of natural rights that people possess by their nature as human beings (or perhaps by the grace of God). Others, like Henry Hazlitt[11] and (arguably) Friedrich Hayek,[12] justify libertarian conclusions on utilitarian grounds; they contend that individual rights provide the social structure most likely to maximize the happiness of the members of society. Neo-Aristotelians, like Douglas B. Rasmussen and Douglas Den Uyl,[13] ground individual rights in classical notions of virtue and human fulfillment.

---

[10] Bram Stoker, *Dracula* (New York: Signet, 1997), p. 186.

[11] Henry Hazlitt, *The Foundations of Morality* (Princeton: Van Nostrand, 1964).

[12] See, for example, Friedrich Hayek, *The Constitution of Liberty* (Chicago: University of Chicago Press, 1960).

[13] Douglas B. Rasmussen and Douglas Den Uyl, *Liberty and Nature* (Chicago: Open Court, 1991).

Welfarism[14] is not a label self-consciously adopted by many thinkers, but a label I have chosen to designate various related perspectives that stand in opposition to libertarianism. Welfarists generally believe that people's basic needs, including survival and health, outweigh or invalidate individual claims to wealth or personal assets. Such wealth or assets may therefore be forcibly transferred from some people to others for the purpose of meeting the recipients' needs.[15] The welfarist perspective usually either rejects individual rights outright or else regards them as interests that can be overcome by the sufficiently weighty needs of others. In some accounts, the needs of others actually create positive rights to certain services or outcomes (such as healthcare or a minimum standard of living) that other people have a responsibility to provide.

As with libertarianism, these are conclusions, not justifications. Probably the most common justification for welfarist conclusions is utilitarian: if some act or policy of coercion generates greater gains for its beneficiaries (say, the recipients of government welfare) than losses for others (those made to pay taxes), then the act or policy is justified because it creates net benefits to society. Peter Singer and Peter Unger—whose views will be examined more carefully later—both represent the utilitarian brand of welfarism. Others, like G.A. Cohen, assert equality of outcome as a valuable goal in and of itself. Yet others, like John Rawls,[16] justify welfarist conclusions on the basis of a contractarian model in which people deliberate over the rules of a just society.

This chapter will not resolve the debate between libertarianism and welfarism. Instead, it will draw attention to a conflict within welfarism that libertarianism avoids. The conflict begins to emerge when we ask the question: are vampires persons?

---

[14] The term *welfarism* has been used for other purposes. It sometimes refers to a specific brand of philosophical consequentialism, without specifying political conclusions. But that is not how I use the term here.

[15] The reference to *recipients' needs* is crucial. Many non-welfarists, including some libertarians, accept a distinct justification for taxation (or other forms of compulsion) as necessary to provide certain public goods that will benefit most or all members of society, *including* those who are made to contribute.

[16] John Rawls, *A Theory of Justice* (Cambridge: Belknap, 1971).

Vampire Personhood

*I Am Neither Good, Nor Bad, Neither Angel Nor Devil; I Am
a Man, I Am a Vampire.*[17]

To put the question another way, do vampires possess whatever characteristics would entitle them to moral consideration? In a libertarian framework, moral consideration would imply the possession of equal rights for vampires; in a welfarist framework, the consideration of vampires' needs and wants would be on equal terms with those of humans. Either way, we need to know whether vampires count as persons from a moral perspective (where "person" means any being that merits moral consideration). Not to put too fine a point on it: if vampires are persons, then hunting and staking vampires constitutes an egregious violation of their rights, a gross indifference to their interests, or both. More provocatively, in the welfarist approach, morality would require providing vampires with regular opportunities to drink human blood.

Robert Nozick summarizes the candidates for characteristics that might signify the possession of rights or morally relevant interests:

> The traditional proposals for the important individuating characteristics connected with moral constraints are the following: sentient [i.e., capable of feeling or perception] and self-conscious; rational (capable of using abstract concepts, not tied to responses to immediate stimuli); possessing free will; being a moral agent capable of guiding its behavior by moral principles and capable of engaging in mutual limitation of conduct; having a soul.[18]

Let's apply each of these criteria in turn. Are vampires sentient? Clearly they perceive the world around them, and they possess the capacity for pleasure and pain. They can suffer from lack of blood, exposure to sunlight, even emotional disappointment. Peter Singer argues that any being that can suffer deserves as much moral consideration as humans: "No matter what the nature of the being, the principle of equality requires that its suffering be counted equally with the like suffering—in so far as

---

[17] Michael Romkey, *I, Vampire* (Greenwich: Fawcett, 1990), p. 5.
[18] *Anarchy, State, and Utopia*, p. 48.

rough comparisons can be made—of any other being. . . ."[19] Under this permissive standard, vampires obviously qualify for moral consideration. Since vampires are also, in most depictions, aware of themselves and the nature of their existence, they still qualify if we require self-consciousness.

Are vampires rational? Like humans, vampires use abstract concepts to impose order on the world around them, allowing them to observe relationships and patterns, to think about the future, and to create plans and execute them.[20] There may exist vampires who, like animals, respond instinctively to stimuli— biting at the first scent of blood—but if so, they appear to be the exception. Unlike killer sharks or deadly viruses, vampires are generally depicted as having minds capable of weighing the benefits of alternative courses of action. According to most accounts, certainly those in *Buffy* and *Blade*, vampires can resist immediate pleasures to obtain longer-term rewards.[21] If they sometimes succumb to their base instincts, the same is true of humans, who sometimes overindulge in food and drink. The difference in rationality between humans and vampires is at most one of degree. Some individual humans have much greater difficulty resisting their passions than the typical vampire. The difference in rationality between the two groups, if any, hardly seems great enough to justify disparate moral consideration.[22]

Free will is more difficult to assess—for both humans and vampires. As humans, we certainly *feel* as though we make free choices, but that feeling could be an illusion. There does not exist direct evidence of free will. What would constitute indirect evidence? The answers turn out to be characteristics already discussed: sentience, self-awareness, rationality. If vampires possess these characteristics, then there is just as much evidence for

---

[19] Singer, 1979, p. 50. Jeremy Bentham, one of the earliest utilitarian philosophers, reached the same conclusion. "The question is not, Can they reason," Bentham wrote, "but, *Can they suffer?*" Cited in Singer 1979, p. 50.

[20] The capacity for planning indicates vampires would also satisfy Loren Lomasky's suggested criterion of "project pursuit" (*Persons*, p. 26).

[21] The vampires of *Buffy* and *Blade* might seem especially human in this regard, but other accounts still show vampires endowed with patience and foresight—Dracula being the most obvious example.

[22] Also, note that humans with limited rationality, such as children, may not be granted the full complement of rights possessed by others, but their interests are still given moral consideration and legal protection.

free will in vampires as in humans. As for the intuitive feeling that one possesses free will, any self-aware, thinking organism will most likely experience the same feeling. We can therefore conclude that there is as much warrant for attributing free will to vampires as to humans (while admitting the warrant may be weak in both cases).

Nozick's next candidate, "being a moral agent capable of guiding its behavior by moral principles and capable of engaging in mutual limitation of conduct," bears a strong resemblance to John Rawls's notion of "moral personality." [23] A being with moral personality is one to whom one can make moral arguments and stand some chance of affecting her choices. This criterion seemingly has greater potential for excluding vampires, at least given popular prejudices about them. Vampires are regarded as indifferent or even hostile to moral constraints on their behavior.

One difficulty with the moral personality standard, as Peter Singer notes, is that it errs by under-inclusion, since infants and young children obviously don't meet it. More importantly, even grown human beings differ in their degree of moral personality. Some humans are more susceptible to moral argument, others less; yet we generally assume the moral agency of humans as a class.[24] Since apparently we do afford consideration to humans with smaller degrees of moral personality, why should we deny such consideration to vampires?

Moral personality is an appealing criterion because it relates to the changeability of behavior: someone with a moral personality can possibly be persuaded to act differently. But there is every reason to believe that vampires can be induced under certain circumstances to behave in a moral manner, even if they do so for purely selfish reasons. In the *Buffy* episode discussed earlier, Anya observes that vampires seek willing victims at blood-brothels to avoid being hunted. Thus, they can be motivated by

---

[23] Rawls, 1971, p. 12. Rawls defines moral persons as "rational beings with their own ends and capable, I shall assume, of a sense of justice" (1979, p. 12). He defines a sense of justice as "a normally effective desire to apply and to act upon the principles of justice, at least to a certain minimum degree" (p. 505).

[24] "Some people are highly sensitive to issues of justice and ethics generally; others, for a variety of reasons, have only a very limited awareness of such principles" (Singer, 1979, p. 16).

strong enough incentives to engage in less harmful behavior.[25] If vampires had greater opportunities to meet their needs without using violence against humans, as would be true if blood brothels and blood banks could operate without fear of attack, the incentive for vampires to eschew violence would be even greater. Without social or legal sanctions, it is likely than many more humans—though certainly not all—would engage in self-seeking behavior at the expense of their fellow humans. If humans and vampires differ in their responsiveness to incentives, it's only a matter of degree.

Nozick's final candidate is possession of a soul. This is, of course, where the vampire literature typically draws the line. But soul-possession is vulnerable to the same critique as free will. Lacking direct evidence of the existence of a soul, we must rely on some other signifier. The most plausible signifiers are characteristics already discussed—sentience, self-awareness, rationality, or moral personality. If it cannot be shown that vampires in fact possess souls, it is because we cannot verify the existence of souls at all, even in humans. We simply *assert* that humans have them and vampires do not.

We need not try to decide among the many possible criteria for moral personhood. There are reasonable arguments for and against each one. Instead, we should simply note the great difficulty of finding any standard for moral personhood that simultaneously *includes* humans and *excludes* vampires.

Ethical and Political Implications of Vampire Personhood

I Was in a Totally Black and White Space, People Versus Monsters, and It Ain't Like That.[26]

If vampires are recognized as persons, how should a just society deal with them? The dilemma is that vampires can't live without human blood.[27] This need seemingly creates an unavoidable

---

[25] The *Buffy* universe provides an even more telling example: Spike, a soulless vampire who nonetheless fights for good because of his love for Buffy.

[26] Marti Noxon, *Buffy the Vampire Slayer*, "New Moon Rising," (2000).

[27] I assume, for the sake of the argument, that vampires need *human* blood for some reason—either for health or for survival itself. The vampire literature differs on this matter,

trade-off between the needs of vampires and humans. The survival and prosperity of vampires requires regular sacrifices—of blood, perhaps lives—by humans. Humans naturally resist such sacrifices. At least on first consideration, vampire-human interaction looks like a *zero-sum game*: the gains to one species are losses to the other. If vampires are just monsters, the conclusion is obvious: humans and vampires will always be at war, and the best interest of humans lies in eradicating the vampires. But if vampires are persons, what then? Could humans justifiably be *forced* to donate blood for the sustenance of vampires?

The welfarist answer is *yes*. So long as the gains to vampires exceed the losses to humans, in terms of life, health, longevity, and personal fulfillment for all persons involved, forced transfers of blood are in principle justified. If a pint of blood could save the life of a human child, while causing the donor only temporary weakness, the moral correctness of the sacrifice would hardly be in doubt. With vampires on equal moral footing with humans, a similar sacrifice would be justified to save a vampire child.

But isn't there an important difference between the obligation to help a particular individual in danger, such as by rescuing a child drowning in a shallow pool, and the obligation to help many anonymous people on a regular basis, such as by making frequent donations to UNICEF? Welfarist authors Peter Singer and Peter Unger both argue otherwise, contending that the two scenarios are morally comparable. Both affirm a simple principle: "If we can prevent something bad without sacrificing anything of comparable significance, we ought to do it" (Singer 1979, p. 169; Unger 1996, p. 8). That principle, when applied to the vampire dilemma, would mandate regular contributions of blood to vampires in need.

The claim is not just ethical, but also political, for while voluntarism might be nice, it is not necessary in the welfarist mindset. Singer and Unger affirm that full implementation of their principle would mandate massive increases in government aid to foreign nations to abate starvation and disease. Doing so would assuredly involve sacrifice by the domestic population—higher taxes and

---

with some accounts allowing vampires to live on animal blood, other accounts positing the importance of human blood.

lower spending on domestic programs. But the same principle that justifies massive aid to needy humans in foreign countries also justifies massive aid to needy vampires at home. Both blood and money donations meet the requirements of Singer and Unger's principle, so long as the amounts donated per capita aren't *too* large. We could easily imagine *Blade*-style mandatory blood banks as the logical implication of welfarist policy.

The libertarian answer to the question of whether humans could be forced to donate blood, however, is a clear *no*. Even if vampires are persons, they do not possess rights that humans lack. Just as humans may not violate others' rights to get money or food, neither may vampires. If vampires wish to sustain themselves, they must find willing victims.

Would libertarian policy lead to the mass starvation of vampires? That's one conceivable outcome, especially if we cannot imagine humans who would be willing donors. But the blood-brothel in *Buffy* raises another possibility: perhaps humans and vampires could coexist peacefully, meeting each others' needs and wants through voluntary exchange. If there's something that humans can do for vampires *and* vice versa, then the vampire-human interaction need not be a zero-sum game. It is actually a *positive-sum game*, in which everyone can come out ahead for having participated. Libertarian philosophers place great emphasis on the capacity of voluntary cooperation and trade to generate happiness and prosperity for the members of society.[28]

While *Buffy*'s blood-brothel scenario had humans paying vampires, it is entirely possible that payments might flow in the other direction. Who paid whom would depend on the relative magnitudes of the human supply and vampire demand for blood. If willing donors were scarce, vampires would have to pay humans, and the market price might be too high for some destitute vampires. If the vampire population grew faster than the human population, the rising demand for blood would push the price even higher. While some vampires might find employment—as club bouncers, nightshift guards, and so on—others might not find a way to contribute enough to society to pay their way. Such vampires would have to subsist on the voluntary charity of other vampires and humans.

---

[28] See, for instance, Schmidtz and Goodin 1998, pp. 14–16.

From Politics Back to Personhood

We Gladly Feast on Those Who Would Subdue Us.[29]

A clever welfarist might claim that the libertarian argument above actually supports his position. Vampires able to pay for their blood would not have to rely on forced transfers. Coercive transfers would only be needed to support those vampires who could not support themselves. In addition, if there were well-developed markets for blood exchange, welfarist moral requirements could be met through transfers of money instead of blood. The government could use tax dollars to subsidize blood brothels or voluntary blood banks, or it could offer "blood stamps" (much like food stamps) for needy vampires. Although everyone would be forced to pay higher taxes, no one would be forced to donate blood.

In this context, it's worth noting that some welfarists oppose policies that involve substantial infringement of bodily integrity, even if such infringement would bring great benefits to others. These welfarists take the more modest position that only *external* wealth and assets may be forcibly transferred for the good of others. They would not, for instance, force a person with two working kidneys to forfeit one to a person with none, though they would force him to pay taxes to pay for dialysis. While this variant of the welfarist position would dodge the possibility of forced blood transfers, it would have to affirm a "blood stamp" program or similar policy.

What would be the economic consequences of adopting such a policy? First, the policy would encourage dependency by some vampires. Given the chance to have blood for free, fewer vampires would find it worthwhile to contribute to society by performing some useful job. There would be a tendency for the burden to grow as more vampires became "hooked" on the system. Second, higher taxes on productive humans and vampires would reduce their incentive to work, because they would get a smaller share of the fruit of their labor. The magnitude of these effects could be small or large, depending on how responsive each group is to its economic incentives.

---

[29] *The Addams Family*, directed by Caroline Thompson, 1991.

More important to my argument, though, are the *political* consequences of the welfarist policy. While it might seem obvious to philosophers like Singer, Unger, and perhaps you that vampires deserve the same moral consideration as humans, that point could easily be lost on a citizenry saddled with providing blood-money to a parasitic underclass. As a result, they would be more inclined to oppose any extension of personhood to vampires.

The claim here is relatively simple: people's willingness to extend moral consideration to the interests of others depends, at least in part, on the burden that results. If the burden is merely having to respect a minimal set of rights, as under a libertarian system, it is likely to be met with *some* resistance, but there is a reasonable chance of overcoming it (witness, for example, the gradual emergence of equal rights for women and ethnic minorities). When the burden rises to the provision of goods and services, however, the level of resistance naturally increases. It is one thing to allow others a chance to succeed; it is another to be forced to support them.

Ample historical evidence supports this claim. One of the earliest and best examples is related by philosopher and economist Adam Smith, in his description of the Poor Law of England.[30] That law of the seventeenth and eighteenth centuries required each parish to raise money for the support of indigent people within its borders. In response, parish officials raised difficult barriers to laborers who wished to settle in their parish, for fear they might come to rely on public charity. A tangle of regulations arose to define the conditions under which laborers could legally settle in another parish. The regulations substantially impeded the mobility of labor, effectively confining most poor people to their places of birth.

In modern times, similar events have occurred with respect to immigration. One of the most frequently invoked arguments against allowing more immigrants into the country is that immigrants will take advantage of the welfare system. Organizations like the Federation for American Immigration Reform (FAIR) routinely point to immigrant claims on welfare to justify restrict-

---

[30] *The Nature and Causes of the Wealth of Nations* (1776, Book I, Chapter X, paragraphs 101–118).

ing immigration into the U.S. One typical FAIR news briefs says, "If we are to have any hope of reducing poverty in the U.S., our immigration laws must be revised and returned to the sensible practice of excluding aliens who are likely to become public charges and to deport those who do."[31] The perception that immigrants depend disproportionately on welfare may or may not be correct, but that is not the point. Even the appearance of dependency can generate opposition to the inclusion of new members in society.

In short, when people believe their pocketbooks are endangered by the extension of public support to some group, they become more willing to exclude that group from the community. The prospect of paying for the upkeep of outsiders stokes the fires of xenophobia.

Possibilities for Human-Vampire Co-operation

These People are Our Food, Not Our Allies.[32]

Philosophers should not blithely assume the good will of man toward his fellow man and proceed from there to a discussion of the morally best public policy, because public policy influences the degree to which people are willing to extend such good will to others. As economist Ludwig von Mises observed, feelings of sympathy and friendship are not the *cause* of social co-operation, but the *result*. Without opportunities for mutual gain, Mises says, "Each man would have been forced to view all other men as his enemies; his craving for the satisfaction of his own appetites would have brought him into an implacable conflict with all his neighbors. No sympathy could possibly develop under such a state of affairs."[33] But voluntary co-operation transforms this zero-sum game into a positive-sum game; it transforms war into commerce.

What kind of society, then, creates the greatest room for the acceptance of vampires? The welfarist vision creates the distinct possibility that humans will have to support vampires with

---

[31] FAIR website, http://www.fairus.org/news/NewsPrint.cfm?ID=1221&c=15, accessed March 5, 2004.

[32] *Blade.*

[33] *Human Action: A Treatise on Economics*, third edition (New York: Regnery, 1966), p. 144.

blood and money, and without compensation for their sacrifices. The resulting resentment would only exacerbate the intolerance of humans toward vampires, possibly driving vampires to have even less regard for the interests of humans. The libertarian vision, on the other hand, emphasizes the potential for humans and vampires to work together and to improve the condition of all—at least, all those willing to do their part. Only in the latter scenario will humans and vampires be likely to develop the sympathy and good will necessary for them to treat each other as persons and moral equals.

15

Rousseau and the Vampires: Toward a Political Philosophy of the Undead

PHILLIP COLE

"No Evidence Is Lacking": A Plague of Vampires

Vampires have not always been works of fiction. At the start of the eighteenth century, reports came out of eastern Europe about plagues of vampires—the dead were rising from their graves in vast numbers to inflict terror and death upon the living. These epidemics began around 1670 and ended around 1770, throughout what was then the Hungarian Empire. The best source of information is the official reports written by representatives of political and religious powers sent to the regions afflicted by these outbreaks of "revenants," as the Undead were called, to discover what was really going on.

One especially notorious case was that of Arnold Paole, a peasant who died in 1726, the subject of an official report published in 1732.[1] According to that report Paole returned from the dead and tormented the people of the village of Medvegia, causing the death of four of them. The villagers decided to disinter his body, which they did forty days after his death. The report reads: "His flesh was not decomposed, his eyes were filled with fresh blood, which also flowed from his ears and nose. . . . His fingernails and toenails had dropped off, as had his skin, and others had grown in their place, from which it was concluded he was an arch-vampire." The report continues that the villagers decided to drive a stake through his heart. As this was done,

---

[1] Christopher Frayling, *Vampyres: Lord Byron to Count Dracula* (London: Faber and Faber, 1991), pp. 20–22.

Paole "gave a great shriek, and an enormous amount of blood spurted from his body" (*Vampyres*, p. 21).

But it didn't stop there, as the victims of vampires were believed to become vampires too. The four people thought to have died from Paole's attacks were disposed of in the same way, as were other people who died from eating the contaminated flesh of animals also thought to have been attacked by him. Those, too, had to be disinterred, staked, and their bodies burned. These included a woman who had died in childbirth three months before who had claimed she washed in the blood of a vampire. The report states: "She was in an excellent state of preservation. Cutting open her body, we found much fresh blood . . . her stomach and intestines were as fresh as those of a healthy, living person . . . fresh and living skin had grown recently, as had finger and toenails" (p. 22). And a sixty-year-old woman who had eaten contaminated meat was, after ninety days of burial, "much plumper," and "still had much liquid blood in her breasts" (p. 22).

These reports were received with incredulity in western Europe. This was the time of the Enlightenment, when philosophy and science were supposed to have won the struggle against superstition and dark fantasies. Vampires certainly had no place in the modern world view, and philosophers tried to explain them away in terms of science or of the primitive state of eastern Europe. Jean-Jacques Rousseau was the exception. In a famous passage he says: "No evidence is lacking—depositions, certificates of notables, surgeons, priests and magistrates. The proof in *law* is complete" (*Vampyres*, p. 31). In fact Rousseau was noncommittal concerning whether vampires existed—this was not the point. Rather, the epidemics were important because they revealed something about the nature of political authority.

The explanation Rousseau sought was political, because in the end the epidemics were a political phenomenon. First, we can take the vampire as standing for our social and political condition, for the exploitative relations that arise from private property (p. 34). Second, we can see the ways in which religious and political authorities seek to control populations by appeal to popular myths and superstitions, by exploiting irrational fear of imaginary monsters (p. 33). In this chapter I follow Rousseau's lead in placing such imaginary monsters at the center of political philosophy. If political philosophy's focus is on the nature and purpose of political communities, then Rousseau has shown the role of fear in constituting those political communities. Vampires and other Undead beings represent some of our deepest insecurities, and so can tell us something crucially important about the politics of fear. So this essay takes a first step towards developing a political philosophy of the Undead.

Hunting Satan's Brood: The Enemy Within

Rousseau claims that authorities—religious or political—seek to create and exploit panic in order to gain and hold on to power. An earlier panic, the witch craze of the sixteenth and seventeenth centuries in Europe and North America, shows the same pattern, and is useful because it has received far greater attention from historians. Hugh Trevor-Roper, in one of the best treatments of this period, concludes that the witch crazes arose because of a struggle for power.[2] They flared most strongly between 1560 and 1630 when religious warfare blazed across Europe. In the Reformation and Counter-Reformation, both the Catholic and Protestant sides identified their enemies as being in league with Satan. Trevor-Roper observes: "Every crucial stage in the ideological struggle of the Reformation was a stage also in the revival and perpetuation of the witch-craze" (*European Witch-Craze*, p. 88).

These were times of great fear and insecurity, and, as usual when a society is in the grip of a panic, it fixed upon a stereotype of the enemy within. This stereotype, once established, "creates . . . its own folklore" (p. 120). Here, then, we have a treatment along Rousseau's lines, in terms of the struggle to assert authority over resistant communities, and there is evidence that similar forces were at work during the vampire craze. What seems to have happened in the vampire case is a struggle between local religious and regional secular authorities, with local religious figures invoking fear of the diabolical supernatural to reassert their power, and the regional authorities seeking

---

[2] *The European Witch-Craze of the 16th and 17th Centuries* (Harmondsworth: Penguin, 1978).

to understand and control that fear. But a puzzling question remains: why are communities so responsive to this kind of strategy? Why are we so easily "spooked" such that we join enthusiastically in the "witch hunt"?

Beyond Hunger

Vampires—and the Undead in general—generate a particularly deep horror. Sigmund Freud, in his famous essay on "The Uncanny,"[3] identifies "anything to do with death, dead bodies, revenants, spirits and ghosts" as "perhaps the most potent" example of the uncanny, and argues that "in hardly any other sphere has our thinking changed so little since primitive times or the old been so well preserved under a thin veneer, as in our relation to death" (*The Uncanny*, p. 148). One commentator on the essay, Michiel Scharpé, makes the insightful point that what is crucial is not so much our relationship with death, but our relationship with the *dead*.[4] The boundary being challenged is not that between life and death, but between the living and the dead. These are, of course, connected, but not all journeys between life and death and vice versa are disturbing. What strikes us as most uncanny, or rather, as we might say, spooky, is the return of the dead themselves into the realm of the living.

The fear of vampires, ghosts and zombies becomes clearer when we see it as a fear, not of death as such, but of the dead. What is at stake is our relationship with the dead and the fear that they are going to return. Fear of our own death is, of course, connected, because they bring the threat of our destruction with them from beyond the grave. But there is something special about this particular form of death. Death is to be feared in many forms. Flying, disease and illness, acts of war, road accidents, murder, old age; these can all give rise to fear of death. But death can also be welcomed; death holds the prospect of peace. In the HBO television series *Six Feet Under* the Fisher family run a funeral home and encounter death and dead people each week. In one episode, David—one of two brothers who run the business after the death of their father—is con-

---

[3] *The Uncanny*, translation by David McLintock (London: Penguin Books, 2003).
[4] "A Trail of Disorientation: Blurred Boundaries in *Der Sandmann*," in *Image and Narrative: Online Magazine of the Visual Narrative*, Issue 5. *The Uncanny*, guest editor: Anneleen Masschelein (January 2003), at www.imageandnarrative.be/.

fronted by the violent prospect of death when he is sadistically robbed at gunpoint.

But in the same episode we get a radically different picture, as his art-student sister Claire displays her self-portrait photographs to the rest of the class for comment. One of the students says of them: "Dead. That's what I like about them. This girl who's, like, dead, and beyond everything—beyond hunger, beyond sex, beyond boredom. And really it's so beautiful to be in that state. Like, nothing can reach her, nothing can get to her." The dead people in the funeral home have a serenity even when they have met violent ends, and occasionally they return in a benign way to have discussions with family members. Quite often these discussions are comforting and revealing, as the dead seem to have acquired a depth and a wisdom lacking in the living. Here, then, both death and the returning dead hold, not fear, but an attraction. By contrast the Fisher family's lives are filled with disappointment and torment. The attraction is, perhaps, that of being absorbed into a greater whole, even if that whole is a complete nothingness, an emptiness. But even in this attractive, beckoning form, death must be resisted, and the Fishers do resist it, stubbornly sticking to the living despite their seemingly remorseless misery. In *Six Feet Under* existence appears in all its absurdity, but in the end the program, despite its darkness, is a comedy, albeit without a laughter track, and represents one of the traditional existentialist responses to the absurdity of existence: wry amusement.

Itchy and Scratchy: Cartoon Cannibalism

The point is that death is not necessarily something to fear, and in the forms in which we *do* fear it this is not necessarily based on anything to do with the uncanny or the spooky. So we are left with the question: what is so especially chilling about the dead in the form of vampires and zombies, and what is especially horrifying about the prospect of death they offer? Perhaps what they represent is motiveless malignity, evil intent to destroy us for no reason. The dead, then, bring with them a supernatural malice towards us, which is inexplicable and irresistible. And so there is something especially disturbing about the death these creatures offer, in contrast to the death we encounter in *Six Feet Under.* Here, again, there is absorption, but this time it is not a promise but a threat, a violent absorption—

we will be consumed. The vampire will drain our blood; the zombie will eat our flesh. We are reduced to blood and flesh in this act of absorption. Here we become nothing, not by entering a pool of greater nothingness, but by being eaten. But what's the difference between this and dying, say, in a traffic accident? It may seem a nonsensical question, but it has a point—in both cases we are dead, whether we enter the Fisher's funeral home or the vampire or zombie's digestive tracts. Why should the latter be so horrific?

One answer, oddly enough, lies in the cartoon series *The Simpsons*, and in the cartoon-within-a-cartoon, *Itchy and Scratchy*. Itchy and Scratchy are cat and mouse, a parody of *Tom and Jerry* and of its extremities of violence. In each episode Itchy the mouse kills Scratchy the cat in an imaginative and shocking act of murder—but the true appalling horror only starts after Scratchy's death. For whatever Itchy then does to Scratchy, Scratchy's eyes always remain present, watching the whole process. Whether the cat is liquefied in a milkshake and then drunk by the mouse, or whatever other cannibalistic or brutal act Itchy perpetrates, Scratchy's eyes blink and widen in shock and horror as he watches. And it is this—that throughout whatever is happening after his death, Scratchy is a witness, conscious and aware of it— that is most deeply and horribly disturbing about this cartoon- within-a-cartoon. Horror films and literature disturb us so deeply because as the vampire drains us or the zombie eats us, as we are reduced to the blood and flesh and skin that make us, we are aware, we are watching, we are not yet really dead. Despite our death we continue to watch, our eyes wide and blinking in horror, as the cannibal Undead eat us; we are dead, but not dead, the Undead audience, being violently consumed by our malignantly evil pursuers. At the center of this disturbance is a problematic relationship, not so much with our own death, although this is ultimately implied, but with our own dead bodies.

Revulsion: Our Dead Bodies, Our Selves

Here, a psychoanalytic narrative, that of Julia Kristeva, can help us to understand the forces at work.[5] For Kristeva the key idea

---

[5] Kristeva, *Powers of Horror: An Essay on Abjection* (New York: Columbia University Press, 1982).

is that of the *abject*, which has its source in the moment that the infant child separates itself conceptually from its mother—the infant experiences horror at its dependence on the mother's body, and at the way in which its identity is consumed by that body, but it is also fascinated by it and clings onto it. This horrified fascination is what Kristeva calls *abjection*. The mother's body, indeed anything to do with the physical body, has become abject. Our physical bodies embody death; we are already in the process of dying, and the dead bits of us (discarded hair, fingernails, skin, and shit and piss) are sources of revulsion and we flush them away in panic. But the abject has the power to disrupt the boundary of the body because it is both inside and outside of that boundary. However much we try to expel it and keep our borders secure, the abject undermines all such attempts. The abject is precisely that which connects us with death and shows us that death is already within the boundary, however much we try to expel it.

Barbara Creed uses this idea to psychoanalyze the horror film,[6] and notes that all sorts of religious taboos, such as sexual perversion, physical decay and death, human sacrifice, murder, bodily wastes, the female body, incest, are things that threaten our identity as a member of humanity. We want to expel them behind a border which will protect us from them, but they are all part of who we are, so this process of expulsion has to be constant. Perverse sexual desires, our bodies themselves and their waste products, our own violence and ferocity, are all things we place beyond a border in order to preserve our humanity, but they constantly erupt inside that border.

These encounters with abjection are played out in horror fiction and film, and were also played out during the witch trials and the vampire epidemics. The woman as witch is abject because she represents human sacrifice, sexual perversion, perverted sexual relations with animals, and cannibalism (*Monstrous-Feminine*, pp. 74–76). The vampire too is such a disturbing figure. It is because the corpse is the ultimate representation of abjection (p. 9). The physical body is the site of the struggle between the subject and the abject, and the dead body

[6] Creed, *The Monstrous-Feminine: Film, Feminism, Psychoanalysis* (London: Routledge, 1993).

is the representation of defeat. It is, in Kristeva's words, "the most sickening of wastes" (*Powers of Horror*, pp. 3–4). The corpse is a body without a soul, and so the vampire is the ultimate form of body without a soul. Creed finds it significant that "such ancient figures of abjection as the vampire, the ghoul, the zombie and the witch . . . continue to provide some of the most compelling images of horror in the modern cinema" (*Monstrous-Feminine*, pp. 9–10).

The corpse, then, is the most powerful symbol of the abject, but even in this extreme form the abject both horrifies *and* fascinates. Émile Zola captures this perfectly in his novel *Thérèse Raquin*,[7] in Laurent's visits to the morgue to seek the corpse of Thérèse's husband, Camille, whom they plotted to murder and whom Laurent pushed from a boat into the Seine and drowned. When there are no drowned corpses to see, "He then became a mere sightseer, and found a strange pleasure in looking violent death in the face, with its lugubriously weird and grotesque attitudes." He sees the body of a young woman who had hanged herself: "He lingered over her for a long time, running his eyes up and down her body, lost in a sort of fearful desire" (*Thérèse Raquin*, p. 109). But the two lovers are doomed by the horror of Camille's corpse, which is with them, haunting them, constituting an impossible boundary between them:

> When the two murderers were lying under the same sheet, with eyes closed, they seemed to feel the slimy body of their victim lying in the middle of the bed, and it turned their flesh to ice. It was like a loathsome obstacle, separating them. A feverish delusion came over them in which this obstacle turned into solid matter— they could touch the body, see it spread out like a greenish, putrefying lump of meat, breathe the horrible stench of this mass of human decomposition. . . . (*Thérèse Raquin*, pp. 175–76)

The theme of the corpse that won't go away is a recurring one in the horror film, especially the drowned corpse returning from the depths. In *The Fog* and *Pirates of the Caribbean* these are literally corpses come to life. In *What Lies Beneath* Michelle Pfeiffer's character is haunted by the ghost of a young woman her husband has drowned and dumped in a lake, but in the end

---

[7] Harmondsworth: Penguin Classics, 1962.

it is the corpse itself that intervenes and drags the husband (Harrison Ford) down to his death in the depths.

Oceans of Time: The Romantic Vampire

In the end, our physical bodies are our source of fear because they are the site of the struggle between life and death, humanity and inhumanity. We can now see the special horror that the vampire epidemics represent, as corpses rose from their graves to destroy the living, transgressing the boundary between the living and the dead. But this connection with death and the inhuman is a source of both horror and fascination, for both death and inhumanity offer different forms of freedom. While death offers freedom from everyday life in the sense of peace, inhumanity offers freedom from the mundane moral constraints of everyday life, so that we can be powerful and ferocious monsters. This is a romantic freedom and vampires represent this as well, and contemporary vampire narratives have perhaps stressed this aspect over that of death. In Francis Ford Coppola's film *Bram Stoker's Dracula* (1992), the Count is a romantic hero searching for his lost love, Elisabeta, and his pursuit of Mina is an expression of that love and devotion, as he has "crossed oceans of time" to find her. Anne Rice's series of novels *The Vampire Chronicles* also pursue the romance of the vampire figure, and in Neil Jordan's film version, *Interview with the Vampire: The Vampire Chronicles* (1994), the vampires are the romantic leads: Tom Cruise as Lestat de Lioncourt, Brad Pitt as Louis de Pointe deLac, Antonio Banderas as Armand. The vampire therefore combines both the corpse and the "romantic" monster who defies morality. The point, however, is that *we* combine both. *We* are the living dead.

Alien Invasions: The Vampiric Immigrant

At the psychoanalytic level the vampire represents the threat of being consumed, and at the political level this is most often expressed by the fear of invasion—what is consumed is our territory, our culture, our identity. The invader here can take various forms but in contemporary political debate the most potent are the immigrant and the global terrorist. However, the connection between the vampire and the immigrant is an older one,

going back to the late nineteenth century when Jewish migra-
tion from eastern Europe was thought to present particular
problems of assimilation, and therefore a particular danger to
the identity of the political community. Ken Gelder points to the
figure of Count Dracula in Bram Stoker's novel, noting that
Stoker represents the Count as "a tall, thin, man, with a beaky
nose and a black moustache and pointed beard" who hoards
riches and moves across borders evading regulation.[8] The person
who helps him escape from England is Immanuel Hildesheim, a
Jew who arranges illegal entry and exit, "a Hebrew of rather the
Adelphi Theatre type, with a nose like a sheep, and a fez."[9]

So here the vampire is the unassimilated immigrant who
threatens the identity of the nation. National identity is lost
through unregulated movement across borders and growing
diversity within them, as one's nation "dissolves," and in Stoker's
novel this becomes "the fear of dissolving into vampires"
(*Reading the Vampire*, p. 12). The British Empire was going
through an uncertain period with economic competition from
the United States and from Germany, and Stoker's novel, published in 1897, was just one reflecting this theme of vulnerability. H.G. Wells's *War of the Worlds* was published in 1898, with
alien invaders who live off human blood (*Reading the Vampire*,
p. 12), and the central theme of another of Wells's famous stories, *The Time Machine*, published in 1895, is cannibalism. The
current trend in American popular culture for vampires, zombies
and hostile alien invaders may also reflect this fear of degener-
ation, as the United States enters a similar phase of economic
vulnerability. Both *The Time Machine* and *War of the Worlds*
have been made into major Hollywood movies in recent years.

The Evil Enemy

At the center of the witch trials and the vampire craze, and our
contemporary fascination with the Undead, is this fear of invasion by an evil enemy who will consume us—take our territory,
our identity, our culture, our bodies. Politically, in Europe there
is a growing hostility to immigration of any kind, and in the

---

[8] Ken Gelder, *Reading the Vampire* (London and New York: Routledge, 1994), p. 14.
[9] Bram Stoker, *Dracula,* edited by Maurice Hindle (Harmondsworth: Penguin, 1993), p. 448.

United States the evil enemy is the global terrorist. Both high-light the fragility of borders. What is fundamentally disturbing about the vampire and the witch is their ability to pass among us undetected, to appear to be one of us, but to be secretly scheming our destruction. The person sitting next to you now as you read this could be a witch or a vampire, and this possi-bility undermines the foundations of our world.

Vampires and other supernatural enemies have the power to render borders meaningless, and it is this that takes us to the beginning of a political philosophy of the Undead, because they draw our attention to the nature and importance of boundaries, political or otherwise. What they reveal is how important these boundaries are to us, and also how arbitrary and fragile they are. Political philosophy has had little to say about boundaries. It usually assumes that the limits of the political community are given, and that all political questions concern those who are already legitimately members of that community. This means the political philosophy has rarely addressed the question of the outsider, and it is this figure that the vampire represents in its most demonic form.

The immigrant is therefore a threatening figure, who will drain away our resources, destroy our identity, bring disorder and disease, or, in the shape of the terrorist, plot our murder. But just as the vampire is an imaginary monster, so is this figure of the immigrant. When we free ourselves from these night-mares we can see the outsider in different, non-threatening terms. The vampire should warn us against such demonization and the representation of those we fear as malignant monsters who only wish to destroy us.

We need to question how borders and boundaries are con-structed and note their deeply arbitrary nature and so no longer mistake them for *moral* boundaries. We also need to question how those on the outside are constructed and so no longer mis-take them for mortal enemies. What is at work here is a two-world picture of demonic evil—that here is an evil enemy intent on destroying us, and they enter from another world, distinct from our own so that all we have to explain is their journey, not their nature. In taking this view we draw a boundary between us and them, so that we are not infected with this kind of evil. Although this conception obviously has its place in the worlds of mythology and fiction, we see it erupt again and again as a representation of actual human agency—migrants, Jews, and those engaged in global terrorism, for example. Once these take on the dimension of the demonic, then there can be no negotiation, no understanding, and no possibility of redemption.

In the Borderlands of Buffy World

The television series *Buffy the Vampire Slayer* plays with the fragility and fluidity of these boundaries, as the vampires and demons cannot be condemned as malignant enemies in any simplistic sense. Some of the demons Buffy and her friends battle against live in our world, but the most dangerous and potentially apocalyptic enter from a demon dimension through the hellmouth over which the Californian town of Sunnydale is situated. In the early episodes of the series, the demons that are found in Sunnydale are exterminated brutally and quickly, and there is something faintly disturbing about the way in which Buffy and her comrades perform this task with relish and very little evidence of what we might call thinking.

However, as the series progresses a more complex view is taken, and the vampires and demons take on other dimensions. They have their own underworld in the back streets of Sunnydale, where they lead their lives out of sight of humans for the most part, running businesses and performing services— in other words, a typical community of illegal immigrants. Angel, the vampire with a soul, is an ally in the struggle against evil, and Spike, a vampire without a soul, eventually joins that struggle and performs heroic acts of self-sacrifice in attempting to protect Buffy's younger sister Dawn from a ferocious enemy that seeks her destruction. In the series finale he has acquired a soul and is the figure who saves the world from the ultimate apocalypse.

The most shocking moments in the series, however, are not demonic at all. The first is the killing by the slayer Faith of a human being who works for the demonic mayor of Sunnydale, and who is actually trying to assist the Buffy gang in their struggle against this latest apocalypse. She kills him by mistake, believing herself to be under attack by supernatural enemies. It is a moment of misjudgment in a battlefield, when a tragic mistake is made which has enormous consequences for all the characters in the series.

The second occurs when Warren, a human attempting to be a supervillain, shoots and kills a member of the Buffy gang, Tara. He is in a state of irrational rage, having had his masculinity humiliated. Warren takes a gun and, in his rage and humiliation, lets off a stream of bullets at Buffy, hitting her and wounding her—but a stray bullet kills Tara. This plunges the narrative into darkness, with the shock of the suddenness of death caused by irrational anger. Neither Faith nor Warren are demonic, and neither are their victims. Faith is eventually redeemed, but Warren never gets the chance, killed in an act of terrible revenge by Tara's partner, Willow, an act for which Willow herself must seek redemption. And so within all the demonic and supernatural dangers, the most shocking moments are human, all too human. This is Freud's uncanny in reverse. Here the supernatural world is disrupted and disturbed by the ordinary—what is most shocking is what ordinary people do. In the end, *Buffy* forces us to look away from the comforts of the demonic conception of evil, with its clear boundaries and sharp distinctions.

A Political Philosophy of Vampires

And so we should no longer take the boundaries of our political community as given, but recognize the extent to which they only become important to us because of fear of what is outside—and, of course, the alien inside. Political authorities seize upon these figures or create them through the language of abjection, in terms of pollution, of sexual perversion, of disease and death: the witch, the vampire, the Jew, or in contemporary times the immigrant, the asylum seeker, the terrorist. Driven by this horror, we join forces with the authorities in hunting down those who have found their way inside our community already, and in erecting more secure fortifications to prevent further invasions. This means they have to be policed more stringently and frantically when they are threatened; imaginary enemies are always the hardest to protect ourselves against. The border is constituted by fear of the abject, but the abject is such that it exposes that border as a fabrication, as no protection at all. The vampire, the witch, the terrorist, already pass among us. This is not because of the lack of secure borders, but because the enemy is always within us, in the form of our deepest fears and insecurities about who we are, fears that are exploited in the struggle for power and legitimacy. What Rousseau shows us in his perceptive analysis of the vampire epidemics is that the real subjects of the ever more elaborate and encroaching powers accumulated by the authorities in the name of protecting the "genuine" members of the community from their "enemies" are those members themselves. And he shows us that, if the task of political philosophy is to subject our political communities to reason and clear thinking, then a political philosophy of the Undead—of the vampire as the "demonized" outsider—reveals the extent to which political philosophers have, so far, failed us.

16

The Undead Martyr: Sex, Death, and Revolution in George Romero's Zombie Films

SIMON CLARK

A figure lies prone on an operating table, its bloodied rib cage exposed and empty. All of the vital organs have been surgically removed. But this body is not dead, not completely. It is struggling against the restraints that pin it down, straining to bite a doctor whose hand is just out of reach. "See, it wants me. It wants food, but it has no stomach—it can take no nourishment from what it ingests," says the doctor, toying with the Undead corpse. "It's working on instinct—a deep dark primordial instinct." Suddenly the corpse breaks free. The Doctor grabs a surgical drill and bores a hole deep into its skull. Only now is it completely dead.

In this scene from *Day of the Dead* George Romero unveils human instinct as the true star of his zombie films. Throughout *Night of the Living Dead* (1968), *Dawn of the Dead* (1978), *Day of the Dead* (1985), and *Land of the Dead* (2005), human instinct is the motor that drives the endless ranks of Undead corpses ever forward. From this we can straightforwardly deduce that Romero portrays pure and unrefined instinct as a dangerous force that is threatening to human life. But why should our most natural urges be seen as hostile, and why does Romero visualize them as stumbling Undead corpses with an insatiable appetite for human flesh?

Repressive Civilization

The Austrian psychoanalyst Sigmund Freud (1856–1939) states that civilization, since its origins, has demanded the constant control and repression of the primary human instincts. Civilization's main job, he says, is to overcome the inhospitable forces of nature. The necessities of human survival—food and shelter—are not in natural abundance, but they become easier to procure when people team up and work as a group. This is the beginning of civilization. Everyone develops a role, and as long as they stick to it they guarantee their own survival within the larger group. This contribution to the group's cause is what we now call work. It is what we *have* to do, rather than what we *want* to do.

Work basically means sacrifice, compromise, and a lot of unrewarding toil, but it is necessary (for the vast majority of us) to ensure our inclusion within the civilized order. But Freud says that the primary human instincts reject this order. They demand constant and unadulterated pleasure—they want to be freely and completely gratified at all times. Therefore civilization is unable to grant what the instincts crave, and the two forces fall into direct conflict with each other. Civilization attempts to control this conflict by offering its citizens attractive substitutes for pleasure such as wages, security, and leisure time. None of these compensations quench the instinctual thirst for absolute pleasure, yet the individual accepts them so that he or she can survive within the civilized group.

But Freud goes on to state that deep down, the individual rages against the injustice of this deal. There is part of the individual's mind that still longs for instinctual pleasure, even though it is banned. Freud says that this unlawful desire sometimes bubbles up within the social order and manifests itself as the dark and murky underbelly of civilization. Freud calls this lawless presence the "return of the repressed."[1] It is a blister on the social order—an unwanted by-product of authoritarian control. Civilization is therefore in a constant state of hostile negotiation, always trying to manage the chaos that it created by repressing the instincts in the first place.

So the instincts are dangerous because they nurture an unlawful desire for pleasure that haunts the repressive order of civilization. Romero's zombie, as an embodiment of these pleasure-seeking instincts, becomes nothing less than a visual

---

[1] Sigmund Freud, *The Uncanny* (New York: Penguin, 2003).

metaphor for the return of the repressed. The conflict between humans and zombies in Romero's films can now be understood as a dramatization of the struggle that exists between civilized individuals and their own repressed instincts. The basic instinctual urges are ripped out of the civilized population by repression, and are manifested in a separate body altogether—the Undead corpse. Freudian theory therefore invites us to conceive of the zombie as a drooling embodiment of an instinctual pleasure that refuses to give in to the repressive forces of civilization—that quite literally refuses to stay dead. A zombie can only be completely killed off when the part of its brain that generates instinctual impulses is destroyed. But throughout Romero's films there are always more zombies, so repressive civilization never manages to totally subdue the instincts. Crucially, it is civilization's repressive squeeze on the instincts that forces the zombies to come oozing out into the social order in the first place. So in Romero's films the Undead corpse is the nemesis, but also the product, of a repressive civilization.

Freud says that repression is not only carried out and enforced by powerful institutions; it is something that individuals do to themselves as well, like an internalized self-censoring mechanism. This develops when the individual's infantile fear of his or her father is converted into an adult sense of reverence towards authority in general. The father's stern morality manifests itself inside the individual's own mind, and this internalization of authority is the basis of the individual's conscience. Freud calls this the "superego."[2]

In his first two zombie films Romero presents scenarios in which the individual's superego—the sense of servitude to a higher authority—is overtaken by an aggressive and unlawful quest for power. In *Night of the Living Dead*, Mr. Cooper is the traditional patriarchal figure, but he is weak, selfish, and disrespected. He is constantly undermined by the other individuals who are struggling to survive the night on their own terms. This lack of a common authority leaves them vulnerable and accelerates the zombies' advance.

Ben, who survives until daybreak, is mistaken for a zombie by other humans. The sheriff's men shoot him dead and then

---

[2] Sigmund Freud, *The Dissolution of the Oedipus Complex* (The Penguin Freud Library, Volume 7, *On Sexuality*, London: Penguin, 1991).

throw his body onto a pile of zombie corpses. This scene subtly suggests that Ben's disrespectful and violent struggle with Mr.
Cooper actually puts him in league with the zombies.
Consequently he is shot by the repressive patriarchal regime and
disposed of in the same way as the Undead corpses.[3]

In *Dawn of the Dead*, those who normally serve the controlling order abandon their posts in an effort to ensure their own
immediate survival: Stephen and Francine work for a television
network, and Peter and Roger are both policemen. They all
desert their civil duties and escape together as the zombie chaos
swells out of control. This collapse of common authority creates
a void in civilization's defenses that sucks in the advancing
hordes of zombies. In both films Romero presents a battlefield
in which the struggling humans are effectively caught in a no-
man's land between civilization and instincts. Those who reject
the civilized hierarchy and plot a course towards their own
immediate gratification are either consumed by the Undead or
murdered by other more civilized humans. As the unlawful individuals attempt to reclaim their prohibited desire, the zombies,
as an embodiment of this desire, close in on them. The only survivors are those who surrender their immediate pleasure and
attempt to crawl back to civilization's front line.

In *Dawn of the Dead* the civilized economy is now redun-
dant. Within the mall, Francine, Stephen, Peter, and Roger are
able to take whatever they want for free. The mall has become
a domain of lawless pleasure. The zombies in the mall may have
been destroyed, but an Undead throng is steadily gathering outside. Once the gang of bikers violently force their way through
the barricade, destructive incivility takes hold and the zombies
return to wreak their bloody havoc. Stephen refuses to surrender the luxurious mall to the marauding bikers without a fight.
Because he gives in to his selfish instinctual desire, he is savaged by the Undead hordes and becomes a particularly flam-
boyant zombie himself. Francine and Peter only survive because
they leave the mall behind and fly off into an unknown, but
more civilized, future.

---

[3] There is a subtext of racial identity and conflict being played out in this scene too.
Romero's casting throughout the four films touches on significant race issues and war-
rants more investigation.

The presence of zombies becomes inversely proportional to civilization's ability to enforce its repressive regime. The more we see humans violating civilized law, the more the zombies close in and destroy the social order. The number of zombies steadily increases throughout the four films, so Romero effectively portrays a dysfunctional society that is descending into unlawful chaos. It is unable to cope with the forces it has unleashed against itself. A reading of Freud allows us to state that the horror of Romero's films is founded in this nightmarish vision of a civilization that is losing its repressive grip on instinctual pleasure.

The Destructive Union of Eros and Thanatos

But what is this instinctual pleasure that the zombies embody? What is pleasurable about being a moaning, mindless corpse? Freud claims that the human instincts are composed of two primary drives. He refers to them by the names of the Greek gods that personify them: Eros and Thanatos, the life and death instincts respectively. Freud says that every human pleasure, from passionate love to sadistic violence and greed, can be boiled down to one or both of these primary instinctual drives.

Eros is the urge to create and reproduce—to unite, nurture, and protect all human life. It embodies the basic principle of survival and growth. Eros is the instinct that brought humans together and created civilization in the first place. But as Freud establishes, civilization represses the raw human instincts, so Eros is in fact betrayed by its own creation. This is because Eros not only creates all the emotional and psychological bonds that pull groups of people together, it fuels a more extreme desire for immediate sexual gratification as well. Within this sexual dimension of Eros, reproduction and the continuation of the species are only incidental by-products of the overwhelming urge to obtain total physical bodily pleasure from other humans.

This is where Eros starts to come into friction with civilization. The repressive order decrees that the body must be primarily engaged as a tool of labor, and this immediately alienates the individual from his or her erotic pleasure. Civilization would soon grind to a halt if everyone constantly pursued their own physical gratification, so any manifestation of erotic desire that is not an act of civilized reproduction is heavily repressed by the social order. This allows us to recognize the zombies' thirst for pleasure as a specifically sexual urge.

In Romero's films the repressed Eros returns to haunt civilization in the form of the zombies' rampant desire for flesh. The Undead refuse any sort of curfew on their erotic pleasure; they want it bad, and they want it all the time. They will bite any flesh they can sink their teeth into. This reactivates the entire body as an erogenous zone and takes the focus away from civilized genital contact. This desire to bite and consume human flesh is an act of reproduction that causes the Undead population to grow at a terrific speed. But as Freud establishes, this reproduction and self-perpetuation—the hallmark of Eros—is merely a by-product of the immediate urge for total sexual gratification.

Thanatos, on the other hand, expresses the instinct to regress—to return to the inertia of inorganic matter. It is the urge to reduce life to something base, crude, and simple, and so becomes associated with destruction and violence. Thanatos yearns to reverse the turbulent process of growth, and summons the universal inertia of death to stifle the friction of organic existence. Civilization represses this destructive instinct by channeling its energy into socially useful aggression and competition. Some examples of this are aggressive contact sports, hostile economic rivalry, and the entertainment industry's commercialization of violence and gore.

In Romero's films the repressed Thanatos returns in the form of the zombies' violent bite that transforms civilized humans into rotting corpses. Everyone who is bitten will sooner or later turn into a zombie. So the Undead bite is not only erotic; it aggressively reduces individual identity to a crude and base level as well. Living people, as the working parts of the civilized infrastructure, are dismantled. The zombies stumble around, wearing the uniforms that used to define their roles within civilization when they were still alive. These uniforms speak of a civil function that is rendered obsolete under the reign of the destructive instinct. The individual regresses to dead matter—becomes no more than walking decay—and is therefore released from the tension of civilized human life.

The repressed instinctual pleasures of Eros and Thanatos are therefore both manifested in the zombie's erotic and destructive behavior. This sheds more light on the main characteristics of the Undead corpse. The zombie walks in a very striking way. The zombie shuffle, as I shall call it, is stiff and awkward, motored by a single and overwhelming urge to consume flesh. If this urge is specifically erotic as we have discussed, then the zombie's body is effectively engorged with desire—bloated by its own sexual appetite. The awkward, stumbling zombie can therefore be compared to a swollen erection, stiffly swaying this way and that in its quest for pleasure. It is an unruly swelling of desire within the civilized order—an erotic presence within the very institution that tries to stifle, like a tight pair of pants, all manifestations of sexual arousal. Civilization demands that the body be soft and malleable, but the sexually primed and defiantly stiff zombie refuses to be molded into a pliable and subservient human tool.

The Undead corpse's sexual desire is realized when it bites into human flesh. But as we have discussed, this bite is more than just erotic; it also satisfies the instinctual urge to regress—to turn life into base and inert matter. Freud says that the regressive desire of Thanatos can be compared to that of a consuming and all-encompassing womb that wishes to draw life back into itself. In response, Barbara Creed suggests that this idea of a devouring femininity conjures up the notorious and mythological image of the *vagina dentata*—the toothed vagina—that literally consumes life and returns it to the womb from whence it came.[4] We have seen that the zombie is a manifestation of the urge to reduce and destroy life. If this instinct to regress plays out the desire of the devouring womb, then the zombie's mouth—the very thing that consumes living flesh and turns it into decaying mater—becomes nothing less than a manifestation of the vagina dentata. The bloodied mouth of the Undead corpse can be interpreted as a horrific depiction of the consuming female genitals, whose deadly bite removes the individual from the tensions and frustrations of civilized life.

And so the zombie's bite, in Freudian terms, unites the sexual component of Eros with the violently regressive urges of Thanatos. This coalition nurtures a double-barreled instinctual pleasure that is in direct conflict with the civilized human body.

---

[4] Barbara Creed, *The Monstrous-Feminine: Film, Feminism, Psychoanalysis* (London: Routledge, 1993).

Freud emphasizes the fact that repression squeezes Eros and Thanatos into a destructive union against civilization. The repressive order therefore triggers its own demise, and Romero's zombie films take this proposition to its horrific conclusion. In *Day of the Dead*, Romero presents a scenario in which the traditional, hierarchical, and repressive model of civilization is outmoded. He shows a civilization at breaking point, in which the individuals in the army base no longer adhere to the repressive principles of the social authority. Disorder gains the upper hand, and the full force of the repressed Eros and Thanatos is eventually unleashed. The resulting wave of zombies swiftly consumes all that remains of the tattered civilization. There's no going back for the survivors; their only option is to disregard the previous repressive system and move on in an effort to pioneer an alternative social order.

The Possibility of a Non-Repressive Civilization

The German philosopher Herbert Marcuse (1898–1979) came up with a new relationship between civilization and the instincts that goes beyond Freud's version.[5] The mere existence of the return of the repressed testifies to civilization's inability to harness the instincts effectively. Marcuse says that this point alone justifies the quest for a new and more successful model of civilization that can accommodate the instincts without repressing them. He highlights the fact that civilization is a product of the historical processes that have molded it through the centuries. If it has evolved to become what it is today, then it can evolve again to become something else. Marcuse focuses on the dissident content of the return of the repressed—on the fact that the instincts refuse to be culled, modified and channeled into something they are not. He says that the primary instincts hold onto the memory of a time when they were free—a time prior to their subjugation by civilization. It is this memory that makes Eros and Thanatos constantly challenge civilization's repressive conquest, and keeps alive the prospect of a reality that is built entirely on pleasure. The Undead corpse, as an embodiment of

---

[5] Herbert Marcuse, *Eros and Civilisation: A Philosophical Inquiry into Freud* (London: Routledge, 1956).

the return of the repressed, is transformed by Marcuse into a tireless campaigner for non-repressive civilization. So beneath the rotting surface of Romero's zombie we can now discover a revolutionary blueprint for freedom.

Marcuse says that a non-repressive civilization would prevail once the curfew on instinctual pleasure is abolished. In a free society, the instincts would no longer be the enemy of the state. A liberated Eros and Thanatos—total and unrestrained instinctual pleasure—would be the currency that holds the new order together. Within this order, work would be transformed into a sense of play. Whereas work is the perpetual delay and repression of pleasure, play is gratifying in itself—it serves no purpose other than that of creating pleasure. This playful pleasure would form the basis of a non-repressive civilization.

This initially seems to take us back to the beginning of Freud's argument. He claims that civilization would soon crumble if total pleasure were suddenly unleashed. The social order would experience a fatal resurgence of destructive sexuality and violence. Marcuse crosses this impasse by stating that a vital transition must take place before a new non-repressive civilization can be realized. He argues that sexuality is only destructive because it is distorted by the regime of repression. If sexuality is freed from the clutches of repressive civilization, it manifests itself in an entirely different way. Liberated sexuality becomes re-united with the pure version of Eros—the instinct to "combine organic substances into ever larger unities." [6] The task of building and maintaining a free civilization now becomes erotic and therefore instinctually gratifying in its own right. This civilization would be an entirely pleasurable institution, free from all repressive frictions. Thanatos, as the urge to be relieved from suffering and tension, would now pull away from death and find total satisfaction in staying alive instead. Eros and Thanatos would write a new constitution—a mandate for freedom and pleasure.

In *Day of the Dead*, Sarah, John, and McDermott escape from the army base and finally end up on a deserted beach. John is fishing, and this can be understood as a relaxing and enjoyable activity that provides food for the group at the same time. They

---

[6] Sigmund Freud, *Beyond the Pleasure Principle* (New York: Liveright, 1950) p. 57.

have finally stopped struggling with their repressed instincts—in the form of the zombies—and have discovered a situation in which surviving is pleasurable in its own right. Zombies only exist under a repressive regime, so the absence of zombies in this scene equates to an absence of repression. This fledgling society on the beach can therefore be recognized as a portrait of a free civilization. In an entirely pleasurable social order Marcuse says that repressed sexuality transforms into Eros. This is played out on the beach as we see that the zombies' engorged and selfish desire has been replaced by the living humans' newly released erotic instinct to survive pleasurably as a group.

Eros is symbolically released from the Undead body, and is reunited with the human individuals from whom it has been separated throughout the entire film. The jerky zombie shuffle is ironed out into the smooth-flowing and fully-functioning human bodies that are completely satisfied by their own playful survival on the beach. We have seen how Thanatos targets death as the only way of being rid of the pain and tension of a repressive existence. But the beach itself can now provide this release. Death and destruction are no longer needed to free the individual from his or her suffering, because in a non-repressive order he or she is already free. The gratified survivors have an intimate and pleasurable connection with their idyllic environment without having to return to the devouring womb.

The previously subjugated and alienated instincts, as embodied by the Undead corpse, are now freely reunited with the three survivors. The return of the repressed transforms into the very fabric of the free order, so the zombies in this scene are effectively vaporized and re-constituted in an entirely new form. Eros and Thanatos are still visible, but they are no longer manifested as a sexually destructive and regressive desire; they exist instead, and are completely gratified, within the pleasurable relationships of a non-repressive civilization.

The zombie yearns for freedom. It refuses repression and strives instead for an entirely liberated future. Yet this future is at the same time the zombie's downfall. The Undead corpse might herald a new dawn, but it will never see the sunrise. The zombie, as the manifestation of a violent cry for instinctual emancipation, is eventually decommissioned by the very freedom it campaigns for so fiercely. Marcuse's philosophical framework allows us to cast the zombie as a self-sacrificing martyr; its demise sparks a new beginning for civilization.

Romero's survivors pioneer a pleasurable reality in which their instincts are entirely gratified. For the moment at least, the survivors have found their instinctual paradise, but as Sarah looks out to sea, we can't help noticing the clouds gathering on the horizon. At the end of the film Sarah has a nightmare. She cannot simply forget all the zombies that are still roaming around and feasting on dead flesh in the underground army base.

Marcuse states that the memory of all those who suffered painful deaths in the past "darkens the prospect of a civilization without repression."[7] This is near the end of his book. It is decidedly downbeat, and seems almost to retract everything that he has argued before. The remaining zombies become this blemish that Marcuse speaks of—they are literally a walking reminder of all the people who died violently under the previous order. And so in *Day of the Dead* the legacy of a repressive civilization still remains. The zombies cannot be forgotten; they haunt the survivors as a memory of the old regime and threaten to return at any time.

In subsequent writing, Marcuse states that his vision is unrealistic—that there will always be some form of repressive order dominating human life. If we now jump to *Land of the Dead*, any semblance of the harmonious civilization depicted on the beach has disappeared and been replaced instead by another repressive regime. The zombies are fenced out of the city, and so civilization is segregated from the instincts once again. As in the previous films, the zombies eventually bring about the demise of the controlling order. The skyscraper owned by the power-hungry business man Kaufman becomes the primary target for the advancing Undead corpses. Kaufman has illegally hoarded a massive wealth for himself and his cronies at the expense of the underprivileged majority living on the streets. He ignores the growing zombie threat and focuses instead on his own selfish plans. As we have already seen in Romero's films, greedy and unlawful individuals open up a fatal gap in civilization's defenses. This chink in the armor is soon exploited by the growing zombie army.

---

[7] *Eros and Civilisation*, p. 237.

At the end of *Land of the Dead* the human survivors are still fighting with their instincts even though Kaufman's regime has been overthrown. Mulligan and his revolutionaries still wish to inhabit the walled city—the traditional seat of repression. Riley and his gang drive off to the north because they want to escape the city altogether. Even though they want to survive harmoniously, they are still inside "Dead Reckoning," their zombie-killing armored vehicle. They continue to be alienated from the zombies outside, and therefore reject the possibility of a peaceful reconciliation with their own instinctual pleasure.

Kaufman is only overthrown because the zombies themselves evolve and work out how to penetrate the city's defenses. Throughout the film we see zombies being taunted, abused, and massacred, but this all changes when they rise up and march together on the city. The zombies display a newfound sense of cunning and ambition. They are communicating with each other and learning how to use tools. Social organization emerges within the zombie population; they are becoming civilized on their own terms.

At the end of the film, it is not the humans but the evolved zombies who seem to be drafting the plans for a non-repressive marriage between civilization and the instincts. As a manifestation of the dissenting return of the repressed, the zombies have broken through the barriers, cages and chains that used to keep them imprisoned. Motivated by the constant persecution of instinctual pleasure, they have finally overthrown the repressive regime. Now that they are free, the future is theirs to pioneer on their own terms. The zombie garage attendant, who kick-starts the Undead revolution and eventually kills Kaufman, turns away from Riley and leads his new breed of zombies off into the unknown. We cannot see where they are going among the tattered remains of the city, but Romero makes it clear that they are no longer closing in on the surviving humans with ravenous intent. Instead of pursuing their appetite for flesh, the zombies have turned their backs on humans and are stumbling towards their new collective existence together.

The repressed Eros, previously manifested by the violent sexual bite, is liberated. Released from the clutches of repression, Eros expresses itself in the zombies' newfound desire to survive, grow as a community, and organize a new harmonious way of existing. The evolved zombies now embody the transformation of repressed sexuality into Eros that is the hallmark of Marcuse's non-repressive civilization. Thanatos—the urge to regress and be rid of all tension—is also liberated because the zombies are free to rot away pleasurably, untroubled by the constant burden of being alive. They reject the struggle with other humans in favor of creating their own community in which they can decay in peace. Both Eros and Thanatos are released. The zombies no longer embody repressed instinctual desire; they embody fully-gratified instinctual pleasure—the bedrock of a non-repressive civilization.

We previously understood the zombie as a martyr whose eventual demise signifies the end of repression. The zombie is still a martyr because it can only serve the cause of freedom once it has given up its human life. But now it is the continued presence of the zombie, and not its absence, that hails the new order. So the martyr is no longer completely dead; the martyr is Undead.

We can finally claim that the evolving zombies represent the beginnings of a pleasurable union between civilization and the instincts. So Romero is able to create the very system that Marcuse reluctantly deems impossible. Romero's work is no more than a fantasy, of course; so too, it would seem, is the prospect of a free civilization. But let's not end on a sour note. Imagine, for a moment, a possible scene from Romero's next zombie film. Imagine leagues of living humans lining up in front of their Undead counterparts, happily sacrificing their flesh so that they might be liberated from repression and delivered into a realm of instinctual pleasure. The erotic and regressive bite would no longer be hostile; it would become a caring gesture that heralds a sensuous release from the tribulations of life. There would be a renegade band of humans who resist this journey to utopia and reserve their right to be unhappy and repressed instead. This would set up a fascinating philosophical question for Romero to explore: is it better to be Undead, happy, and free, or alive, miserable, and repressed? In this emerging new order, to give oneself to a zombie would be a radical act of self-initiation; it would be a rite of passage into the land of the dead—into a realm of pleasure and freedom.[8]

---

[8] Many thanks to Kasey Mohammad, Richard Greene, and William Irwin for their helpful feedback and assistance.

17

When They Aren't Eating Us, They Bring Us Together: Zombies and the American Social Contract

LEAH A. MURRAY

George Romero's series of zombie films, *Night of the Living Dead* (1968), *Dawn of the Dead* (1978), *Day of the Dead* (1985), and *Land of the Dead* (2005), engages one of the fundamental questions of the last two centuries in American political philosophy: which is the superior position, *individualism* or *communitarianism?*

Individualism is the idea that the success of a society depends on self-reliance—individual hard work, ingenuity, and entrepreneurship. The individualist's America is a place where individuals can reach their full potential unfettered by overreaching government or the constraints of traditional societal norms and hierarchies: in essence, a place where the individual shapes society, not *vice versa*. Individualists tend to reject communism, for example, because it limits individual freedom, especially by placing too much emphasis on the needs of other people.

Communitarianism is the idea that societies prosper most and best when citizens co-operate. The Civil Rights Movement in America succeeded, on this account, because many citizens worked together to put the needs of the society above their own individual desires. Communitarians embrace neighborhood connectedness and group activities. They believe that a good society results from a sense of community and self-sacrifice, according to John F. Kennedy's famous dictum: "Ask not what your country can do for you, but what you can do for your country."

Individualism and communitarianism represent two dominant American political tendencies that have been fundamentally at odds since the founding of the nation. Both these strains
are found at the heart of the American *social contract* (more on
this term in a little while). Indeed, much of American political
philosophy is committed to the ideal of individualism and the
notion that one person standing alone can fight the torrents. Our
political, historical, and literary culture is littered with lone-actor
hero-types who are represented as saving the day by behaving
in a strictly American individualistic fashion. Some political
philosophers, however, have argued that individualism is not
necessarily the best thing for democracy, as it has increasingly
led to detachment on the part of citizens from each other. The
less people feel connected by their social contract, the more
likely they are to allow their sovereignty to slip away. Should
they be self-reliant and only look out for themselves? Or should
they connect with others and develop an ideal of the common
good?

I argue that Romero's *Dead* films evoke the problem of what
should be at the heart of an American social contract, and that
they implicitly advocate communitarianism over individualism.

Civic-Mindedness versus Fear

According to Thomas Hobbes's theory of the social contract, as
developed in his 1660 work *The Leviathan*, people are brought
together because they are terrified. Hobbes famously claims that
life for man in a "state of nature," devoid of government and
authority, is "solitary, poor, nasty, brutish, and short"; that is,
individuals basically go around trying to kill each other, much
like the zombies in Romero's films. The characters inside the
besieged farmhouse in *Night of the Living Dead* demonstrate
how a community can be formed simply out of fear. Most of the
characters have never met before the terrifying events of that
evening bring them together. They quickly form a governing
apparatus in which two male antagonists, one black (Ben) and
one white (Mr. Cooper), vie for a position of power while a
horde of zombies advances outside.

Ben is the hero of the communitarian position, working from
the very start to save as many people as possible. He tries to
make the farmhouse as safe as possible for himself and the trau-

matized, useless Barbara, even when she does nothing to help him. He exemplifies the social contract by drawing all parts of his community into the protective equation. On the other hand, Cooper, who is soon found hiding in the basement with his wife, child, and two other persons, embodies the individualist position of "every man for himself." He admits openly that even though he heard screaming upstairs, he refused to risk his own life by coming up to help. He also advocates not going to the central community location prescribed by emergency broadcasts, in favor of maintaining the relative safety of their basement fortress (Ben argues that if they must remain in the house, it is safer upstairs).

The conflict in *Night* could be seen as representing the beginning of the end of individualism as an appropriate core for the social contract. It is interesting in this context, however, that by the end of *Night* even the predominantly communitarian Ben ends up shouting that upstairs, *he* is the boss, thus reverting to a more individualistic position. When Ben tries to get the gas required to escape from the farmhouse, Cooper locks the door in an attempt to keep him out, and Ben finally shoots him out of rage. Cooper, wounded, staggers back into the basement, where he is attacked by his own daughter, now a zombie. Eventually the zombies overcome all the characters except Ben, who makes it through the night by barricading himself in the basement (Cooper's favored site, ironically), but is mistaken for a zombie and shot by the vigilante mob as he emerges in the morning (it is difficult not to infer that his being black has something to do with it as well).

Alexis de Tocqueville argues in his 1835 treatise *Democracy in America* that democracy will only work in this nation if individuals are civically minded. Note that Tocqueville is attempting to explain how democracy can work to a Europe that has much stronger communal ties, a Europe whose people are connected to each other in a vast hierarchical fabric. For government to work without that vast tapestry, people need to be connected to each other in order to further the aims of a government based on the rule of everyone over everyone—in other words, a society with more Bens and fewer Mr. Coopers. The more Americans join various groups ranging from the political to the religious, Tocqueville says, the more they connect with each other, thus furthering both the ends and the means of democracy. The warning he issues concerning the larger democratic project is against individualism. His concern is not that people might want to be distinct individuals (in fact, Tocqueville champions the personal rights of people to make their own choices), but that they might care more about themselves than about the community as a whole.

In *Dawn of the Dead*, these themes are played out even more elaborately. As the film begins, the zombie threat is in full force. Since the social contract has already broken down, panic has set in and we see Americans reverting to a Hobbesian state of nature. The usual organs of social control, government and the media, are on the brink of collapse. Near-panicked analysts on television attempt to tell people what to do to survive, but no one listens because all, including the "experts," are gripped by total fear of a hideous death. This fear has led to what *Leviathan* envisions: the declaration of martial law in the city. Only by completely giving up our individual freedoms to an outside authority can we hope to survive.

Whereas *Night* depicts the catastrophic failure of individualist isolation, *Dawn* demonstrates the next step in the social contract: coming out of the state of nature, driven by fear of death, to an untenable social living position. First, poor people are mowed down by the military as fear and anarchy give people an excuse to kill whomever they want. Sadly, these are the same groups that society has taught them to fear the most: the blacks and Hispanics who live in the projects. We also see remnants of a more communitarian social contract when the priest tells Peter that he could not kill the zombies, and so has just forced them into the basement. This is the first time in the Romero films that any concern for what happens to the zombies is implied, and the first time we see an explicit non-individualistic tendency given words. The priest says:

> Many have died, last week, on these streets. In the basement of this building, you will find them. I have given them the last rites; now, you do what you will. You are stronger than us. . . . But soon, I think they be stronger than you. When the dead walk, señores, we must stop the killing . . . or lose the war.

When the two military men, Peter and Roger, connect with two media people, Stephen and Fran, they eventually develop a little social contract in the abandoned shopping mall that they occupy together. Immediately they hook into the old institutions of the former world, which has taught them not to think of the zombies as human. The media reports that zombies should be destroyed: despite their human appearance, they should be considered mindless, soulless animals undeserving of respect—exactly the opposite advice of that given by the priest. The team at first takes the offical advice to heart, whole-heartedly taking pleasure in shooting the zombies inside the mall from moving vehicles with high-powered rifles, and using the ones milling outside for target practice from atop the safety of the roof. Eventually, however, the official advice is difficult for our little group to follow, when Roger is bitten and they have to face the fact that he must be destroyed. Once it happens to someone in their group, they cannot be so callous—the "humanity" of the zombie is more difficult to ignore. Whereas the group has taken the other zombies they have killed and put them in the freezer, they bury their friend Roger in a patch of interior landscaping.

When they are attacked by a biker gang, the group reacts in a classically individualistic mode. Stephen says "it's ours, we took it," referring to the the mall and all its resources. Instead of working together, the two different groups fight each other and both end in a bad situation. The biker gang is destroyed by the zombies, and Stephen also becomes a zombie. Because the two competing groups do not display communitarian tendencies, Fran and Peter are finally forced to flee the temporary consumerist paradise of the mall.

Communitarian Impulse

In *Day of the Dead*, the zombie threat has evolved to a near complete takeover of the world, and we see a group of scientists and soldiers holed up in a bunker in an effort to survive. Sarah, one scientist, hopes to solve the problem by curing the zombie virus, while Dr. Logan, another scientist, tries to figure out how to train the zombies not to kill living people (or not just *any* living people; it is suggested that there may be profitable military applications for domesticated zombies).

We feel more sympathy for the zombies in *Day* than in any of Romero's previous films. For one thing, they are rounded up

and subjected to scientific experiments that are very uncomfortable to watch. The more individualistic characters do not feel
sympathy for the zombie plight, while the communitarian hero,
Sarah, does. The soldiers are only able to feel sympathy when
it is one of their own who is being experimented on. Again, the
individualistic instinct only allows you to connect with those like
you—a fatal flaw. All of the soldiers are eventually eaten by
zombies, while Sarah, and two other communitarian characters,
John and McDermott, survive to leave the bunker. The zombies,
meanwhile, are beginning to show startling new abilities. As Dr.
Logan says, "it's the beginning of civil behavior"—the zombies
begin to demonstrate the capacity to develop their own social
contract. We root for "Bub" the zombie to destroy Captain
Rhodes, leader of the soldiers, at the end because Rhodes has
demonstrated such nasty individualistic tendencies.

Land of the Dead, the most recent film in the series, explores
another aspect of the problems with the Hobbesian social contract. The movie begins with the quote "if these people ever
learn to think, to reason in any way, the outcome will be disastrous." This could be a Rousseauian statement made by someone watching humans coming out of a state of nature.
Jean-Jacques Rousseau argues in *On the Origin of Inequality*
(1754) that as soon as humans reasoned and formed societies,
vanity and civilization were born and brought man to a corrupt
state. In *Land*, the corrupt state is the result of a social contract
born out of individualism.

In *Land*, we see that the zombies have clearly taken over, but
pockets of people have formed city-fortresses, and some semblance of order has been restored. Kaufman (Dennis Hopper),
the leader of one of these cities, organizes a social contract that
puts him at the top of a very strict hierarchy—exactly as Hobbes
would predict would happen with a contract born of fear—and
becomes the Leviathan. Only wealthy white people can live in
"Fiddler's Green," where they are fed very well and live in beautiful apartments. They are isolated from the zombie threat, and
also from the unkempt poor who are housed in the slums surrounding Fiddler's Green. Kaufman and his minions provide
vices such as prostitution and extreme (if unsophisticated) gladiatorial games for the poor to keep them distracted. For example, we are introduced to Slack, a communitarian hero, when
she is thrown into a cage with hungry zombies. Surrounding the

cage are poor people cheering the zombies on in a manner reminiscent of the Roman arenas where Christians were fed to the lions. When the poor begin to organize, Kaufman either has them imprisoned or killed. The Tambourine Man, who has been leading protests in the streets, is very quickly rounded up and put in prison (Slack is thrown in the zombie cage because she worked with the Tambourine Man).

Kaufman has also enlisted people to serve in a makeshift military to defend the city and its surrounding environs from the zombies. In his military we find Cholo, a Hispanic individualist, who risks and ultimately loses the life of one of his men to bring back liquor to Kaufman to secure a place in Fiddler's Green. This loss of life is the result of an individualistic instinct and gains Cholo nothing (Kaufman refuses him, implicitly because he is Hispanic).

The communitarian Riley also serves in Kaufman's military. Unlike his colleague, Riley works to make the world a better place for people immediately around him. He strives to bring back goods to the poor people, and saves as many people as possible while putting his own life at risk. The people he saves (Slack, for example) eventually become his community. Riley is rewarded for these choices in this movie when he is able to leave the corrupt city successfully. Note that his community is not formed out of fear but from a mutual bond to make the world a better place. We are led to think that this community might actually be better when Riley tells the Tambourine Man, who gains control of the city after the zombies topple its leadership, that leading the city the way he wants will result in more of the same corruption suffered under Kaufman's regime. The message is that a contract based on the survivalist motive of fear cannot sustain itself and will eventually collapse under the weight of its own individualist contradictions.

The other communitarian leader in the movie, interestingly enough, is a zombie. We are introduced to Big Daddy during a raid on a town controlled by zombies, when he displays sympathy for other zombies who are distracted by fireworks and mowed down by Kaufman's military. This also evokes Rousseau's social contract, as developed in *On the Social Contract* (1762), based on something he calls the general will. Rousseau argues that people do not form communities because we are afraid, but that we connect to each other because of a

common bond—that is, a communitarian contract. Big Daddy
and the zombies demonstrate this type of social contract when
they stop focusing on the fireworks and eating human flesh,
and focus on working together to bring down the Leviathan.
Watching the zombies organize is like watching an emergence
from a state of nature into a social contract. Like Riley, they
form a mutual bond to survive, and their contract is similarly
based on community rather than individual needs. By the end
of the movie, as a result, the Undead form a more sympathetic
community than the living inhabitants of the city. They take out
Fiddler's Green, and we root for them as they do so. We are
thus left with two communitarian heroes: Riley and Big Daddy,
who base their contract not on fear but on communitarian
ties.

Importance of Community Connection

One theme that plays out in all of Romero's movies is the "us
versus them" attitude that develops when the original social
contract falls apart. The introduction of the zombie threat causes
all people to become completely individually driven. Thus the
live people begin to see themselves in compartmentalized
groups as well. *Night* demonstrates this when Cooper refuses to
help anyone that is not his family. In *Dawn* a SWAT team offi-
cer calls the poor people living in the projects "spics" and "nig-
gers." Throughout *Day* the all-white soldiers refer to the other
characters in racist language, and their conversation is overlaid
with a distrust and suspicion of science and intellectuals; in
addition, they constantly subject Sarah to sexual harrassment. In
Land the wealthy white people who live in Fiddler's Green have
pushed the poor minorities out into the city's outskirts.

In all these movies, the implosion of the governing authority
brought on by the zombie threat causes people to revert to a
"protect your own" mentality. This is the basest individualistic
tendency, and it is not a sympathetic position in any of Romero's
films. Each, except arguably *Night*, demonstrates the fatal flaw
of not working together as the individualistic heroes die and the
communitarian heroes survive (and even in *Night* there is the
vague suggestion that Ben's abandonment of his communitarian
ideals somehow precipitates—if only because it precedes—his
death at the hands of the living mob).

Though Tocqueville argues that we need to join groups to begin our deliberative democracy, to fuel communitarian tendencies, we cannot simply join groups where everyone looks like us. Indeed, Romero's films dramatize our need to connect across a diverse range of people in order to survive. Throughout, those groups that exhibit isolationist, racist, and other exclusionary tendencies—the rednecks in *Night,* the biker gang in *Dawn,* the soldiers in *Day,* and the white wealthy people in *Land*—fare poorly.

Another marker of individualistic chauvinism is the inappropriate laughter, elation, and general sense of superiority that attends the living's treatment of the Undead: in *Night,* vigilante hicks treat the mass shooting of zombies like a hoedown; in *Dawn,* the bikers make a macabre game of killing zombies when they invade the mall (to the perverse accompaniment of pie-throwing and circus music); and in *Land,* the urban poor set up humiliating "have your photo taken with a zombie" amusement stands.

These individualistic travesties do not present a pretty picture of human nature, and for Romero, the arrogance they represent is the path to destruction. Conversely, his communitarian heroes are notable for their compassion and empathy. They are leaders who understand that cooperation and not fear of others is the only way to survive. Ben in *Night* says we need to work together and help each other, not hide in the basement while someone is screaming upstairs. Peter stays with Roger until the very end and is the one who shoots him (reluctantly) when he comes back as a zombie in *Dawn.* Sarah in *Day* asks "Why can't we just work together?" when faced with the soldiers' threat of death. Riley in *Land* leaves Big Daddy and his fellow zombies alone, saying, "They're just looking for a place to go, just like us." Throughout these movies, the message is that the communitarian tendency is the preferable position.

No Way Out

And yet this pro-communitarian message might appear to be complicated in a number of ways. In *Night of the Living Dead,* Romero kills off all the characters, on both the individualistic and the communitarian side, intimating that the question has long since lost relevance in our thinking. Romero himself has commented in interviews that what is most scary is one's neighbors. Thus the fact that zombies are the people we know makes them even scarier.

Is it Ben's communitarianism or his individualism that enables him to survive the longest? And which, if either, is most relevant to his ultimate destruction? The suggestion in *Night* is that these two driving concepts in American political thought have wiped each other out, leading to a bureaucratization of our lives. This bureaucratization, symbolized by the police that kill Ben at the end of the film, has numbed our sense of individualism and made it impossible to connect in any real way. Ben's "success" is casually ended by an overwhelming apparatus, and presumably his heroic story is lost forever.

Although *Night* seems to offer an ambiguous understanding as to what is actually the better tendency, individualism or communitarianism, the rest of the movies in the series make a clear case for commitment to a communitarian-based social contract. Indeed, the zombies in *Land* provide the perfect example of a community working and making decisions together in an effort to save their world. For Tocqueville, this is exactly what a democracy needs: a system which allows all members of the community to be accountable for what happens to each other.

The Romero *Dead* films ultimately depict the communitarian social contract as preferable to one based on pure individualism. If there are still some irresolvable contradictions—if it is not clear whether *Land*, for example, should be interpreted as a nightmare vision of the inevitability of Hobbesian totalitarianism, as a Rousseauian rejection of civilization outright, or as a hopeful Tocquevillian gesture toward democratic equality—it still appears clear that even if Romero no longer believes in the viability of communitarianism as a "way out" for humanity, he nevertheless believes it was once the right choice to make.

PART V

Leaving a Good-Looking Corpse

18

The Fear of Fear Itself: The Philosophy of Halloween

NOËL CARROLL

Halloween: The Festival of the Wandering Undead

Halloween is the night of the living dead. In all likelihood, the festival originated in Ireland where it was celebrated on November 1st, Samhain, which was, for the ancient Celts, the first day of winter, the season of death.

According to legend, on Samhain, the souls of all those who had died in the previous year gather from hither and yon to enter the otherworld. The living would put out food, drink, and other offerings to placate the traveling souls of the dead, perhaps to expiate any wrongs that they had done to them. Bonfires were lit and recently harvested food was fed to the flames as a sacrifice.

This should sound somewhat familiar to you. For it is very probable that the practice of going from door to door dressed as skeletons, vampires, zombies, ghosts, mummies, ghouls, Frankenstein's monster, and other assorted living dead in the expectation of receiving candy, money, and the like is a re-enactment of the itinerary of the wandering Undead on Samhain.

Catholic missionaries penetrated Ireland in the fifth century, entering into competition with the indigenous Druidic religion of the Celts. But rather than attempting to stamp out Samhain entirely, they appropriated it. In accordance with a strategy developed by Pope Gregory the Great, Catholic missionaries melded their myths with the local ones. In this way,

pagan fertility imagery, like painted eggs and rabbits, was dra-
gooned into the iconography of Easter, and pre-Christian symbols, like the Germanic *Tannenbaum,* were re-identified as
trees of special significance to Jesus. In Ireland, Samhain
became All Saints Day—the day in which all those saints without feast days of their own were honored—and the day after
that—November 2nd—became All Soul's Day, a day, like
Samhain, dedicated to all of the souls of the departed. Though
now in Catholic vestments, these days were still marked as
belonging to death and winter as clearly as Easter is associated
with spring and rebirth.

Halloween, of course, is the day before All Saints Day. Saints,
needless to say, are hallowed. So, "Halloween," in other words,
is "All Hallows Eve," or more archaically, "All Hallows' Even,"
which was shortened to "Halloween."

The Catholic missionaries also re-described the gods of the
Druids as demons, devils, fairies, goblins, and monsters, and
their priests and devotees as witches and wizards. Their kingdom was identified as the underworld. So, on Samhain, that
enchanted moment on the seam between two seasons, the gates
of hell are opened not only to receive the wandering dead but
also, in the process, to loose onto the world the denizens of the
domain of death, including devils, demons of every monstrous
shape, and witches, not to mention the prisoners of the underworld—ghosts and other Undead in every manner of degenera-
tion from the horrifically mutilated, fraying, and decaying to
bone-dry skeletons. This is, of course, a cast of characters whom
you already know, even if you never heard of Samhain. In their
trail, evil and chaos reigns.

This superstitious belief then was given embodiment by
mummers and maskers who, dressed like the minions of hell, go
from door to door exacting tribute. For whenever the Undead
appear, they typically want something from the living. When the
Irish emigrated to America, they brought this custom with them,
and they came in such large numbers that it became a national
theme. As I recall the Halloweens of my youth, it is easy to re-
imagine them as visions of hellish chaos—with piles of autumn
leaves burning in the twilight, and clusters of witches and skeletons and ghosts scurrying madly in every direction, driven by
too much sugar.

The predominant imagery of Halloween revolves around death. The most traditional costumes allude to the wandering dead—ghosts, ghouls, skeletons, and so forth. The devil, of course, is the lord of the dead and witches are his missionaries. Since they are often members in good standing in the league of the living dead, many movie monsters are naturals—or, perhaps more aptly, supernaturals—for Halloween masking, including the Mummy, Dracula, Frankenstein's monster, zombies, and so on. Likewise, any demon from *Buffy the Vampire Slayer,* especially perhaps from the episode devoted to Halloween, is ripe for masquing.

In fact all manner of monsters can inspire Halloween mumming—even those who hail from outer space—since they would fit into the Christian redefinition of the Halloween universe as demons, soldiers of Satan's armies of hell. Of course, not every costume on Halloween is monstrous. But what is nevertheless very striking is that so many of the most frequently recurring ones are connected to the realm of the Undead in one way or another. Over three-fourths of the Halloween outfits and masks at my local costume shop were of monsters, most of them of the Undead variety.

Halloween decorations also invoke death imagery. The Jack O'Lantern refers to an Undead trickster—a blacksmith named Jack—who, having been exiled from both heaven and hell—wanders the world, some say with his head in his hand. Dummies—sometimes scarecrows, perhaps to ward off carrion feeders—are often set up or hung from porches, and they are joined by effigies of witches, ghosts, corpses, and, more recently, movie monsters. Mock spider webs, replete with rubber arachnids, imitate the interiors of crypts, while various vegetables, like cobs of corn, are hung on doorways. Often these vegetables are already in a state of deterioration, reminding onlookers that they were mowed down in the recent harvest. Leaves, already in the colors of autumn decay, are everywhere, whether intentionally or not. And, of course, there are cut-outs of Halloween figures like witches and ghosts plastered on windows, blackboards, and the like.

Nowadays, many of these decorations are store-bought, rather than homemade. And the entertainment industry uses this celebration of death as a marketing ploy. Horror movies, like the recent remake of *The Fog*, a ghost story, are released around

Halloween, as was John Carpenter's classic *Halloween,* in order
to exploit the seasonal taste for death. You'll recall that Michael
Meyers becomes one of the Undead in the course of that film.
For similar reasons, the DVD of George Romero's *Land of the
Dead,* a zombie thriller, was released on October 18th, 2005, so
as to give everyone who desired a copy time to buy one in
order to horrify themselves and their friends on Halloween
night.

And, of course, broadcast television literally goes into its
vaults to exhume a veritable bestiary of the Undead for the
weeks approaching Halloween night. Starting at noon of
October 23rd, 2005, the American Movie Channel ran a solid
week of horror films. Obviously, the programmers at this station
were quite confident that there are, at any given moment at this
time of year, a sufficient number of viewers eager to have the
bejesus scared out of them to warrant a non-stop fright fest.

Though AMC—and, of course, the Science Fiction Channel—
may be the most extreme examples here, other stations feature
an upsurge of horror fictions during this season. It is, for example, a perfect occasion for marathon re-screenings of *The
Twilight Zone* and *Outer Limits.* Nor was it an accident that
Showtime chose the beginning of the 2005 Halloween weekend
to premiere its new series *Masters of Horror.* For on and around
Halloween has come to be the time of year when people gather
before their flickering hearth not to tell ghost stories, but to
watch them.

And finally, another frequently observed trend is that
Halloween is becoming more and more of an adult holiday—an
opportunity for masquerade parties, where the traditional costumes of the Undead are never far from sight. The fancier parties may even have TV monitors scattered about, re-running
favorite monster movies continuously.

The Paradox of Halloween

A great deal of what I've just said is not news to most of you.
Except for the bits about the history of Samhain, the rest is
widely known and very familiar. But—and this is where this
chapter really begins—it is so familiar that I think we lose sight
of the fact that this is all very peculiar, even paradoxical. Many
derive some strange kind of pleasure or satisfaction from the

horror films that bombard them during this season. Indeed, they seek them out. They revel in spectacles of corpses and decomposing bodies.

But how many among them would jump at the opportunity to spend the afternoon in the city morgue viewing dead and decaying bodies, and, even if they did, would they derive the same sort of satisfaction they get from the horror movies? If some of those stiffs could be re-animated, would they be willing to dance with them? The Undead in reality would be pretty revolting, not entertaining.

Moreover, the paradox extends beyond the motion pictures customarily marketed around this time of year. It pertains to Halloween itself. For, the strange pleasure or satisfaction that we take in these movies prefigures the larger mystery of how we can enjoy Halloween. For, Halloween is about death, perhaps the most fearful aspect of human life. According to the philosopher Martin Heidegger (1889–1976), it's the source of *Angst* so deep that most of us spend our lives denying the inevitable fact of death. Rather than face it, we turn ourselves into social robots.

And yet on Halloween, we appear to embrace death's imagery. Many thrill at the prospect of the representatives of death reeking evil and mayhem in our popular entertainments, and we derive a strange satisfaction from our fellow citizens wandering the streets in the make-up of the Undead. Of course, not all this imagery is, so to speak, "straight." Much of it is parodic, from *Abbott and Costello Meet the Mummy* to the capering skeletons in Halloween parades. In 2005, Tim Burton's *Corpse Bride* and Wallace and Gromit's *The Curse of the Were-Rabbit* arrived just in time to satirize the myths of Halloween horror. But isn't it just as anomalous that we should laugh at mortality as that we should find any satisfaction in being, as we say, "scared to death"? These are the paradoxes of Halloween that philosophy needs to address.

Needless to say, this is not an issue that most schools of philosophy have broached. However, since many of the traditional figures of Halloween are associated with the kinds of creatures who haunt nightmares, and since psychoanalysis has advanced hypotheses about the significance of these figures in our dreams, psychoanalysis is an obvious place to look for suggestions about our attraction to imagery of the evil dead which, one would think, should repulse us. One book that would appear to be especially pertinent is *On the Nightmare* by Ernest Jones,[1] perhaps best known as Freud's biographer and the person responsible for bringing Freud to England in his flight from the Nazis.

A Psychoanalytic Solution

Jones's book employs Freudian analysis in order to plumb the symbolic portent and structure of such nightmarish figures of medieval lore as the vampire, the devil, the witch, and so forth. Since many of these imaginary beings correspond to the recurring figures of Halloween, some may be tempted to adapt Jones's analysis of the relevant dreams to the costumes and entertainments of October 31st.

Jones's account, moreover, seems initially promising, if only because it has the right structure. For he appreciates that the fantastical beings that concern us are simultaneously attractive and repellant. As a hard-line Freudian, Jones is committed to the notion that all dreams involve wish-fulfillment. However, many wishes are for things forbidden. So dreams driven by forbidden desires putatively camouflage their objects in symbolism—often symbolism that makes the objects appear to be anything but desirable—indeed, sometimes symbolism that transfigures the objects of desire into something loathsome. It's as if the dreamer is saying to his psychic censor "I can't be desiring this, because I find it so repulsive."

That is, the selfsame item may be both the subject of a wish and of an inhibition. The inhibition component takes the form of negative imagery or affect. The function of the dreamwork, including the nightmare, is to construct situations that, in a manner of speaking, forge a compromise between our wishes and our inhibitions.

Jones writes:

> The reason why the object seen in a nightmare is frightful or hideous is simply that the representation of the underlying wish is not permitted in its naked form so that the dream is a compromise of the wish on the one hand and on the other of the intense fear belonging to the inhibition (p. 78).

---

[1] Ernest Jones, *On the Nightmare* (New York: Liveright, 1951).

For example, on Jones's analysis, the vampires of lore have two essential characteristics: they are Undead revenants and they subsist on the blood of the living, which they extract orally. According to the vampire legends that serve as the basis for Jones's investigations—and as opposed to the way in which the vampire is represented in contemporary popular culture—vampires first return from the dead to visit their relatives and to feast upon them. This imagery, Jones hypothesizes, can be interpreted initially as the wish, on the part of the living, for the dearly departed relative to return from the dead. But the alleged loved one is a horrific figure. Specifically, what is fearful about the revenant is bloodsucking, something that Jones associates with sexuality and seduction. Moreover, since the revenant is a relative, the sexuality in question is incestuous. So the wish that underwrites the symbol of the vampire is a wish for incest. However, this wish is simultaneously inhibited by the dream-work inasmuch as the vampire is represented as an abominable and dangerous predator.

That is, the forbidden desire for an incestuous liaison with a dead relative is transformed, by a process of denial, into something very different—a vicious attack. Attraction and love for the relative is alchemized into fear and disgust. Instead of yielding lips, the living quarry imagines himself or herself to be penetrated by merciless fangs. The humans portray themselves as passive victims and the Undead as aggressors. It's the vampire who is the active agent, not its prey. This supposedly allows the pretended victim to consummate, in the dream, a sexual, indeed an incestuous, relation with the vampire without blame. For, in this scenario the mortal must be innocent, since she is being ruthlessly savaged. The sexuality here, on Jones's account, is primarily regressive, a blend of the sucking and biting characteristic of the oral stage of psychosexual development. But all this nuzzling can be indulged without guilt, since it has been reconfigured as an unwanted onslaught.

Jones then goes on to analyze the iconography of other fantastic beings, many of whom are the staples of our popular entertainments, including Halloween. Given his Freudianism, in case after case he discovers that the imagery masks sexual wishes. The horrific imagery functions to deflect the sanctions of the psychic censor, also known as the super-ego. For the wish is disguised as its negation, namely as fear and disgust, and delight masquerades as aversion. In the case of the nightmare, the dreamer putatively cannot be charged with sexual transgression, because she is having the attentions of the vampire, the ghost, the ghoul, and so forth forced upon her. As anyone can see, she is not enjoying herself; she is being violated. Her predominant feeling is ostensibly not pleasure, but horror, though, according to Jones, this horror is actually the price that she has to pay for pleasure that comes from the dreamland gratification of her sexual desires.

In favor of Jones's hypothesis is the fact that sexual themes are germane to some of the figures that concern us. Often witches are first encountered as beautiful young maidens, only to reveal their horrific aspect the morning after. And Dracula is usually depicted as a handsome seducer, though not when he sports his Nosferatu look. Satan is a seducer too, but not a carnal one. Some of these monsters abduct women; maybe that is supposed to insinuate rape. Perhaps all the rough-house to which these nightmare figures subject their victims belies the childhood confusion over sexual congress and violence of the sort that Freud maintains occurs when children witness the primal scene.

Furthermore, with special reference to Halloween, the notion that all these figures are fundamentally transgressive fits with the ritual suspension or carnivalesque inversion of the rules on the holiday. For, like April 1st, Halloween is an evening when tricks are permitted, as well as being a time when excessive eating and drinking is the order of the day (or night). One might also say that Halloween is a period when a major ontological role-reversal occurs: the living "become" the dead.

But there are also problems with expanding Jones's hypothesis to cover Halloween. Some of the figures at the intersection of the nightmare, Halloween, and popular culture may have explicit sexual connotations, but just as many do not. Skeletons, on the face of it, are not sexy. The suavely attired Count Dracula may be alluring, but the case is less convincing with zombies, ghouls, milky wraiths, and creatures or demons from outer space like the Predator and the Alien from the film series bearing those names.

The psychoanalyst may reply that these examples are beside the point, since, according to Jones, the sexual significance of these figures is concealed by design. It is precisely the fact that these creatures strike us as the opposite of sexually inviting that enables them to trick the censorious super-ego into admitting them into the bedroom. The advantage of this "black means white" mode of interpretation is that it can account for from whence the pleasure or satisfaction comes with regard to this otherwise vile imagery. However, it does require the presupposition that these fantastical beings *always* stand for a wish, indeed a sexual wish, often one connected to the putatively universal desire for incest, and that the horror that accompanies exposure to these figures is only ever a diversionary tactic cloaking a deeper source of satisfaction.

And yet, might it not be the case that sometimes a zombie is just a zombie, and being devoured by one is simply cannibalism? That is, might it not be that frequently we are just horrified by our Halloween entertainments? When the leprous revenants in the re-make of *The Fog* pummel Mayor Malone into the cemetery to the sound of startling claps of thunder, my blood runs cold, which is not a tingle of sexual arousal. Nor does it seem plausible to speculate that I have any incestuous inclinations toward these ghosts, since they are not my relatives. Likewise, as Moonface drills out the eyes of his victim in "On and Off a Mountain Road" (the first installment of the aforesaid *Masters of Horror*), I am squirming, but not with pleasure. Isn't it possible that I am just horrified by the spectacle?

It may be alleged that I am merely in a state of self-deception here. My ego, along with my super-ego, has been duped; only my id knows and it's not talking. Moreover, if I say that I'm simply horrified by the spectacle, how are we to explain the satisfaction that I take in it? But again, notice that this explanation comes with an expensive theoretical price-tag.

One has to presume an awful lot of hypothetical states, laws, and processes, including a universal desire for incest, the reducibility of all the pertinent desires to sexual desire, the idea that all such fancies are wish-fulfillment fantasies, the mechanics of repression, the homuncular behaviors of the different parts of the psyche, indeed, the supposition that the psyche is partitioned in this way, the existence of the unconscious, and so on. In short, one must accept large portions of psychoanalytic theory in order to get this hypothesis off the ground, including the idea that we are always in a mental state of disavowal regarding what is really happening to us as we consume horror fictions.

This is a very elaborate—some might unsympathetically say "Rube-Goldberg-like"—explanatory apparatus. Would not a simpler model be far more compelling? For example, might not the notion that we are literally terrified by the appropriate moments in *The Fog* be a better account of what is going on, especially if we could say how that terror can be satisfying without resorting to the complex paraphernalia of psychoanalytic theory? All things being equal, a more economical explanation of the phenomenon should make us less confident of the more Byzantine psychoanalytic account. So let us see if we can find one.

The Meta-Fear of Fear

We can start to evolve an alternative explanation to the psychoanalytic one by focusing on part of the phenomenon before us in order to see what the part can tell us about the whole. So let's ask: what is it about the popular entertainments, like horror movies and television programs, that seem to yield pleasure or satisfaction at the same time that they are designed to raise negative emotions—emotions of fear and disgust?[2] It is perhaps useful here to recall the primary audiences for such entertainments—adolescent and young men, though, in recent decades, more young women are joining their ranks. What is it that they might derive from horror spectacles?

The adolescent male viewers—who often tramp to the Cineplex in groups—are engaged in a rite of passage. Speaking as one who enacted this ritual himself, they wish to demonstrate to themselves and to their peers that they can endure spectacles of substantial amounts of violence, carnage, filth, and impurity. They come to the theater with a certain fear of their own fear, namely that their feelings may swing out of control when subjected to particularly gruesome stimulation. For the adolescent horror aficionado, Franklin Roosevelt's aphorism—that the only thing we have to fear is fear itself—might be amended to say "we, untested as we are, are very afraid of being afraid." Exposure to the horror spectacle, then, confirms that the viewer will not lose it, at least in the culturally controlled situation of the movie theater where the viewer

---

[2] For an account of horror that relates it to the arousal of the emotion of fear and disgust, see Noël Carroll, *The Philosophy of Horror* (New York: Routledge, 1990).

has been insulated from genuine danger by the ontologies of fiction and the screen.

Adolescence is a time, at least in our culture, when one is especially prone to anxiety about one's emotions This is true not only of fear but of anger, love, desire, and so forth. The fear is that one will be unable to handle one's emotions—that they will take control of us with untoward consequences. With the changes in our bodies, attendant to adolescence, our emotions and desires begin to seem mysterious to us. We develop a nagging fear of what might occur under their aegis.

A large part of that fear is that we are entering an emotional terrain that is, as of yet unknown, a *terra incognita*. Various aspects of adolescent popular culture enable us to explore that country to a limited degree and to become familiar with it in such a way that we no longer feel utterly "out of it" and helpless with respect to our affects. Perhaps electronic shooter-games enable us to play with rage in this manner. It is my hypothesis that horror fictions, especially audio-visual ones, allow us to test our own fear factor. Its power over the viewer—at least to the extent that that power rests upon the fact that our emotional dispositions are frighteningly obscure for being untried—can be reduced by giving our fear a reassuring trial run.[3]

One objection to this is that an adaptive account like this overlooks the obvious. We are never going to encounter vampires, ghosts, ghouls, Undead skeletons, and the like, so the fears we test at horror screenings are not really relevant to the experience of any kind of fear-producing situation that we are going to encounter in life. What we see in horror fictions are scientifically impossible events; they are not the right sort of things to test our authority over our feelings.

Nevertheless, the imagery of the Undead does combine many elements of legitimate anxiety. First, there is the prospect of death. Halloween spectacles of the Undead invite us to confront the fact of death itself. The Undead, moreover, are often in some pronounced state of decay or deterioration. This too is a fact of life that horror fictions bring to the fore. The impurity of

---

[3] The idea that many entertainments are a means of enabling emotional management, especially for children, is explored at length by Gerard Jones in his *Killing Monsters* (New York: Basic Books, 2002).

the zombie is connected to an automatic fear of corpses that most of us feel, while the misshapen and twisted bodies of many Halloween horrors are exaggerations of actual abnormalities that may affront us in the real world. Likewise the aggressiveness and ferocity of many fantastic beings have real world parallels. The war of the worlds, in the film of the same name, is a form of intergalactic genocide.

So one source of satisfaction to be drawn from typical Halloween horrors is a kind of control or mastery that some can derive from experiencing fear close up. This is not to say that horror fictions inoculate us against fear, but rather that they can alleviate the meta-fear of fear by permitting us to explore the first-order level of fear itself. Extrapolating, then, from the satisfaction that can be found in typical Halloween entertainments to the holiday itself, I speculate that the festival itself, with its convergent horrific iconography of the living dead, is a cultural platform that invites experimentation with the negative emotions that surround death and deterioration for the purpose of palliating the fear of fear.

That the holiday is primarily an affair for the young and for adolescents may be offered as corollary support for this hypothesis, since they are probably especially prone to fear of the emotions. Halloween is a social occasion that affords the opportunity to educate youth in the process of emotional management. It is a folk remedy for the fear of fear whose medium is primarily the iconography of the Undead. Nor is it without efficacy for us oldsters who feel death approaching as our bodies ourselves show signs of decay.

Another piece of corollary, albeit informal, evidence for my hypothesis has to do with a feature of Halloween to which many of you may feel I have not yet paid sufficient attention. As mentioned earlier, much Halloween iconography, including that of the Undead, is offered in a parodic spirit. *Scream* is just as likely to be shown on Halloween night as is *The Curse of Frankenstein*. Halloween parades of the Undead and campy imitations of Bela Lugosi belong to the holiday as much as the imagery designed to make onlookers cringe.[4] This is probably especially true of adult masquerade parties.

---

[4] On the connection between laughing and screaming, see my "Horror and Humor" in my book *Beyond Aesthetics* (Cambridge: Cambridge University Press, 2001).

Halloween levity may, at first blush, appear to contradict my hypothesis about the function of the holiday to mitigate the meta-fear of fear by means of inducing fear. However, as is well known, humor is a widely acknowledged device that is used by people in professions, like medicine, mental health, the military, and law enforcement, which professions bring them into close contact with death, injury, decay, and malevolent behavior. These professionals use laughter—what the philosopher Henri Bergson called the anaesthesis of the heart—in order to control their emotional reactions in such a way that they can get on with their work. That is, laughter too is a well known means of emotional control. That laughter and horror exist side by side on Halloween may be the result of their sharing the same basic function for revelers: both contribute to enhance their feelings of self-control with respect to the emotions, most notably fear and disgust.

The conjecture that Halloween iconography of the Undead—both media-made and handmade—imparts satisfaction and pleasure due to the alleviation of our fear of fear and, thereby, to emotional control, is in competition with better-known explanations like psychoanalysis. But the fear-of-fear hypothesis is not only simpler than its psychoanalytic rival. Its leading assumption—that many of us, at least at certain times in our lives, are prone to the fear of fear—is readily confirmed introspectively, whereas much of the psychoanalytic account relies upon the existence of operations and entities that defy direct confirmation. To its dialectical advantage, then, the fear-of-fear hypothesis of the pleasure taken in the Halloween iconography of the Undead is more economical both with respect to the number and complexity of the concepts and operations it presupposes as well as being simpler in terms of the kinds of observations that contribute to its confirmation.

Fear itself may not be the only thing that frightens us on Halloween; but it is one of them.[5]

---

[5] This chapter's background information on Halloween comes from Jack Santino, ed., *Halloween* (Knoxville: University of Tennessee Press, 1994); Jack Santino, "Halloween in America: Contemporary Customs and Performances," *Western Folklore* 42 (1983), pp. 1–20; Jack Santino, "The Folk Assemblage of Autumn: Tradition and Creativity in Halloween Folk Art," in John Michael Vlach and Simon Bronner, eds., *Folk Art and Art Worlds* (Ann Arbor: UMI Research Press, 1986), pp. 151–169.

19

"Powerful, Beautiful, and Without Regret": Femininity, Masculinity, and the Vampire Aesthetic

JOAN GRASSBAUGH FORRY

"They have forgotten the first lesson. We must be powerful, beautiful, and without regret." When Armand speaks these words to fellow vampire Louis in the 1994 film *Interview with the Vampire*, he is not just talking aimlessly. Rather, he is reciting a truism about how vampires are portrayed.

Perhaps the most familiar form of the Undead, vampires have appeared in many different guises over the past century. From the umpteenth re-telling of the haunting story of Bram Stoker's *Dracula*, to the comedic children's book *Bunnicula*, the story of a vampiric pet rabbit that raids the refrigerator at night and sucks the "blood" from the family's vegetables, all vampire stories play on themes of power, beauty, and moral character.

Vampires are powerful not only because they inspire fear and terror in the living, but also because they escape from the troublesome human burdens of aging and sickness. Vampires are the ultimate affirmation of individualism, escaping from human moral obligation, caring only for themselves, and free from regret or remorse for their actions. But how and why must vampires be beautiful? There's no doubt that they are; even Bunnicula has sleek fur and the most deep haunting eyes one can imagine in a cute little bunny. But just how does beauty work in the conventions of vampire representation? Are conventional beliefs about beauty and appearance operating in the portrayal of vampires, or do these conventional beliefs get shoved out in the sunlight to get dusted?

Conventional standards of bodily beauty, femininity, and masculinity are at work in vampire films and television; however, these standards often shapeshift to challenge cultural norms surrounding gender and sexuality. The female vampire is terrifying because she is a killing machine housed in an ultra-feminine body. For example, Drusilla, from the television series *Buffy the Vampire Slayer,* has long flowing hair and only wears dresses, but she is insane, hell-bent on wreaking havoc on the mortal world, and often bites small children and puppies. Strangely, the male vampire is often feminized while simultaneously represented as masculine. Think of Dracula's stylized coif in Francis Ford Coppola's 1992 film *Bram Stoker's Dracula* or the sensual and refined Dracula played by Frank Langella in 1979. The consequences for these transgressions differ according to gender. Female vampires are usually punished and rendered powerless, either through ridicule or death, while male vampires flourish, or languish, in elegance and style. There are many variations on the visual portrayal of the vampire, and though there are certainly counter-examples to my findings, there are common themes in the representation of the vampire.

Beauty 101

Aesthetics is a branch of philosophy concerned with the observation and interpretation of art. Philosophers of art deal with questions of whether things are indeed art or not, the values of art, and properties of art such as beauty. Generally, beauty is associated with goodness because observation of a beautiful artwork, or object in nature, causes some kind of pleasurable experience. Philosophers of art have long debated the definition of beauty and how it can be detected and evaluated in artworks. For example, Pythagoras (582–496 B.C.E.) and other Pre-Socratic philosophers argue that beauty could be assessed according to a "golden ratio," a mathematical value indicating a degree of balance and symmetry. Plato (427–347 B.C.E.) argues that beauty is a metaphysical property that is always in harmony with goodness, fairness, and the divine. Aristotle (384–322 B.C.E.) separates goodness from beauty, claiming that goodness pertains only to conduct, while beauty pertains to objects. Aristotle instead claims that the forms of beauty are order, symmetry, and definiteness. Immanuel Kant (1724–1804) argues that judgments about beauty are subjective in the sense that individuals make judgments about beauty, but these judgments are objective in the sense that others ought to agree on which things are beautiful. The pleasure experienced in observing a beautiful object is, for Kant, present in the act of observation or judgment and in nothing else.

But beauty gets complicated when we talk about human bodies and representations of human bodies. Is beauty really an intrinsic and natural property, or is it an appearance that can be achieved through some set of practices? Feminists and social theorists criticize the naturalness of the human body, arguing that human bodies are not wholly natural, but are largely constructed through practice. The late philosopher Michel Foucault traces the body's transition from a natural entity to one that can be molded and shaped, using the figure of the pre-modern soldier to discuss the construction of the body through disciplinary practice. The soldier of the seventeenth century, Foucault argues, was "natural": he was "born" a soldier and possessed physical "gifts" and strength of character that could not be acquired. However, a change took place by the end of the eighteenth century: "the soldier has become something that can be made; out of a formless clay, an inapt body, the machine required can be constructed."[1] Anyone (any man, that is) could now be a soldier. The body of an ordinary man would be sculpted into the body of a solider through rigorous physical training; this process is discipline.

The important question for Foucault is how these ideas of naturalness and disciplinary practice function. Vampires get around the disciplinary process involved in cultivating physical strength because they are strong and powerful without practice. Following Foucault, we can question how the vampire goes against ideas of both naturalness and disciplinary practice, how vampire stories function to warn, horrify, and excite us, and why the vampire is so appealing.

Feminist philosophers, such as Susan Bordo and Sandra Lee Bartky, have used Foucault's concept of discipline to discuss how women's bodies are regulated through beauty practices. Beauty is a gender-specific social construct that shifts according to culture and historical period. Women's bodies aren't naturally beautiful; rather, women can make their bodies into beautiful

---

[1] *Discipline and Punish: The Birth of the Prison* (New York: Vintage, 1979) p. 135.

bodies by performing a set of practices deemed appropriate to one's culture and historical moment. Sandra Bartky examines three categories of disciplinary beauty practices that produce contemporary conventional femininity: (1) practices that produce a body of a certain size or shape; (2) practices that produce certain movements or gestures; and (3) practices directed toward displaying the body as an ornamented surface.[2] Practices that produce a body of a certain size or shape include dieting and exercise. Bodily movements and gestures are restricted through feminine clothing such as skirts and high-heeled shoes. Producing an ornamented surface involves hair removal, intensive hair and skin care, cosmetic application and maintenance, and paying attention to the details of one's clothing. All of these disciplinary practices require generous amounts of time and money.

The ideal feminine body that is the result of all this is youthful, thin with ample breasts, and walks with smooth movements, preferably with a moderate swivel of the hips. She possesses long styled hair, flawless skin, eyes and lips appropriately accentuated by makeup, and clothes and accessories that match and enhance her body's shape. Departures from this ideal are seen as unfeminine, or even masculine. Bartky claims that these beauty practices are not applicable to men in the manner and degree that they are to women. However, Susan Bordo analyzes the recent rise in male beauty culture and points out that beauty practices are increasingly marketed toward men, altering representations of men and masculinity in popular culture.[3]

Though women must perform these practices in order to appear beautiful, beauty is still portrayed as "natural." For example, when Kendra the vampire slayer arrives in Sunnydale, California, emerging from the cargo pit of an airplane in Season Two of *Buffy the Vampire Slayer*, her eyeliner and lipstick are perfect, and her provocative clothing is unwrinkled, despite her long trip from some unknown faraway place.

---

[2] "Foucault, Femininity, and the Modernization of Patriarchal Power," in *Femininity and Domination: Studies in the Phenomenology of Oppression* (New York: Routledge, 1990) p. 65.

[3] "Beauty (Re)Discovers the Male Body," in Peg Zeglin Brand, ed., *Beauty Matters* (Bloomington: Indiana University Press, 2000) pp. 112–154.

"I'm Too Sexy for My Mirror"

But how do these concepts of beauty, femininity, and masculinity apply to vampires? Conventional ideals of beauty, femininity, and masculinity are both reinforced and resisted in the conventions of vampire representation, or what I call the "vampire aesthetic." First, vampires are exempt from the majority of beauty practices. In escaping from pesky mortal aging, vampires are always youthful, and the only effort they need to make to keep their youthful appearance is to feed regularly on the blood of the living.

Because most vampires have no reflection, they cannot be too concerned with their appearances. Because vampire bodies stay youthful and relatively unchanged throughout their lease on immortality, vampires don't need to worry about weight or exercise. We rarely see a fat vampire, or a vampire who feels compelled to go to the gym. Their beauty is effortless. But in this effortlessness, conventional ideas about femininity and masculinity are emphasized. One of the tenets of both feminine and masculine beauty is that it must *appear* natural and not contrived. No matter how much effort went into shaping one's body, one must always pretend that this body comes naturally.

Second, vampire movements are elegant and smooth because of their supernatural powers. Vampires can shapeshift into other creatures, such as bats or wolves. They can move without obeying the laws of gravity, floating without touching the ground. Their movements are stylish and elegant; when they move swiftly, they move with precision, not with lumbering, erratic motions, unless they are stupid and easy fodder for a vampire slayer. For the female vampire, moving smoothly and suggestively is in line with conventional femininity. But the male vampire's graceful movements, intended to aid him in seducing his victim, blur the presumed line between masculine and feminine; men are not supposed to walk gracefully and lightly.

Third, male and female vampires are both heavily sexualized. A key part of vampire stories is the seduction of the victim. William Patrick Day writes, "Vampire stories are also tales of sexual sensationalism, the bite that is the kiss, pain that is pleasure, death that is love."[4] A thinly-veiled sexual voracity, the vam-

---

[4] *Vampire Legends in Contemporary American Culture: What Becomes a Legend Most* (Lexington: University Press of Kentucky, 2002) p. 5.

pire's sexuality is synonymous with the thirst for blood. Because the bite functions as a metaphor for sex, the vampire is not only a predator, but also a sexual predator. The promise of a vampire's sexuality lies in the vampire's method, seducing victims so that they become willing participants. The bite is often represented as highly pleasurable for both the vampire and the victim. Often, during the bite, both vampire and victim appear as if they are in the throes of orgasm.

The vampire's sexuality works with constructed norms of gender and sexuality. For the male vampire, seduction is not a transgression according to constructed masculinity, which takes sexual initiation and aggression to be the norm. Also, vampire stories challenge heterosexuality and monogamy. The male vampire often keeps a harem of female victims that he has turned into vampires. Jonathan Harker's encounter with the three sisters in Dracula is an example. Most vampire stories in which the main vampire character is male are heterosexual; the male vampire seduces and drinks the blood of female victims. In *Interview with the Vampire* we see homosexual overtones among male vampires. Louis and Lestat are companions for some time until they turn Claudia, a girl child, into a vampire and form a family of sorts. Louis and Claudia eventually leave Lestat, but Louis is soon compelled (seduced?) by Armand, another male vampire, and he arranges to leave Claudia for Armand.

Lesbian vampire portrayals are more common and hence, more widely accepted. The 1983 film *The Hunger* and film adaptations of the novella *Carmilla* portray lesbian vampires as the main characters. In addition, a distinct subgenre of lesbian vampire pornography arose in the 1970's and continued into the 1990's, with titles like *Barely Legal Lesbian Vampires,* and *Dracula's Dirty Daughters.* The female vampire's sexual appetite can be interpreted in two ways. First, for the lesbian vampire, her appetite is another invocation of a stereotype because lesbians are popularly represented as sexually aggressive, and thus deviant. But, second, the female vampire's aggressive sexuality is a transgression because she is female. Conventionally, women's sexual desire is supposed to be passive.

The Female Vampire as *Femme Fatale*

Usually presented as accessories to the male vampire main character, few female vampires take center stage in vampire films and television. But those female vampires that we do see generally conform to ideals of femininity. Consider Queen Akasha from the 2001 film *Queen of the Damned,* the second film adaptation of Anne Rice's novels in the series *The Vampire Chronicles.* Queen Akasha, played by the late pop singer Aaliyah, is scantily clad throughout the film, despite the moderately cool climate (other characters wear heavy coats). Her hair is long, with elaborate knots piled on top of her head. Her belly is exposed to highlight her sexuality. When she moves, she seems to slither, and with one graceful arm gesture, she can burn other vampires to ashes. There is only one scene in the film that shows Akasha's carnage involving any physical contact. This lack of contact, and reliance on some supernatural power, is a feminine way of killing because it is passive. This reliance on supernatural powers and not on physical contact is a common theme in portraying female vampires.

Drusilla is similarly feminine. The vampires in *Buffy* are either animalistic automatons or sophisticated and developed characters. Drusilla falls into the latter category; she was a recurring character through Season Two of *Buffy* and she made two guest appearances in Seasons Three and Five. Drusilla and her peroxide-headed companion, Spike, arrive in Sunnydale ready to wreak havoc and kill Buffy. Drusilla always wears long dresses or nightgowns, never pants. Her hair is long and is always styled and her nails are perfectly manicured. Drusilla is cruel and insane to boot, presumably from being tortured prior to becoming a vampire.

Drusilla is often portrayed as if she were a child, and she is treated like a child as well. For example, in one scene from Season Two, she talks to a dead bird in a cage. She asks Spike why it won't sing to her anymore and he replies, in a father-like tone, that it's dead and that she kills every pet that's given to her. She whimpers and Spike comforts her. Drusilla conducts tea parties with blindfolded dolls and rips apart the ones that anger her. Her irrational and emotional tendencies, conventionally associated with the feminine, make her threatening because there is no logic to her wrath. But, because she is portrayed as childlike, her threat is neutralized. However, because these childlike qualities are embodied within an insane creature that ultimately wants to destroy the world, her character is even more uncanny and threatening. In the Season Two finale, Drusilla manages to kill Kendra, the other vampire slayer. Drusilla kills Kendra in a feminine way: like all vampires on the show, she possesses incredible physical strength and well-honed fighting skills, but she kills Kendra by first hypnotizing her, and then slitting her throat with her long, polished fingernail.

Claudia in *Interview* played by a young Kirsten Dunst, is also portrayed as child-like and incapable. However, unlike Drusilla who is a grown woman, Claudia is actually a child when she is turned into a vampire. Claudia also plays with dolls and is dressed like a doll in frilly dresses. Despite her childlike body and her girlish appearance, Claudia is a vicious killer. The film's comedic moments center on her child-vampire escapades. When she kills the seamstress and disposes of a number of piano teachers, Lestat reprimands her and reminds her, "Not in the house!" But as Claudia becomes older and begins to understand that she will never grow up into a woman, she becomes bitter and blames Louis and Lestat for stealing her womanhood from her. She deceives Lestat into drinking the blood of a corpse, a form of death for a vampire, in an attempt to kill him. Her childlike face as she lies and deceives Lestat is especially frightening and uncanny because such dark intentions are embodied within a small child.

The feminine appearance of these three characters, like many others, serves to enhance their characters as devastating, threatening women. Ultra-feminine appearance, expressed through conventional dress, movement, and youth, offsets the female vampire's excessive sexual or vampiric desire. The female vampire has, then, two interpretations. First, her feminine appearance neutralizes her as a threat. Or, second, her feminine appearance adds to her threatening nature; she is more dangerous because her body appears unthreatening. Barbara Creed explains that female vampires are horrifying and attractive because they threaten to undermine the dominant position of men in patriarchal, or male-dominated, society.[5] The female vampire is represented as a femme fatale, a "fatal woman," shrewd, cunning, and hell-bent on leading men to utter ruin. The femme fatale embodies a set of fears and anxieties about the place of women in general: women might rise from the dead and devour all those who ever wronged them with gross irrationality, emotion, and violence.

The female vampire is also a character that inspires liberation. She threatens patriarchy, even when she appears ultra-feminine, her feminine body performing cruelty and violence. But this liberatory reading doesn't work, because the *femme fatale* doesn't survive; her evil nature is punished through death, or she is made powerless through ridicule. For example, in *Queen*, Akasha chooses Lestat to be her king, but her desire to dominate the world is too much even for the egotistical and arrogant Lestat. He is horrified when she litters the beach with corpses, and he conspires to kill her in the end. Claudia's attempt at murdering Lestat in *Interview* is punished by death when Armand's crew kidnaps her and she is left to turn to ashes in the morning sunlight.

Drusilla, on the other hand, is made to look foolish. Drusilla and Spike escape Sunnydale at the end of Season Two, and in subsequent seasons we are updated on her story. She dumps Spike for a disgusting chaos demon, a half-man, half-deer creature with large oozing antlers and no personality. She is foolish and juvenile for dumping Spike for a revolting creature with no powers. She returns to Sunnydale in Season Five, only to be made to look foolish again when Spike rejects her and she flees in disgrace. Drusilla's whereabouts are currently unknown.

The female vampire as *femme fatale* provides a powerful social message for women. Being bad, beautiful, and immortal might be fun for a while, but girls, in the end it doesn't pay off.

The Male Vampire as Metrosexual . . . Sort Of

Beauty is connected to power and self-definition in the vampire aesthetic. Vampire characters range from human-like to pure evil snarling monsters. Take the vamps on *Buffy the Vampire Slayer*,

---

[5] *The Monstrous-Feminine: Film, Feminism, Psychoanalysis* (New York: Routledge, 1993), pp. 3, 61.

for example. Vampire protagonists, or those vampires that have some kind of character or sophisticated power, appear human-like, usually embodying elements of conventional beauty, until they are angered or about to strike, when they uglify, their fore-heads going bumpy, eyes turning yellow, and fangs appearing. Those vampires that are subordinate or less powerful, or driven purely by lowly hunger (such as Harmony's minions), are always ugly and usually meet their demise at the hands of the vampire slayer or flee in a cowardly fashion, never to be seen again.

Sophisticated male vampires usually play the role of vampire protagonist in vampire films and television. In this role, the male vampire is usually a character struggling for self-definition. Having retained some semblance of humanity, he tries to navi-gate between the loneliness and boredom of immortality, and the ethics of killing humans. Often a self-divided character, the vampire protagonist struggles with delight in killing, need for bodily nourishment, and moral shame. Louis from *Interview*, Angel and post-soul-restoration Spike from both *Buffy* and *Angel*, and some portrayals of Dracula are examples. Because immortality has given him many years to reflect, the male vam-pire is often wise, articulate, and, last but not least, concerned with maintaining a distinctive image.

The popular slang word *metrosexual* denotes a stylish het-erosexual male who is in touch with his feminine side and pos-sesses "good taste." Similarly, the male vampire protagonist is in touch with his feminine side, as expressed not only through his appearance and movements, but also in his surroundings. Whereas less important vampires live in "nests" where they feed in filth, and leave the bodies to rot where they sleep, the male vampire protagonist is usually surrounded by gothic elegance, and languishes in a castle or mansion, or at least a well-fur-nished apartment. Even the masculine Spike from *Buffy*, who lives in a dirty crypt, is comedically feminine and image-ori-ented. Buffy catches him painting his fingernails black in one fifth-season episode, and he maintains a love for the soap opera *Passions*. Commonly, the struggling male vampire is challenged by some situation, like falling in love with a human, and this becomes an opportunity for him to express his emotions, which have been constipated by years of killing without regret. Though he is incredibly strong, the male vampire protagonist is rarely represented as overly muscular, or overtly aggressive. Because he is an Undead creature of the night, he is forced to be subtle, and is persuaded to hunt by his emotional inclinations.

But when the male vampire embodies typically feminine traits, it works not to render him less frightening or less powerful, but instead allows his audience to identify with him. No longer evil incarnate, if he dies, it's a tragedy. More often, he lives, either to torture himself and do penance for his wrongs, or to live a life of vampire happiness after he has learned his lesson. He expresses his emotions, struggles with them, and he does so with some kind of "good taste" or aesthetic sensibility. He is able to see beauty in everyday worldly objects, even if not in himself, and this brings him solace. He takes comfort in the harsh world that troubles him so deeply; this is the ultimate lesson for the human audience.

Symbolizing a wish fulfillment for immortality, freedom from the mortal coil, carnivorous animalism, and a sexual voracity, the vampire has given us something to both fear and to embrace. The image and appearance of the vampire serves to question a number of boundaries, between real and unreal, dead and Undead, masculine and feminine. Beauty plays varying roles in the vampire aesthetic. Vampires are themselves beautiful and their beauty fits with standards of human beauty. Their visual appeal makes them seem less threatening, as beautiful entities are commonly thought to be pleasurable to gaze at or engage with. However, a vampire's beauty also works to make him or her more frightening; encountering a beautiful vampire usually means one will meet one's end. Not only are vampires often physically beautiful, but they seek beauty in their vampiric struggles with immortality. Beauty, especially for the male vampire protagonist, is a comfort, a shield from the bane of immortality. But, as we have seen, beauty functions differently according to gender in the vampire aesthetic. In the realm of the Undead, the male vampire becomes a beautiful martyr while the female vampire becomes a disastrous woman whom we love to hate.

Philosophers by Day . . .

ROBERT ARP is Assistant Professor of Philosophy at Southwest Minnesota State University, where it's too damn cold for any of the Undead to haunt!

ADAM BARROWS is a doctoral candidate in English at the University of Minnesota. His research explores the connections between time and imperialism. Adam teaches courses in British and Postcolonial literature, and always worries about getting midterms graded before sunset.

NOËL CARROLL has reincarnated the ideas of so many dead philosophers that he has been re-animated as Andrew Mellon Professor of the Humanities at Temple University. Some of his tombstones include: *The Philosophy of Horror, Beyond Aesthetics, Engaging the Moving Image*, and, most recently, the Blackwell anthology, *The Philosophy of Film and Motion Pictures*, co-edited with the vampire Jinhee Choi.

SIMON CLARK is an artist, musician, and writer from Britain. He graduated from Goldsmiths College in 2003 with an M.A. in Fine Art. He regularly performs a one-man show called *Sad, Sad Songs of Wretchedness and Death* in which he sings a repertoire of country 'n' western dirges from inside his homemade coffin. With song titles such as *Cold Hole for Your Bones, Surrender to the Worm*, and *I'm Doggone Dead and I'm OK*, he has become something of a self-styled authority on all things morbid and miserable. If commercial success is an Undead figure rising from its grave, Simon's body of work remains very much buried. He remains hopeful however that one day his obsession with death might actually earn him a living.

PHILLIP COLE is a member of the Undead until he gets coffee in the morning. After that he is Reader in Applied Philosophy at Middlesex University, London, but still retains the power to turn students into zombies during his lectures. During his research into the spirit world he tried to strike a happy medium. His book, *The Myth of*

Evil, published by Edinburgh University Press in 2006, and, fortunately, contains no attempts at humor.

JOHN DRAEGER is Assistant Professor of Philosophy at Buffalo State College. His research interests include ethics, political philosophy, and philosophy of law. He doesn't think that he's ever met a vampire. But if he does, he says he'd welcome the opportunity to talk some philosophy over coffee and a cinnamon roll. After all, decency may demand it.

JOAN GRASSBAUGH FORRY is a Ph.D. candidate at Temple University where she is completing her dissertation on gender, subjectivity, and sport culture. Her research interests include feminist theory, Foucault, ethics, and critical race studies. She teaches philosophy and women's studies at Temple, where she must regularly reprimand her students for gnawing on each other's brains.

RICHARD GREENE is Associate Professor of Philosophy at Weber State University. He received his Ph.D. in Philosophy from the University of California, Santa Barbara. He is the Executive Director for the Society for Skeptical Studies. Richard has taught corpses in logic, metaphysics, and epistemology.

LARRY HAUSER, when not lurching around Leelanau County in search of brains and feasting on the fine ones there, partakes of the brains of philosophy students and colleagues at Alma College and Michigan State University. His specialty is the philosophy of mind. He believes that computers really do think. Their electronic brains, however, are still too dry for his taste.

DALE ("FULL-METAL") JACQUETTE, otherwise unemployable, is Professor of Philosophy at the Pennsylvania State University. There he teaches logic, metaphysics, and philosophy of mind to legions of the Undead, and, between episodes of going ballistic (hence the nickname), attends endless committee meetings featuring wildly implausible plots, fatuous, lusterless dialogue, and pathetically wretched action sequences that couldn't be re-animated even by supernatural powers.

WILLIAM S. LARKIN is Associate professor of philosophy at Southern Illinois University, Edwardsville. As a result of having pretty badly misunderstood the idea that philosophy is the pursuit of the "Good Life," Professor Larkin went into philosophy primarily for the money and the ghouls. Since at least half of that has not worked out nearly so well as he'd hoped, he's trying to get out of philosophy by writing, directing, and starring opposite Kyra Schon in *Romero and Juliet*—a stage play about the undying love between two star-crossed and scab-encrusted Undead lovers set in suburban Pittsburgh.

K. SILEM MOHAMMAD once played Dracula on stage (don't get too excited, it was a junior college production in Modesto, California). He is Assistant Professor of English and Writing at Southern Oregon University, and has taught courses on zombies and the horror film. He is the author of three books of poetry: *Deer Head Nation* (2003), *A Thousand Devils* (2004), and *Breathalyzer* (2006). His blog {lime tree} (http://limetree.ksilem.com) routinely addresses such topics as "dead kitten poetics." Spooky!

LEAH A. MURRAY is Assistant Professor of Political Science at Weber State University. She earned her Ph.D. in 2004 at the University of Albany, focusing on American Politics and Political Theory. While her students are pretty sure she is not Undead, the black cat and broom in her office make them suspicious of her witchy status.

TED M. PRESTON is the current head of the philosophy program at Rio Hondo College in Whittier, California, and received his Ph.D. from the University of California, Riverside. His philosophical interests include Nietzsche, self-fashioning, and martial artistry. Despite being one of the "children of the night," he finds himself routinely teaching early a.m. classes. Only by sheer force of will (and coffee) does he refrain from bursting into flame when greeted by the dawn, and collapsing into dust when stepping foot into the classroom. When not reflecting on Unlife, he extols the practical benefits of philosophy, and believes firmly that an unexamined life is not worth Undeath.

HAMISH THOMPSON obtained his doctorate from the University of Edinburgh in 2002 in Philosophy of Mind after many "zombified" years as a student. He currently teaches a wide range of courses as a part-time instructor at the University of Louisville and Western Kentucky University. Since arriving in the US in 2001 from his homeland of Scotland, he has driven the equivalent of four times round the globe, commuting often in a state of being "awake, but unaware," or perhaps conscious "of" rather than conscious "that." His main goal is to become a stationary reflective educator.

MANUEL VARGAS is currently working as a philosophy professor in Northern California for some folks known as the Society of Jesus, a clandestine wing of an obscure group known as the Roman Catholic Church. While one of his teachers in graduate school was reputed to be a vampire, and while Vargas can be killed by a silver bullet or wooden stake through his heart, holy water does not harm him. Yet.

MATTHEW WALKER grew up in Pittsburgh, where he hung out at malls and longed to star as a pasty-faced extra in a George Romero zombie film. Instead, he ended up as a pasty-faced philosophy graduate student at Yale University, where he's currently writing a dissertation on Aristotle's ethical theory.

DOUGLAS GLEN WHITMAN is Associate Professor of Economics at California State University, Northridge, where he feeds on state taxpayers. His office is located atop a Hellmouth, as the College of Business and Economics doubled as Sunnydale High during the final season of *Buffy the Vampire Slayer.*

WAYNE YUEN received his M.A. in Philosophy at San Jose State University and is Professor of Philosophy at Ohlone College in Fremont, California. His primary philosophical interest is applied ethics, but he has recently rediscovered alchemy. He is currently researching a cure for zombification, largely consisting of caffeine and sugar, the secrets to life itself.

Index of Rigor Mortis